ASCENSION OF A WOMAN
A Memoir

By Karen Moreno Scott

ASCENSION OF A WOMAN

a memoir

KAREN MORENO SCOTT

Copyright © 2021 Ascension of a Woman.

All rights reserved. No part of this publication may be reproduced, distributed without the prior written permission of the publisher, except in the case of brief quotations embodied in critical reviews and certain other noncommercial uses permitted by copyright law. For permission requests, write to the publisher, addressed "Attention: Permissions Coordinator," at the e-mail address below.

davina@alegriamagazine.com

Library of Congress Number: 2021922108
ISBN: 9781737992745

Published by Alegria Publishing
Book cover and layout by Sirenas Creative
Photography by Aurelie Davis
Edited/Proofread by Polished Words, LLC.

DEDICATION

This book is dedicated to every inner child in need of healing and feeling seen, heard and loved.

And of course, the most loving thank you goes to my rays of light…

my creator and father, God
mi mamita linda and muse, Elsie
my beautiful baby girl, Samantha
my partner and angel, Michael
my twin sis, Karla
my munchkin, Elsie Victoria
my soul sisters, Verenice and Gissel
and my Alegria family

You are forever a part of me.

PREFACE

It is said that *silence is golden*. That is certainly the standard by which I was taught to live from a very young age. I learned to keep what I saw to myself, to never repeat what I heard, and to be seen but not heard--even when it meant silencing my pain and suffering and compromising my well-being.

As a direct result of this conditioning, my childhood trauma went unnoticed, unhealed and carried over into my adulthood. Before my healing journey began, I walked around life sweeping my troubles under any rug I could find, pretending I had life all figured out, leaving pieces of my soul scattered everywhere I went.

That was until I decided the time had come to set myself free.

Ascension of a Woman is a culmination of all the blessings in disguise that have saved me, taught me, lifted me up, and carried me to the beautiful place I find myself today. This is my inner child gently raising her thundering voice and reclaiming the years she lost nurturing wounds that simply needed a little love, grace, and gentle care. My mother has passed on, but I lovingly take the torch and carry the light forward, paving the way for my future generations for whom I have paid the price so that they wouldn't.

This is my life story which is an ebb and flow of highs and lows, wins and losses--my evolution and ascension into womanhood.

What gives my book purpose is realizing wisdom seldom comes from an easy life, and storytelling is what connects us at the most basic human level. I hope you will find pieces of yourself in the pages of my revelations which are both haunting and beautiful.

Thank you for going on this journey with me. This book has been a great healing tool for me and I hope it will inspire you to raise your voice, and to empower those around you to raise their own voices, in order to continue shedding light on our struggles as people of color and the issues that plague our communities.

I am living proof that through faith we can rise from the ashes and ascend into the light--not because we have died but because we have come alive!

FOREWORD

"I am like a drop of water on a rock. After drip, drip, dripping in the same place, I begin to leave a mark, and I leave my mark in many people's hearts."

— Rigoberta Menchú

What an honor it has been to witness week after week in the last year the creation of *Ascension of a Woman* by Karen Moreno Scott.

The book that you are now holding was created over 12 months during a global pandemic, and it took tremendous willpower from Karen to bring it to life.

She knew that it would only be through her unfiltered vulnerability that she could do justice to her story while honoring her soul and her ancestors.

I have no doubt the pages you are about to read will invite you to examine your own life with all of its tears and laughter. As Khalil Gibran so wisely once said:

"Tears that purify my heart and reveal to me the secret of life and its mystery, laughter that brings me closer to my fellow men; tears with which I join the broken-hearted, laughter that symbolizes joy over my very existence."

Ascension of a Woman is a courageous memoir where Karen gifts us her story with a sincere heart. We go on the journey of a woman who has survived loss, abuse, and her own share of tribulation and heartbreak. *Pero a la vez, nos regala una hermosa oportunidad de conocer su linaje y su alma*: a precious opportunity to witness her gracious tribute to her heritage, her immigrant mother's legacy, and a brave examination of her own process of forgiveness, healing, and self-love. Her story becomes a mirror in which to look at our own trauma and liberation.

Davina A. Ferreira
Founder/ALEGRIA Media & Publishing

Ascension of a Woman

I am no longer a broken soul walking among broken souls
I am a woman on the mend having walked
a thousand miles to reach the light
My rightful destination

I look back at my shadow and wait for her patiently
I extend my loving hand to let her know she is not alone
I can see her shy away for she has much healing yet to do

Even in darkness I see her innocent beauty clear as day
From a distance I blow sweet kisses to her mending wounds
Hoping they will tear down her walls and break her
heart wide open

Until our final lesson is learned and the time to
integrate should come
My shadow and I walk together side by side, not yet hand in hand
Staring into each other's eyes, we will do a song and dance

My shadow is my companion
The ruler of my unconscious mind
She has unknowingly led me down a path of destruction
Yet I recognize she has sacrificed her happiness
for the sake of mine

She is my greatest ally and my worst enemy
She is my friend and also my foe

My shadow is me
She and I are one
We are true soul mates
Walking the earth on this journey called life

I have fallen and also risen
I came undone to come alive
I am a woman on the mend
I am a goddess in the making
I am in my totality…
Ascension of a Woman

"...this is my story and if I'm going to tell it, it has to be done with integrity and raw honesty."

1

As an adult, I have often heard people say that I appeared to be well put together and seemed to have life all figured out. What those folks didn't know is that much of what they saw was, in part, a great illusion I created and a role which I learned to play very well in order to hide the pain I was in. You see, underneath the exterior layers of my nice clothes, high heels, perfectly manicured hair and nails, and made-up face, was a little girl in a great deal of pain who had spent most of her life silently crying for help that never seemed to come.

I wrote this book for so many reasons, but the most important is to share with you how, through my own healing journey, I have shifted the narrative of my story and turned my emotional pain into my emotional strength. I can only hope that in sharing my story, I will be able to help others do the same. I'll admit I have so much to say that I'm not quite sure where to begin. I know, I'll start by saying this.

What I am about to share with you is not meant to sound like a tragic tale. In fact, my intention is quite the opposite. I like to think of my story as one that defines the true meaning of being a woman. As women, we often go through the unimaginable and endure experiences that shake us to our core--yet we are conditioned to sweep our feelings under the rug, to carry on with a smile on our faces and hold up the world with our strength despite whatever struggles we may be facing behind the scenes. By the grace of God, we somehow always manage to find the will and strength to push forward in our journeys through life that can sometimes be immensely challenging and cruel.

I say this because it seems a bit cruel that becoming strong and resilient is dependent upon how much we are willing and able to endure. That the harder the fall, the bigger the lesson, even if it means that in the process you are broken in almost every way. For me, the hard lessons came by way of growing up fatherless; of enduring rejection and abuse at the hands of people who were supposed to love and protect me; of having to overcome homelessness, not once but twice; and of having to endure the loss of my beloved mother in my early thirties. My mother was not only my biggest supporter, my shero, but also the woman who taught me to love hard, forgive harder, and fight like hell to protect Samantha, my daughter.

This is my coming of age story, four decades in the making. A story of learning to become resilient, tough, and most of all, determined. To weather the storms of life, learn to roll with the punches, and get back on my feet to keep pushing forward, because what other choice do we have?

In the chapters ahead, I will share with you my journey and the wisdom I have gained along the way. Although some of my experiences brought me to my knees, they have also been an essential part of my awakening. So here it all is, in black and white. This is me bearing my soul to you and the entire world. You may find some of what I share difficult to read, but this is my story and if I'm going to tell it, it has to be done with integrity and raw honesty. I will share about my coming out of the ashes of abuse--sexual, physical, and emotional. Of overcoming poverty, infidelity, divorce, and loss. How even though I was taught as a young girl to be seen but not heard, I came to find a voice, *my voice*. How I broke free from all those who have in some way attempted to silence me into submission, to silence the voice of my inner child. She is no longer willing to cry alone, waiting for help to arrive, because I am her rescuer who will no longer allow her to drown in sorrow.

This is the story of my evolution and my ascension into the spiritually divine woman I find myself to be today. Of my journey toward personal freedom and bittersweet awakenings that would have me come undone in order to discover the woman I was always meant to be.

As my history professor would often say, "To know where we're going, we must first look back to where we've been." So let's go back to my beginning. A beginning that almost did not come to be.

2

I am the daughter of an illegal immigrant. A woman born and raised in her beloved Guatemala, a country in Central America encircled by its bordering countries, Mexico, Honduras, Belize, and El Salvador. Elsie is her name. She was born in the late 1930s, a time when there was little opportunity for women to think independently and strive for a life of professional success. They were instead groomed into a life of servitude. Servitude to the men they would have the great honor of marrying and to however many children God willed them to bear. This was the life my mother was destined for, and proud to live, until the tragic death of her husband, a police officer killed in the line of duty whose dead body was dumped at her doorstep. Widowed and traumatized by her husband's untimely death, and left with a small pension that would not nearly be enough for her and her seven children to survive, she became determined to find a way out of the impoverished life that a woman like herself would be destined for.

Beautiful as she was, with soft brown skin, elongated brown eyes that were Egyptianesque, black silky long hair, and a body that defied child-bearing odds, there was not a shortage of eligible bachelors courting her, willing to take her and her children in. Still grieving the loss of her late husband, this was an option she was unwilling to accept. Instead, she decided to follow in the footsteps of her brother and sister, and join them in the United States, where she knew she could start a new life away from the painful memories she would be leaving behind, not only a grieving widow, but as a woman still recovering from the loss of her beloved mother, whom she had also recently lost to an aneurysm.

Without the means to get herself and her seven children across the border, my mother would have to leave her children behind for now. She had no other choice. If she was determined to give her children a better life, this was the sacrifice that had to be made. With a shattered heart, my mother prepared to leave behind the life she knew and loved and her babies--the only ones she had left to live for, and embarked on a solo journey toward the land of promised opportunities.

As I think about that day in my mother's life, I cannot begin to imagine what it must have been like to say goodbye to her young children without knowing for certain what the future would hold. Those final gut-wrenching minutes of clenching them and putting on a brave face as she explained why she must go. Asking the older ones, who were no more than babies themselves, to look after the little ones until she could come back for them. She comforted them with nobody to comfort her or ease her pain and doubt, because she knew all too well that her journey was dangerous, which meant there was a possibility she would never see her babies again. What would become of them if she could not keep her word and return for them as she was promising she would? The thought must have been unbearable, but she knew this was the only way.

The unfortunate reality is that women like my mother, who are determined to make the journey to the land of opportunity, become sacrificial lambs who risk their lives to embark on a journey with the promise of returning for their children. Yet as we know, far too often and in many tragic cases, they don't ever make it at all.

But thankfully, she did. Make it, that is.

After weeks of arduous and brutal traveling by land through the vast country of Mexico, including much of its harsh and unrelenting deserts, my mother arrived in Tijuana, the final destination before crossing over into the U.S. Her coyotes, the masterminds behind what I call "operation crossover," gave her final instructions on how, when, and where her crossing of the border would go down. I picture it being a lot like taking a deep breath before plunging into a cold body of water. Although it was nothing short of challenging, crossing the border in those times was not nearly as dangerous as it is today. This was long before human trafficking, Immigration & Customs Enforcement (ICE), and cages. If you were caught illegally crossing the border in those days, border patrol would detain and process you, and immediately release you back to your country of origin. It was nothing like the horror stories you hear of today. Thankfully, at least not for my mother.

She successfully completed her journey and arrived in California in the early 1970s, making this the first of many new beginnings for her. My mother arrived feeling nervously excited about the future but also saw it as an opportunity to reinvent herself as a single working mother, ready to begin living on her terms and embrace the opportunities she would not have been afforded in Guatemala. Unbeknownst to her, the chapters ahead would come with their share of struggles and tragedies, yet she would somehow find the strength to overcome them, one by one. My mother was a woman determined to do whatever was necessary to accomplish her goal, and even though it would take her a few years to do so, she returned to Guatemala for her children just as she promised she would.

As you can imagine, my mother's journey by land with other illegals and their coyotes was by no means a lavish and luxurious expedition through the countryside of Mexico. But, unwilling to be a burden to anyone, she arrived in California prepared to work as hard as was necessary and quickly found employment as a domestic worker. Having nowhere else to go, she temporarily moved in with her brother, whom she describes as a temperamental man who was not always kind to her. Nevertheless, she was grateful to him for taking her in.

My mother was in her mid-thirties then and, despite being a young widow, she was full of life and subtle beauty, and it was not long before men took notice of her. In particular, there was a man named Leon who was a friend of my uncle's. I'm not quite sure how they met, but I know the attraction must have been instant because not long after meeting, Leon and my mother became romantically involved.

This is where my story begins. You see, Leon is the man who fathered us, my twin sister and me, only to abandon us before we were even born. I hate to introduce my father to you in such a way, but that's how he was introduced to me. As my mother put it, he abandoned us upon her refusal to terminate the pregnancy. *Is that really all,* I wondered, *or is there more she isn't telling me? I guess I'll never know.*

The one thing I know for certain is that my mother was not one to beg. If Leon wanted out, she would find a way to manage without him. As a widowed mother of seven, my mother had to have known that life would only get harder with two more mouths to feed, but that did not stop her from moving forward with the pregnancy, and from that day forward, she became both my mother and father.

" I worked very hard at pretending
to be something I wasn't."

3

I grew up fatherless. It is a truth I was often ashamed to admit. I mean, it's one thing to grow up having two parents who are not together or even to have an estranged father, but to literally know almost nothing about the man who is in part responsible for your existence is a travesty, if you ask me. It didn't help that my mother was unwilling to share anything about him. I had so little to go by that he almost didn't seem real at all. The only bit of information my mother felt comfortable enough to share was his first and last name, that my twin looked like him, and that he was a man of little patience who could be quite moody. Oh, and of course, that he abandoned us before we were born. This is something no child should ever have to hear, yet sadly, so many of us do because not all men who father children are equipped to become dads, so they bail and flee from responsibility. According to my mother, Leon didn't just abandon us, he actually attempted to convince her to terminate the pregnancy altogether. When my mother refused, he left. That was the abrupt ending of their relationship and the beginning of my existence.

Even as a child who could barely understand why adults did what they did, I couldn't help but feel incredibly guilty knowing that Leon left simply because I came to exist. I carried the burden of believing I was somehow partly responsible for his departure and my mother's heartbreak. It is one of the many reasons I grew up never wanting to disappoint her and needing to please her at any cost. This included avoiding asking questions about Leon because even though I felt I had a right to ask, whenever I did ask, I was met with resistance and asked never to mention *that man*. She was so adamant about not ever mentioning him that the mere thought of him often made me feel as though I was somehow betraying her.

I remember being a teenager and standing in the kitchen talking with my mother and twin one afternoon, when suddenly my twin blurted out that one day she hoped to be able to locate our father because she wanted to meet him. I had secretly wanted the same, but I would have never admitted it. Especially not after seeing the look of disbelief and disappointment on my mother's face. My twin was typically the quieter one and I was the one who was always pushing the limits, but even I knew better than to talk about him. I know my twin's intentions weren't to hurt our mother's feelings, but it did hurt her so much that even years later she would still bring it up from time to time.

That is the one thing I did feel was unfair about my mother. Her refusal to address, or even just talk about, the trauma of Leon leaving her while she was pregnant caused her to project her anger onto my twin and me any time we mentioned him. I also think a part of my mother wanted us to feel the same anger toward him that she did, but how can you be angry at somebody who only lives in your imagination? Even though I knew the circumstances were different, I found it incredibly unfair that my other siblings got to openly talk about their father, while my twin and I were forbidden to talk about ours at all. I never did tell my mother this, but her unwillingness to share anything about Leon made it impossible for me to feel confident because I lacked self-identity. I felt as though I was only a part of a whole, an incomplete version of myself.

I couldn't understand then that this was about so much more than my mother's unwillingness to talk about Leon. This was about the shame that a woman like herself, who had been raised Catholic, who had saved herself for marriage and had the misfortune of losing her husband, was now a woman who had birthed illegitimate children with a man unwilling to stand by her and unwilling to take his share of responsibility. What kind of man asks an expectant mother to choose between him and her unborn children? I don't blame her for being scorned and angry at him, and I also understand why she felt ashamed to talk about that chapter in her life.

As a kid, however, I didn't understand any of the complicated adult stuff. So there I was, this young and curious girl left with many unanswered questions about my father's identity. The most challenging thing for me was navigating around people's curiosity about my racial identity, because it was obvious I was mixed-race, but I had no clue what races I was a mixture of and, therefore, couldn't give anyone a straight answer. To be honest, I don't think my mother really knew either, and that complicated things for my twin and me because it fueled some of my siblings who deliberately used our dark appearance to tease us and make us feel like less than. In fact, the first time I ever heard terms like *nigger* and *blackie* were from my eldest and youngest brothers who relentlessy used my dark skin against me. People outside my home always told me I was beautiful, but I didn't believe them because within the walls of my home I was constantly reminded that I was different, and it made me feel ugly.

I spent decades blocking the bullying I endured at the hands of my two brothers, and it wasn't until recently that I was able to connect the dots and realize that for my eldest brother, this was a way of breaking down my self-esteem and laying the foundation for others things to come. As for my twin, she didn't endure the jokes about her darkness as I did because she was a little lighter than me, but she endured bullying for a slew of other reasons. You see, it is an unfortunate fact that if you come from a Latino family, you have more likely than not been teased or bullied at the hands of your own family members. What these family members who are supposed to love and protect you do is take the vulnerable parts of you and your insecurities and use them as weapons to tease and bully you. They act as though it's all in loving fun, but it often has the opposite effect and it breaks down your self-esteem to the point that instead of loving the parts of you that make you different, you loathe them, and that self-loathing becomes a part of your identity which leads you to self-rejection. It's quite sad, actually, and I can attest to how much that toxic humor can affect a person's ability to love themselves.

The name calling and teasing was yet another layer that fed my insecurities and fed my need to know more about my father. I figured that if I at least knew what he looked like, I would see the similarities and feel like less of an outcast. I couldn't help but wonder whether I had other siblings who looked more like me. *Would they accept me? Would they think I am perfect in all my darkness? Why doesn't my mother take notice of all the emotional pain that is being inflicted on my twin and me for being different? Why do we have to be punished for simply being ourselves?*

What hurt the most was discovering that Leon had actually made attempts to meet my twin and me, only to have our mother turn him away. I can't recall how or when the subject came up, but by my mother's own admission, Leon had made contact with my uncle because he wanted to make arrangements for us to meet. We were about nine years old then, but my mother turned him away because she felt it was too little, too late for him to come into the picture. I couldn't believe that we had a chance to meet him and my mother robbed us of that experience without ever asking us what we wanted. After she shared this with us, I was angry with her for some time. *How could she do that to us? How dare she not ask us what we wanted?* I had so many questions and all of them would go unanswered because she thought she knew what was best for me. I was angry and yet I couldn't express my anger for fear of hurting my mother's feelings. *Why do I always feel the need to put other people's feelings before my own? Don't I matter too?*

I became so tired of being questioned and feeling ashamed about not knowing my father's identity that instead of admitting that I had no father, I began telling lies. I decided that I'd tell people that my father was my siblings' father, my mother's deceased husband. It was an easy lie to tell because all my life I had heard stories about him and what he was like, and I felt like I actually knew him. So I went with it. My mother even encouraged it. One afternoon, I walked into the dining room where I found my mother hammering a nail into our dining room wall. When I asked what she was going to hang up there, she very proudly responded that she was going to hang up a picture of my father. Surprised and confused, I asked whether she had found a picture of my father and how come I hadn't seen it. My question must have stopped her in her tracks because she put the hammer down, slowly turned to me with an annoyed look on her face, and very sternly replied that it was not a picture of *that man* she was putting up, but of her deceased husband. Infuriated, I reminded her that he was not my father, to which she responded that as far as she was concerned, he had not only been her husband but the father of *all* her children, so I might as well call him my father. *Is she actually giving me her blessing to lie? Perfect.*

I liked this version of my story and for a moment in time I got quite comfortable in telling my lie. The best part for me was that it was sealed with a kiss from my mother and all. This made me feel less guilty and made my story that much more believable. Mostly, I liked how confident it made me feel to act as though I knew exactly who my father was--to have a face, a name, and a story to go with it. You have no idea how many times I sat at our dinner table staring at that black and white photograph of a well-groomed man in a suit and tie, daydreaming about the imaginary father I could say

I shared with all my brothers and sisters. This made me feel like a part of a whole family, complete with a mother and father. How beautiful that fantasy was.

I worked very hard at pretending to be something I wasn't. At first I thought I was doing it to avoid being rejected by my peers, but it was hardly about that at all. What I was doing was perpetuating my self-loathing and rejecting myself for everything I actually was: an illegitimate daughter of a man who didn't want me and a sibling to my brothers and sisters who sometimes loved me and sometimes made me feel like the half-sister. Just as Leon had rejected me upon learning of my existence, so too was I living in self-rejection.

It took decades of soul-searching, spiritual healing, therapy, and so much other self-work (including writing this book) for me to understand that Leon's abandonment had nothing at all to do with me or with me not being enough. My story was simply meant to start out the way it did in order for me to go in search of myself and learn to decipher the code to my own happiness rather than searching for it in anybody else. Yes, my arrival into this world was unplanned and unexpected, but I know now that I was a creation of love and by no means an accident. My parents were two imperfect humans who came together for a purpose, to create my sister and me, and I'm grateful that from the moment my mother learned of our existence in her womb, she fought for our lives regardless of her circumstances and regardless of whether Leon would stay or go. Many women in her shoes, especially having seven other children to care for, would have absolutely chosen the man over their unborn child(ren). But not my mother. She chose my sister and me, and for that, I will forever be indebted to her.

Despite Leon's absence in my life and the emotional pain he caused my mother, I have come to make peace with him and honor him as my biological father. Without him, there would be no me. That is a truth I can never deny, nor do I want to. Through his absence I learned a great deal about myself and the depth of my mother's love for me, and I choose to see the beauty in that.

Today, I no longer live feeling ashamed about growing up fatherless, because it isn't something to be ashamed of, nor is it a reflection of my self-worth. If I am truly to love myself for who I am, fatherless and all, I cannot at the same time hold any resentment toward Leon for deciding to walk away. In fact, I no longer look at his departure as abandonment because I can see now that he gave me the only thing he had to give, his absence. He wasn't equipped to be the father I would have needed him to be, and for that I forgive him. As far as I'm concerned, I would rather have had an absent father I never knew, than to have had a father I loved who was in and out of my life because he was emotionally unavailable.

Besides, as you will later come to find, Leon does eventually make his way into my life in the most unexpected way.

4

 My childhood memories come in waves, some which are beautiful and some not so much. I'm easily frustrated when I search my memory bank only to get lost in a deep ocean of darkness. Memories that my twin can recollect with ease, I struggle to find at all. I have come to depend a great deal on her memory for me to know what happened throughout different periods of our early childhood. Although I appreciate her willingness to share it all with me, I can't help but feel sad that those memories she's recounting are her own, from her perspective, and not as I lived and experienced them for myself. The hardest thing for me is accepting that if it were not for my sister, I would have little memories to go by and the happy chapters of my childhood would feel as though they never happened at all.

 Apparently, blocking periods of one's life is not uncommon for adults who've experienced trauma early in their lives, because it is part of the flight or fight response which the brain activates to help us process the pain. In my case, even though I know I lived many happy moments throughout my childhood, the memories of them are so deeply buried under the rubble of my trauma that I have difficulty accessing them. I have spent the last several years in the trenches, with a steel shovel in my hand, digging out and confronting my unhealed wounds so that I can pull the goodness out and begin to bury the bad stuff.

 Something which I can actually remember, and brings me much joy, is the memory of growing up a twin. It's difficult for me to put into words what it feels like to have someone to grow up with at every stage of your life, but what I can say is that there is a bond so deep it would be difficult, if not impossible, to break. After all, she is the one person with whom I've shared some of my greatest and happiest moments, as well as some of my darkest and most painful moments.

Now don't get me wrong, it hasn't always been peachy keen between my twin and me because our personalities have always been quite different. While she is taller in stature than I am, she tends to be a quieter and more sensitive person than me. For the most part, we balance each other out, but every now and then those differences can also be the root cause for our sibling rivalry. Yet, no matter how much we bickered, we have always been inseparable. How could we not be when, since childhood, she has been a constant presence in my life. She was my first playmate, companion and confidant, and my favorite dance partner because we knew all the same dance moves. Whenever we'd have gatherings and music would start playing, we'd goof around and make up silly dance moves that would get everyone laughing. She is an introvert and I am an extrovert, which has always made us the perfect blend of both sugar and spice.

Speaking of balance, my sister and I are Libras who came into the world by way of c-section in a Los Angeles hospital one late Tuesday night in the fall of 1973. It should come as no surprise that the section of our birth certificates where the father's name goes was left blank. At birth, we were given our mother's maiden last name, Moreno. Eventually, upon moving to a predominantly white neighborhood, my mother insisted that we use Leon's Jewish last name in order to be more accepted by our teachers and peers. Kids at school found my white name and the contrast of my dark skin to be very confusing. I mean, let's be honest, if you saw the name Karen Katz, you would never guess it belonged to a little dark multiracial girl who spoke Spanish and ate black beans and tortillas. Going by that name was as foreign to me as Leon was, but we went along with whatever our mother thought was best for us. By the time we got to middle school and had moved to a predominantly Latino community, my twin and I begged our mother to change our last name back to Moreno, a name which seemed more suitable for two brown girls like ourselves. She agreed and we were grateful. I also felt a weight lifted off my shoulders because, as I came to find, growing up fatherless is not uncommon in the Latino community and therefore, I didn't have to lie about it anymore. Isn't it sad that it took me living amongst other fatherless kids to finally feel like I belonged? Isn't it sad that it's a reality for far too many of us? I certainly think so.

When it comes to twins--yes, even fraternal twins--people get very curious. Wherever we went, if people discovered we were twins, they would always ask us a ton of questions, from who was a better student to which one of us was born first. You name it, we were asked. In our case, I came into the world first. My sister followed seven minutes later. She was a perfectly round bundle of joy, and I was a tiny firecracker who was probably born kicking and screaming. From our personalities to our physical appearances, we have always been recognizably different in almost every way--polar opposites, some might say. Yet no matter how different we are, we have always been very close. Even though we were always bickering, if one of us got into any trouble, the other would cry. Our mother fully embraced being a twin mom. She enjoyed dressing us alike until just before we started junior high. Yes, we were the dorky girls with matching outfits. I remember how wonderful it felt to finally reach an age where I could dress in whatever style I wanted rather than having to look like my twin's carbon copy. In some ways, it felt a lot like we were our mother's real-life dolls and she enjoyed playing dress up with us. It was fun but also a little depressing for a young child who just wanted to be carefree, run around, and play with other kids without a care in the world. My twin and I were always the kids at parties who were dolled up in fancy outfits and dressy shoes, hardly ever getting to play or run freely like the other children. Instead, we sat there next to the adults like dolls on display, bored out of our minds, feeling like outcasts and wondering when we could go home. I know my mother only did it because she was proud to show off her beautiful twin girls, but it was such torture for us.

My mother worked a lot, which meant that we were usually left in the care of my two older sisters who attended night school in order to help our mother with childcare during the workday. They were wonderful to us and showered us with lots of love and affection. One of my first memories of my early childhood is of my eldest sister, who was the first of my siblings to come from Guatemala. She used to love nibbling on my pudgy nose and chubby toes, and she'd always find my reactions amusing. Her laughter was infectious. She was always nurturing, gentle, and patient with me. Just the way a child can get attached to their nanny, I became extremely attached to my eldest sister. I vividly remember when she became a mother for the first time. I was six then and not ready to let her go. Boy was I angry at her! At first, I didn't want to go anywhere near my nephew because I thought of him as the kid who'd stolen my second mother from me. But he sure was cute and, over time, I realized he wasn't so bad and I grew to love him like a little brother.

On those rare occasions when my mother had a day off, she filled our home with the sweet aroma of her cooking, which she took much pride in. My mother made everything from scratch, down to the batter she deep fried her chicken in. Every meal was a feast and every bit of it was made with love. I can remember looking up at her as she cooked with her apron on, cutting, chopping, blending, and roasting whatever was on the menu for the day. I was a picky eater and my mother was not the type to force us to eat anything we didn't like, so she would always prepare something special on the side for me. My siblings did not like that our mother did that. In fact, on a few occasions while my mother was at work and we were left in the care of my older sisters, I remember tossing eggs between the wall and stove because I didn't like my sister's cooking. I got caught, of course, and in a lot of trouble with my sister, but I didn't know what else to do!

Besides loving to cook, my mother loved music, which meant that there was always something playing in the background. From traditional Guatemalan *marimba* to *cumbias, romanticas* (ballads), *y viejitas pero bonitas* (oldies but goodies), my mother had an eclectic taste in music that shaped my world. Over time, she grew to love English music, but her first love would always be the Spanish music that connected her to her roots in Guatemala. If a song she loved came on the radio, she would grab my sister with one hand and me with the other for us to dance with her and twirl us around. We grew up loving to dance because my mother made it a part of our daily lives.

Despite working long hours, having a house full of kids and having a long list of daily to-dos, my mother managed to keep a tidy home. She'd always say that it was better to keep a clean house than to have to deal with the embarrassment of excusing our mess if unexpected guests showed up at our doorsteps. Personally, I think cleaning was a coping mechanism for my mother, to help keep her sanity and relieve some stress for having a house full of people to provide for and to tend to with no time left for herself. Sadly, this was a time when self-care was not encouraged or made a priority for anyone, especially not a single mother of nine.

I can certainly attest to the fact that growing up in a house full of people with little to no privacy felt incredibly overwhelming and I eventually developed anxiety, which I wasn't even aware I had until just recently. Much like my mother, I too seek refuge in cleaning. At family functions, whenever I start feeling overwhelmed, I'll go into the kitchen and start cleaning up, doing the dishes, sweeping the floors--even if I'm tipsy. My sisters used to think of it as rude, but they couldn't understand that was never my intention. It was simply how I coped with my anxiety and still do to this day. The only difference now is that I am aware of my anxiety and have learned healthy coping mechanisms that help me be more present rather than feeling the need to escape.

    I think that if it had always just been my mother and her children living together under one small roof, it wouldn't have been so bad, but that was hardly ever the case. Our small place was almost always invaded by some distant relative or complete strangers (to me, anyway) who would come over from Guatemala in need of a place to stay while they got on their feet. Some would stay only briefly while others would get very comfortable and completely overstay their welcome. The worst kind were the ones who would leave without ever giving my mother a proper thank you for feeding them, doing their laundry, and putting them up for free. It was frustrating to watch people take advantage of my mother's kindness, generosity, and hospitality. More so, it was incredibly uncomfortable to live in a household that often felt chaotic and out of control because people were either coming to live with us or showing up at our doorstep unannounced, expecting my mother to feed and entertain their entire family. Of course, my mother always did as she felt was expected of her, but it felt incredibly intrusive to me and I cannot recall a single occasion where my mother asked if we were okay with this type of living arrangement. If she had ever taken the time to ask, she would have discovered how detrimental this was to my mental health, and I would venture to guess that my siblings felt the same. But as they say, *silence is golden*--because as a child you are to be seen but not heard.

My saving grace was the few glimpses of alone time my twin and I got to spend with our mother. Although we were very close to our older sisters who helped care for us, our mother was our everything and we were very attached to her. She was so beautiful, elegant, loving, and incredibly affectionate, and she always made an effort to carve out time for my twin and me. Her love language was *acts of kindness*, which meant that if she had a little extra money or could afford to do something nice for us, she would take us to Disneyland or to the Million Dollar Theater in downtown Los Angeles to watch a beloved Spanish-speaking clown named, Cepillín. I vaguely remember our trips to Disneyland, but I definitely remember jumping out of my seat to dance along with Cepillín who, looking back, was a silly looking clown.

My mother and sisters worked as cleaning ladies in a motel owned by my aunt's partner. It was located somewhere on the westside of Los Angeles, and seeing as my mother and sisters didn't have a means of transportation, my mother jumped at the opportunity to move closer to work when a two-story rental property became available across the street from the motel. The house seemed enormous to me; it was certainly larger than any place we had ever lived in. But as big as it was, it lacked warmth and never really felt like home to me. Come to think of it, of all the places I have ever lived (and I have lived in many), very few actually ever felt like home. They say *home is where the heart is*; I guess that's why the only place that ever really felt like home was my mother's arms.

These are the few and scattered memories I am able to pull from my mind as it relates to my early childhood. The next vivid memory I come to is being six years old, wearing a dress with a beige faux fur coat, with my doll in my hand, surrounded by family saying goodbye at Los Angeles International Airport. Apparently, we--my mother, two sisters, and two brothers were preparing to board a flight leaving for Guatemala where we were going to live indefinitely.

"...bigotry and colorism seem to know no bounds, even amongst families."

5

My twin and I sat next to our mother on the big plane flown by Pan Am, an airline that no longer exists other than in period pieces depicting life in the 1960s and 70s. This was a time when the only men on the flight crew were the pilots; the female flight attendants were called airline stewardesses and were a well-regarded part of the flight crew. The pilots wore dark suits with hats and the stewardesses dressed in skirt suits, with scarves around their necks and a matching hat. They appeared so refined, perfectly manicured and incredibly welcoming with infectious smiles that seemed to be painted on their faces. I was in awe of them and I definitely added this to my when-I'm-a-big-girl-this-is-what-I-want-to-be list. We were served a full meal and got to drink whatever we wanted. It all seemed so fancy and high-class for a kid who didn't have a luxurious upbringing. Oh, and believe it or not, it was still legal to smoke in airplanes then, so the armchairs were equipped with silver-plated ashtrays.

Because we were the youngest, my mother wanted my twin and me close, so we sat in the seats next to her. I observed my mother and could see she had done this before. She was always well prepared with a bag of tricks to fix any situation that might arise. She used to get nauseated on flights and carried slices of lime, which she proceeded to pull out of her hardcover burgundy toiletry case. It was then that I noticed her soft manicured hands and polished nails. My mother had never been rich in her life, but she had an elegance about her. She wore a corduroy blazer over a silk top with her Jordache jeans and heels. Her silky black hair and made-up face were right on point. She was a lady with great taste and always looked her best. People often thought we came from money even though half the things we wore and owned were from thrift shops. But, as my former boss once told me, when you have good taste you can make ten dollars look like a million bucks, which is exactly what my mother did.

In the seats next to ours sat my two eldest brothers and one of my sisters, all three who were in their teens. The youngest of the boys stayed with our aunt, and my older sisters worked, so they stayed behind. They did come with us to the airport to say their goodbyes, because back in those days, the entire family could walk through the airport to the boarding area. I was excited for my first-ever plane ride, but I was very sad to have to say goodbye to my sisters who I had never been apart from since being born. I remember the heaviness I felt in my heart and since then, I find airports incredibly nostalgic because I remember how it felt not knowing when I would see my loved ones again.

At this point you're probably a little confused, wondering why the heck we were going back to the country my mother had journeyed so long and hard to leave many years before. As I see it, she was acting in love and taking a leap of faith, but here is how she told the story.

When my mother first brought my siblings from Guatemala, she knew it would take them time to acclimate to a new way of living. Life was different in the U.S. than in Guatemala, especially for the two older boys who had gotten used to having no real adult supervision while my mother was away. They had freedom there that they didn't have with my mother around. She made her expectations clear, set ground rules for them to follow, and fully expected them to obey her. She had heard stories of immigrant parents who'd lost their kids to gangs, violence, and drugs, and she wanted to do whatever was necessary to keep them from going down that road. Her only request to them was that they stay in school or get a job or do anything they wanted as long as they stayed off the streets. She warned them that should they start veering from this plan, she would not hesitate to send them back to Guatemala.

My brothers must have thought our mother was bluffing or that she wouldn't dare send them back to Guatemala after how hard she had worked to bring them over, and they carried on with their shenanigans. Particularly the eldest who tended to be more defiant, temperamental, and incorrigible. It was as though he was angry or carrying resentment but instead of voicing it, he acted out. I was too young to understand the scope of what was happening, but it was obvious he was on the wrong path and this had my mother worried. She was left with no choice but to intervene.

This is how we came to be on that plane with one-way tickets headed for Guatemala indefinitely. It may sound drastic, but it was my mother's radical act of love for her sons. She was determined to save them from themselves at any cost.

Upon arriving in the very early morning, we were met by my mother's cousins, the children of my mother's only living aunt. As we walked through the airport, it was plain to see that we were in a very different world here, because everything looked, felt, and smelled quite different than in California. Instead of luggage, some people carried large boxes held together with rope, and some were dressed in regular street clothes while others wore traditional Indigenous attire. At only six years old, and never having traveled anywhere before, I was in a total state of culture shock. Not to mention the fact that my mother seemed to have turned on her *chapina* switch, which I hadn't really seen before. *Chapina* is a slang word used to describe a Guatemalan female, and my mother was playing this role to a tee. She suddenly appeared to be very

Guatemalan, speaking in a tone and using slang words that made her sound different to me. I realize now that although this was a side of her that was unfamiliar to me, Guatemala was home to her, and here is where she was most herself. As strange as it felt, it was fun seeing my mom in this new light.

We made our way to my great-aunt's house where we would be staying until we found a place. She lived in a community called *La Colonia Primero de Julio*, which is located in *la zona 5* (zone 5) just north of the capital. The *carreteras* (roads) were very bumpy and the *camioneta* (our transportation) seemed very squeaky, but we managed to make it just fine. My mother was quite fond of her aunt, who was her mother's only living sibling, and must have been young when my mother was born because my mother referred to her by her first name.

From the moment I met my great-aunt, I didn't get a warm feeling, but my mother loved her dearly and that's all that mattered. She was a fair-skinned woman in her late fifties who lived with her husband and their adult son in a relatively nice neighborhood. I don't know what my great-aunt's husband did but I knew he was the sole provider, and he must have done well for himself because, unlike some of my mother's acquaintances whom we later visit, they seemed to be able to afford a nice lifestyle. I mean, my mother once took us to meet an acquaintance of hers who lived in a hut without running water or electricity and would have to cook in the same room that she lived and slept in over firewood. *I don't see a kitchen sink or a bathroom. Where does she wash her dishes or shower?* I'm guessing she must have had access to an outhouse for restroom use because there was no bathroom in sight, at least not that I could see. I had never truly seen poverty until then and I realized how fortunate anyone who could afford to live in a house with a kitchen and bathroom really was. These are luxuries not many are afforded, yet they are basic life necessities most of us could not live without.

Although only one of my second cousins lived with my great-aunt and uncle, she had a few other adult children, three daughters and two other sons, although one of them was out of the picture. When I asked her why he wasn't in the picture, my mother explained that he had moved to the U.S. to get away from his family because they had always rejected him for being dark; they were ashamed of his dark skin and dark features and had treated him poorly because of it, so he decided to leave and never return. I couldn't believe that family would do that to family, but that was only because I was too young to recognize that even within my own family structure, the color of my skin was used to describe me and/or make me feel less than, but we will get to that later. What I will say for now is that bigotry and colorism seem to know no bounds, even amongst families.

This also makes me think about a story my mother once shared about my grandfather, her father. As my mother told it, the story goes that he had been born the darkest in his family, and because of it, had been on the receiving end of ridicule and rejection. His upbringing had been so painful for him that he deliberately married my grandmother who had a very fair complexion with sandy brown hair and light eyes. My mother was the eldest, and while she was dark herself, she was a shade my grandfather was accepting of. He adored my mother and showered her with much love. Sadly, the same could not be said for her younger sister, who was born with much darker skin and kinky curly hair. Unwilling to accept my aunt, my grandfather accused my grandmother of being unfaithful and left her because of it. After abandoning my grandmother, he quickly moved on and married another woman who also had light skin, except she had blue eyes. When they were newlyweds and had not yet started their own family, my mother enjoyed the best of both worlds because she was adored by her stepmother as well and got to spend a lot of time with them. That all changed when they had their first child together. According to my mother, he became so distant that he even stopped providing my grandmother financial support for their children. My mother, who had been so attached to him, was devastated. Especially because his lack of financial support caused her, her mother, and her siblings to endure many hardships. Things became so difficult for them that my grandmother had to find different ways to make money, sometimes as a seamstress, and even washing other people's laundry, just to be able to buy my mother necessities such as shoes for school. I can still remember how much my mother cried as she told me this story. It wasn't until she began working with a therapist that she even remembered those painful memories, which she didn't realize were still very painful for her to recount.

The irony is that much like what happened with my grandmother, the children my grandfather fathered with his second wife all took after him. Not a single one had been born with light skin or features like their mother. Although my mother never stopped adoring her father, I know she held a lot of resentment toward him and she hardly ever talked about him. I never got to meet either of my grandparents, but I have wondered whether my grandfather would have disliked me for being dark. It really doesn't matter now anyway, but it's a thought that has crossed my mind.

The only grandparent figure I did actually meet was my mother's stepmother, who was a poor reflection of what I always envisioned a grandmother to be like. I can still see her passed out cold on the couch--still sitting--so inebriated she could hardly open her eyes. Apparently, after my grandfather's passing she began drinking heavily and became an alcoholic. Her children seemed to enable her by buying her the alcohol and the woman was just wasting away one swig of her bottle at a time. It was really quite sad and although I never got to know her because I only met her a few times, I did feel quite sorry for the old woman who was passed out on the couch with her disheveled white hair, her skirt over her knees, her stockings showing, and a bottle of vodka in her hand. *Mi mamita linda--my beautiful mommy, I will forever wonder what you must have felt seeing the woman your father abandoned you for in such a state. Was she worth losing you? Did you feel as sorry for her as I did?*

I don't know whether it was a generational issue or whether it is a common occurrence in Latin American countries, but alcoholism was prevalent amongst the different people in my mother's extended family. It was something I wasn't used to seeing because my mother hardly drank at all. I think the most I ever saw my mother drink was during our time in Guatemala, because every time we were around her family she was pressured to drink. Although my mother never drank with the intention of getting drunk and she would take her time sipping her drinks slowly, I can still remember the first time I saw her drunk. I hardly recognized the person she had become in that state. *I don't like seeing you this way, Mami! These people may be your family, but they are practically strangers to me and if you keep getting drunk, who's going to look after us? I don't feel safe with these people. I don't even know them.*

Sadly, it seemed no matter where I turned, alcohol was a problem. My great-aunt's husband was also living with alcoholism, and as much as everyone tried pretending it was normal, there was nothing normal about it. Every day when he arrived home from work, still wearing his suit, he would walk into the kitchen, grab a tall bottle of vodka and a glass, and he would sit there until he was so drunk he'd barely make it to their bedroom. I found it so interesting that in the mornings when he was sober, he was a serious man, suited up, looking clean and proper; yet, once he got home and sat on that one chair at the kitchen table, he would drink himself to oblivion. While his daily drink of choice was vodka, he was a heavy drinker of any alcoholic beverage he could get his hands on. But that tall, slim, clear bottle seemed to be his faithful companion every evening after work. While their life may have looked perfect on the surface, there was clearly a lot of emotional torment going on within. Personally, I think it was the shame and guilt of having pushed away their first-born son for having been born dark, because he would sometimes cry or mumble things under his drunken breath. It was quite sad to see but impossible to ignore. During our stay in their home, my great-aunt was obviously embarrassed by her husband's behavior, but she enabled it too. Perhaps it was because he was a functioning alcoholic and was still a good provider despite his illness.

My great-aunt was not a warm person at all, and she was also a control freak; I think mostly because she couldn't control her husband's drinking. And during our stay with her, she even controlled my mother's parenting, especially as it related to my twin and me. She criticized my mother for "spoiling" us, and constantly voiced her disappointment in my mother's weak approach to our finicky eating habits. Unwilling to accept that my mother did not believe in forcing us to eat anything we didn't like, especially when it came to more traditional Guatemalan foods that we weren't used to eating, my great-aunt began force-feeding us. When we cried and refused to eat, she would demand that my mother leave the dining room and would force us to sit at the dining table for hours in order to teach us a lesson about what happens to spoiled little girls who don't want to eat the food that is being offered to them while there are kids starving everywhere. My twin and I spent many long evenings going hungry and crying at the dinner table as the food on our plates got progressively colder and inedible. Being in a new country, surrounded by people we hardly knew, and being forcefully introduced to foods we were not accustomed to eating was torture, and I longed for the day when it would come to an end. Eventually, my mother was allowed to come get us off the table, but the damage was done.

These experiences were so traumatic for me that still to this day I cannot eat much of the traditional Guatemalan cuisine my mother took such pride in cooking for us; it just brought too many sad memories. I can still remember staring at the bowl of *caldo* (stew) watching a thick layer of lard form as it cooled down, with tears in my eyes and hunger pangs in my stomach. I would sometimes feel such anger toward my mother for not standing up to her aunt and allowing her to treat us in such a cruel and inhuman way. But I knew, even at my young age, that my mother complied out of respect for her elder. This was my mother's only living aunt and she obeyed her as she had been conditioned to do. Thankfully, it seemed as though my mother grew tired and we finally moved out of my great-aunt's house and into our own place. I was relieved to get away from that wicked lady.

We moved into a home in a nice middle-class neighborhood. It was a two-bedroom house on a cobblestone street with no yard to play in but large enough for us to live comfortably. When we arrived, our furniture that my mother had shipped over from California was there waiting for us. Having our own belongings helped make things feel a lot less strange and a lot more like home. I also really liked that in this house, my mother made food I actually liked. As is pretty common in Guatemala, we would make daily runs to the local *mercado* (street market) to purchase groceries and produce my mother would need for the day. She also hired a milkman to deliver freshly squeezed milk to our doorsteps every morning. I didn't like it much because it was fresh cow milk, which meant it was not only lukewarm but would also have milk fat around the rim of the glass bottles. There was a lot of adjusting for me to do in this new world.

Seeing as we were there to stay indefinitely, enrolling us in school was the next logical step. My twin and I spoke Spanish because it was our first language, but my mother really wanted us to also be able to fluently read and write it as well. I'm actually really grateful she did that for us. My Spanish skills have been instrumental in both my personal and professional life, as well as my education. We got enrolled at the local public school which was run a lot like a private school; we wore uniforms and the school staff seemed like drill sergeants to me. The school faculty also felt that in order for my twin and me to become more independent of each other, it was in our best interest to be separated and assigned to different classrooms. We were fine with that, although it seems my sister got the better end of the deal with a much nicer teacher than the one I had been assigned to. My teacher was more like an evil drill sergeant who was grouchy and short-tempered and didn't seem to know how to speak without yelling. My mother had warned us that teachers in Guatemala were allowed to use corporal punishment in the classroom, but I never thought I'd see it with my own eyes.

    One morning, a girl who sat in the back of my classroom eagerly asked to be excused to go to the bathroom. The teacher seemed annoyed at this request, ignored her, and kept writing on the chalkboard going over our lesson for the day. After about the third or fourth time she had asked, the girl was visibly uncomfortable and began wiggling in her chair. She pleaded to be excused to no avail; the teacher thought she should have gone before class instead of disrupting it. I felt so bad for this girl and seeing the defeated look on her face was disheartening. Then, without saying another word, her shoulders dropped as she began to urinate right there in her seat. We were six years old, what did the teacher expect? She became infuriated to see what was happening and marched over to the girl. Upon reaching the girl's desk, she pulled her up by her hair and let her have it. Humiliated, the girl just stood there with tears running down her face and urine streaming down her legs. It was devastating to watch. To add insult to injury, the teacher made her sit back in the chair until break. The chair was still dripping with urine. I was horrified and told my mother what I had witnessed.

Furious to hear this, my mother marched into the classroom the very next day and warned my teacher that if she ever touched me, she would have to answer to her. My mother may not have been brave enough to stand up to her mean aunt, but she sure stepped up for me in school. It was something she would do many more times in the years ahead, and I loved her for it.

I hadn't realized how immensely popular my mother was in Guatemala; she was a woman with many admirers, and those who were still single came out of the woodworks to court her the minute they heard she was back in town. Although she didn't seem interested in dating, she did enjoy having friends to talk with, whom she never kept secret from us and would even invite over for coffee or a drink. We saw nothing wrong with it because we were always present. There was one gentleman in particular who we actually liked and hoped she would date; he was handsome, a professional, very respectful, and well spoken. He would show up with flowers and other little gifts for her and made her smile a lot. *I think my mother has a crush on him, even if she never admits it to us. Maybe she thinks we're too young to understand that adult stuff, but I am smart enough to see she likes him. She is too shy to talk about love interests, past or present, but I wish she would be willing to share because I know she's more than just a mom. Aren't moms and dads also allowed to have crushes?* I only wish my brothers would have been as open to the idea of my mother finding love again as we were, but they weren't and they made it abundantly clear.

One evening, while my brothers were out, my mom's friend was over for a visit. They were sitting on the couch in deep conversation when my brothers walked in and completely lost their minds seeing him sitting there. I felt that the younger one of my brothers was just following the older one's lead, but together they were really awful to my mother's guest; they rudely interrogated him, said awful things to my mother, and eventually ran the nice man out of our house. He made several failed attempts at reasoning with my brothers, but they were unwilling to listen and began throwing rocks at him. My eldest brother even threatened to hurt him if he ever showed his face around our house again. If I was embarrassed by my brothers' behavior, I can only imagine how humiliated and infuriated my poor mother must have been, but she still chose to do nothing about it. I'm sure they felt great satisfaction knowing our mother's friend never came back to visit again. Regardless of what my brothers thought, I always felt our mother was deserving of love and companionship. I only wish they would have been more selfless and less selfish; it was the least she deserved.

As our lives continued on, we all fell into a comfortable routine. It's actually surprising how easy it was to adapt to life in Guatemala once we got our own place. Perhaps it was because we were so young and as long as our mother was around we were happy. She actually seemed more at ease here because she wasn't working all the time. Here, she was so much more present and available to us, which was a welcoming change.

My mother would even have my twin and me baptized again in Guatemala. She wanted us to feel connected to her homeland and we were not opposed to it because we knew how much it meant to her.

Then, just as we were warming up to the idea of staying in Guatemala permanently, our circumstances quickly took a turn, and all the joy we had been experiencing came to a screeching halt. Life as we knew it would never again be the same.

"I don't know how my mother did it, but she somehow always remained an indestructible pillar of strength."

6

Although it had been several months since we had moved to Guatemala, it seemed as though my mother was not fully committed to the idea of making our stay permanent. I'm guessing it was in great part because she was missing my siblings who had stayed in California. Having our family split again couldn't have been easy for her, especially because she had always been very close with my sisters. Communicating with them was also a challenge because, for whatever reason, our mother never had a phone installed in our house. This meant the only two options my mother had to reach my siblings were to either write them a letter or wait until we visited my great-aunt so we could borrow her phone. The calls must have been expensive to make because whenever my mother made them, they were usually very brief.

One afternoon, when we were all home, my mother received an urgent piece of mail, also known as a telegram. To this day, I don't exactly know what the telegram read, but I know she received bad news from back home.

The next part gets a little blurry for me, but here is what I can remember.

There had been an accident back home and my mother needed to return to California immediately. There was not much more she could tell us for now. She must have been able to make special arrangements to fly home because she was issued an expedited passport and prepared to leave. I never imagined this meant that she would be leaving without us, but it did. My two sisters and I were to stay in the care of our great-aunt and our brothers would go to their paternal grandmother's ranch. Until that moment, my twin and I had never been away from our mother for more than a few hours while she worked; and now, here she was leaving without being able to give us any definite return date or a time frame of any kind. I can still see her standing in my great-aunt's living room crying, pleading with her to take good care of us, and my great-aunt assuring her we were in good hands. As life would have it, the same story my mother had lived years prior when she prepared to leave her babies was now repeating itself as she prepared to leave us.

She left one October day around my twin's and my seventh birthday. With all the chaos and confusion surrounding the news she had received, we had all forgotten it was our birthday at all. She would be gone so long that she would also miss Christmas, New Year's Eve and Day, and my sister's fourteenth birthday in mid-January. It was the longest few months of my life and, with each passing day, life only seemed to get more difficult to bear. Although my great-aunt had promised our mother she would take good care of us, she would soon begin to show her true colors, especially as it related to my twin and me. She was, after all, the same woman who had no relationship with her eldest son because of the darkness of his skin, and my twin and I, with our own dark skin, were reminders of that. She made it so obvious that our presence displeased her that we would often just choose to stay locked in our room, which only made us feel more isolated and alone.

Our big sister, who was just a kid herself, tried her best to keep us distracted with storytelling and reminiscing about our days together as a family in California, but we could only escape our reality for so long. The truth is that we had received no word, either by mail or phone, since my mom had left and we were too young to understand why we couldn't be with her. *How much longer will we have to live here? Why can't she send for us? What is holding her up? Mommies aren't supposed to just leave their kids.* With each passing day, we would eat less, experience less joy, spend less time outside; we were becoming depressed and our aunt showed us little kindness or compassion. We hated everything about being there and not knowing when our mother would return for us only made our sadness more profound.

Then finally, after several months of being away, my mother returned for us.

I remember what it felt like to run into her arms that day. It was a lot like coming up for air after having been underwater for too long and letting out a sigh of relief because you didn't drown. Do you know that feeling? I remember not wanting to let her go for fear she would leave me again. I didn't think I could survive being away from her again. I cried. We all did. We wept for how much we had missed being away from her for all those months, for all that we had endured in her absence, and because by the look of her, we knew that whatever it was that had kept her away from us for so long must have been awfully terrible. You could see the pain and sleepless nights in her face; she was thinner than ever, with her cheeks sunken in and dark circles under her eyes. The heaviness she was carrying was palpable. Somehow, however, she still managed to look like an angel from heaven. With tears in her eyes and a warm smile on her face, she said there was no reason to cry because she was with us now. She commented on how much we had grown and promised not to leave us again. In her absence, my twin and I had turned seven, and our sister fourteen, but it felt as though we had aged many more years.

She had returned, but it wasn't to stay, it was to take us back to California. She had to return as soon as possible and we had little time to make the necessary arrangements to get us all back home.

During my mother's absence, we had not been allowed to go home and I don't know whether my mother had made arrangements for anyone to check in on the house at all. As you can imagine, we were excited to finally be back in our place and start preparing for our return to our first home: California. Unfortunately, our excitement quickly came to a halt when we walked through the doors and discovered our home had been burglarized. There were papers and things thrown everywhere; the house was a complete mess. Not that anyone would expect burglars to be nice people, but they literally showed us no mercy and took everything of any value we had--down to our dolls. As if we had not already endured enough, we also had to endure this violation of our privacy. It was such an awful and vulnerable feeling. We were actually scared to even be there but we couldn't just abandon the house and run.

As devastated as my mother was, she did not have it in her to fight the battle of pursuing an investigation. If anything, this only made it easier for her to sell what was left. All she really cared about was getting us home to California as quickly as possible.

I don't know how my mother did it, but she somehow always remained an indestructible pillar of strength. The more life knocked her off her feet, the more determined she seemed to get back up. She was not only resilient but incredibly forgiving of others. Despite knowing how much our great-aunt had mistreated us during our time in Guatemala, and even though she had some inclination that her aunt may have had some involvement in the burglary, my mother never held it against her. Years later, after my great-aunt became widowed, it was she who was in dire need of a place to stay and arranged to come live in California with us. My mother graciously and lovingly opened the doors of our home to her, allowing her to stay as long as she needed.

I, for one, was happy to be leaving Guatemala; I could see why my mother had left that place to begin with and I hoped I would some day forget all about it. As much as my mother loved her country, I hated everything about it--the food I was force-fed, the bigotry and unkindness displayed by my own relatives, the distance it drew between me and the people I loved--all of it. That is all my child self remembered and held on to about our time in Guatemala, and I swore never to return to that dreadful country which had brought my family and me such pain and misery. I was elated and ready to say goodbye to all of it.

As we prepared to embark on our journey home, my mother delivered more devastating news. It turned out that the two-story home we had been living in before leaving for Guatemala, the home two of my sisters had remained living in, had burned down due to what appeared to be an electrical malfunction. Although both my sisters had been home at the time, only one was able to jump out and be rescued by firefighters. The other, who was seven months pregnant at the time, was not able to jump out from the second story window and never made it out. By the time the firefighters were able to gain access to the second floor and reach my sister, she had sustained third-degree burns throughout her entire body, yet miraculously, both my sister and her baby survived. All those months my mother had been away from us she had spent at my sister's bedside, waiting for her to make enough of a recovery to return for us. She never expected to be away as long as she was, but she couldn't leave our sister's side until she knew for certain that she was stable.

You are so strong, Mamita. You must feel so sad that my sister is hurting so much and you can't make her all better. Now I understand why you've been gone for so long. My poor sister, she must be in so much pain. I'm so sad for her. To this day, I cannot begin to imagine what it must have been like for my mother to have seen her daughter come close to death. More than anything, I cannot imagine what it must have been like for my sister to endure such emotional and physical trauma, to lose her physical identity, and not even be able to enjoy the birth of her first child.

I cannot fathom how much grief my mother must have been feeling, because despite not losing my sister, my mother had lost so much in such a short period of time. Between the house fire in California and our home being burglarized in Guatemala, she lost so much more than just things. She had lost decades of memories, letters, photographs, and precious mementos which were irreplaceable. How she was able to hold it together, I will never truly know.

While I was sad to hear my sister had been injured, I was too young then to truly comprehend the gravity of this devastating news. And I wouldn't understand until the moment I saw my sister for the first time in the hospital, which had become her home since the accident. Between that and learning that we had no home to go to upon returning to California, it felt a lot like I was getting my head dunked under water without a chance to catch my breath. At this point, the only thing we had left was faith. Faith in God and faith in our mother who, more than a matriarch, was a warrior ready to take on the world and whatever situation came her way. She may have been breaking on the inside for all we knew, but she never showed it. She cried every now and then, but she somehow always got back up, ready to carry on and stay the course. Every difficulty we endured made us stronger for her and for each other. We were by no means a perfect family, but we were surviving together, pulling each other through and leaning on each other along the way. That is what my mother always wanted: for us to be a united family regardless of the circumstances. And we did our best to remain that way until her passing.

Being that my twin and I were American born, my mother informed us that she would be arranging for us to fly home and have somebody pick us up at the airport. She and my siblings would join us at a later time because they had to travel by land, as they were not able to reenter the U.S. legally. After having been separated from our mother for all those months, we couldn't bear the thought of being separated again and we begged her to let us stay with them. She wasn't thrilled about the idea and, to get us to change our minds, even warned us that this journey would be long and difficult. But there was no changing our minds. Although nothing could have prepared me for the journey we were about to embark on, nothing seemed more painful to me than being away from my mother. I also know that I wouldn't be half the person I am today had I chosen to take the easy route home. I may not be an illegal immigrant, but I am proud to say I walked alongside my mother who was. I got a first-hand experience of what her journey toward the American dream looked like from her perspective. I wouldn't trade that for anything in the world.

7

Have you ever taken your index finger and traced it over the lines of an image or over the wrinkles of a person's face or over the lines imprinted on the palm of somebody's hand, trying to read the map of their story? Those are the images which come to mind as I prepare to take you through the journey I embarked on with my family from Guatemala through Mexico into the United States. This was a truly life-altering moment which not only tested my mental and physical endurance but also shaped me into the person I am today. I invite you to sit back and get comfortable as my seven-year-old self guides you and provides details that may be somewhat blurry or out of order, but which I hope you will find as remarkable as I did.

The first memory my mind comes to is being on a bus, riding through different towns of Mexico. Along the way, my mother told us stories of the different places we passed through, like Guanajuato, where there is a museum which holds the bodies of people who died and were mummified during the 1800s after a cholera outbreak. *Wow, mummies! I've heard about mummies before. They scare me because I can't see their faces. Mamita, how come I'm not allowed to ask you all the questions I want, like when did you first see the mummies? Have you ever touched one? Do they scare you as much as they scare me? You're always telling me not to ask so many questions. My teacher told me it's okay to ask questions, but you always make me feel bad when I do. Why? Don't you see I want to know everything about you because you're my favorite person? Is it because you want to keep it a secret? Why do big people keep so many secrets? It's so unfair. Am I supposed to grow up keeping secrets too? I don't want to.*

When we arrived in Guadalajara, we went to a cathedral to pay a visit to Santa Inocencia (Saint Innocence). She was a young girl who was killed by her father after going behind his back to receive her first communion, which he had forbidden her to do. Since her death over three hundred years ago, the young girl's body, which is preserved in wax, lays in rest in a glass case and is dressed in ceremonial clothing. Being a woman of strong faith, my mother asked us to pray to this saint because she was known to make miracles happen. *Please help us get home safely. I'm scared.*

While in Guadalajara, my mother had arranged for us to stay at the home of a former neighbor from the states who also owned a home there. Generously, the woman allowed us to stay for a few days which gave us an opportunity to rest, do laundry, and regain energy before continuing on; the road ahead would be the most challenging yet.

In order for us to stay on schedule, we stayed only a couple nights. When the time came for us to head out, we must have left in the middle of the night because it was still dark out. The street the house was on was lined with trees with an abundance of leaves which gently rustled with the light breeze. As the branches swayed, they almost appeared to come alive and it scared me a little.

The next thing I remember is my family sitting on an open platform of a train station. It was still dark out, but there were other families and individuals there waiting, some sleeping, some awake, and a few kids running around. As my mother covered us up to keep us warm, she began instructing us on what we would need to do next. She said there would be a train coming and we needed to get on it; however, it would never actually come to a complete stop, which meant that we had to jump onto a moving train.

Hearing this made me feel scared and suddenly my stomach felt sick. How were we supposed to jump onto a moving train?

Was that even possible? My mother must have seen the frightened look on my face because she quickly assured my twin and me that everything would be okay; in fact, she promised it. She said the train would not be going too fast, but it would be going fast enough for us to need to run in order to keep up with it and be able to jump on board. As soon as we heard the train coming, we were to get up and start running as fast as we could until one of the adults could grab hold of us and get us onto the train. She said it was very important that we follow her instructions and stay close to her because if we didn't keep up, we could be left behind. *What if one of us doesn't make it onto the train? What if we get separated? I don't want to do this. Please, I want this to stop! Don't make me do this!*

As the sound of the unsuspecting freight train got closer, my heart began pounding so hard I thought it would jump out of my chest. Hurriedly, everyone picked up their belongings and prepared to run. Some people panicked and forgot to take their belongings, while others were carrying too many things to run fast enough, but my mother grabbed us and we all just ran. As the train caught up to us, those running ahead threw their belongings onto the freight car, grabbed hold of the rails around the openings, and quickly jumped in. The men who made it in first began helping the children and women jump on board.

I did just as my mother had instructed and ran as fast as my tiny legs would allow, holding on to her hand as tightly as I could. At first, I was running forward but looking backward to see how far behind us the train was. As we ran, my mother said I should never look back because it would only slow me down. Those words would become embedded in my brain and be my guiding light throughout my healing journey. While my logical brain understood what she was saying, fear had set in because I didn't want to be the one left behind. I began to cry but I never stopped running. Suddenly, I was being lifted up into the air, then arms grabbed hold of me and placed me inside the freight car. I cannot tell you who made it onto the train first or last, but I can say that my mother and her children all made it into the train safely. *Thank God.*

Next, I remember my family and I walking through the desert. Although we had gotten an early start, the sun, relentless and unforgiving, seemed to be wearing us down with every step we took. There was no shade in sight, just a wide and open space that seemed endless. We had several people in our group, and everyone seemed equally exhausted and in desperate need of water to quench our overheating bodies.

By some miracle, we came upon a home in the middle of this vast desert. As we got closer, my mother walked ahead of us and knocked on the door. She didn't want any of the men to knock for fear the homeowners would think they were being robbed or something. We did look a bit disheveled and I could see why someone might think that. A middle-aged couple came to the door and my mother asked if she could please have water for her thirsty family who had been walking for some time. I'm not sure how many others like us they had seen before, but without hesitation, they generously shared. I have always believed in miracles and as far as my seven-year-old self is concerned, that couple was heaven-sent and God had been looking out for us that day, because they could have just as well not been home or been unwilling to share their water with us. People often make fun of me because I am always looking for ways to conserve water and I cannot stand watching people run faucets or hose down their driveways, or anything which is wasteful of water. But that's mainly because I have personally experienced what real thirst feels like. When you have gone thirsty in the middle of a blazing desert, you very quickly become aware of just how precious water really is.

We walked until we reached what appeared to be a truck stop for drivers to rest, eat, and refuel. The adults gathered to talk business with some of the truck drivers and made arrangements for them to take us into Tijuana, Mexico. This would be our final stop before crossing over the U.S. border into California. My mother was no stranger to this arena, that was plain to see. She carried herself with confidence and knew exactly what to ask and what to say. It was a dangerous mission to carry out with young children, but she was fearless and handled herself like a pro. Traveling in this manner required that we put our lives in the hands of complete strangers, which was frightening but we had no other choice. During my time in Guatemala, I caught glimpses of graphic news reporting about violence committed against unsuspecting women and children. I was scared to think how vulnerable we were to be trusting these men who were complete strangers, yet I had no choice but to trust that my mother knew what she was doing.

The adults decided it was best for us to split up into different trucks to avoid overcrowding and attracting attention. My mother asked us to follow her as she walked behind the driver who would be transporting her, my two sisters, my cousin, and me. The driver was a middle-aged man who spoke softly and said he had a family of his own. This gave me comfort and I could see that it also put my mother's mind at ease. Nevertheless, she never left us alone or took her eyes off us at any moment, especially not my big sister who was now a young lady.

Our driver gave us a quick tour of his trailer, which had an extended cab making it a lot roomier than it appeared from the outside. In the front were the driver and passenger seats. Immediately behind that was a long back seat that had been converted into a sleeping area equipped with blankets and a pillow. He had pictures of his loved ones taped along the interior wall of the extended cab. The third compartment was accessible only through a side door outside the truck. It was a small enclosed space with a tiny window that was about the size of a 5x7 picture frame. He explained that for most of the ride we would be able to sit in his sleeping area, but eventually, we would have to move into this small compartment when we reached the inspection point. He warned that while we were in there, it would get hot due to lack of ventilation but we had to be as silent as possible to avoid getting caught.

We drove the rest of the day, into the evening, and overnight. My mother seemed to have stayed awake all night. When morning came, the sun was already beaming and making its presence known. There was not a cloud in the sky and it got warm pretty quickly. We pulled over. The driver turned to us and said we had come to the point where we would have to move into the enclosed cab with the tiny window. As we proceeded toward the cab and he opened the door for us to get in, I began to panic. The thought of us all being crammed into such a small space made me afraid. *What if he forgets to come get us? What if it gets too hot in the cabin and we can't breathe? I don't like small crowded spaces. This feels more frightening than jumping onto a moving train.* As soon as we were all in, crammed like sardines, the door closed and then locked. We must have looked frightened because my mother asked us not to be afraid and assured us everything would be alright. It was very warm in that cab and with five bodies crammed tightly, the sweating began almost immediately. The only thing that gave me hope was knowing that if anything bad happened, at least we were together.

The loud engine turned on and we drove some distance away. With the cab being right up against the large engine, combined with the hot air coming in through the 5x7 window, it was difficult to breathe at all. We began gasping for air when my mother suggested we each take turns putting our faces up to the window to try to catch our breath. *I hate everything about this space. It's loud and hot and I want* out. *I hate how helpless it makes me feel.* We were suffocating and all we could do was pray that this would be quick.

The truck slowed down and eventually came to a stop. My mother whispered for us to sit still and be as silent as possible. We heard the driver get off the truck; there were different male voices and footsteps going around the semi. I couldn't make out what they were saying but I prayed the driver would hurry. *What would be worse, suffocating to death or getting caught?* We must have only been there minutes but it felt like an eternity. Our mother began pulling us so that we could take turns breathing through the window. After a couple deep breaths, she would pull us down for the next person to go. *I wish I had the window all to myself, but it wouldn't be fair to the others. I don't know which is worse, being deprived of air or water, but this trip is most certainly testing my endurance.* A few seconds later, the engine turned back on and we were driving away. *Thank you, God.* As soon as it was safe to do so, the driver pulled over, let us out of the coffin--I mean cabin, and asked us to move up front where it was nice and cool for us. I had never felt so relieved.

I don't remember arriving in Tijuana, but I know we had not been there long when my mother sat my twin and me down for a conversation about what the next leg of our trip would look like. She explained that because the two of us were born in the U.S., we would be able to return without having to cross the border as illegals. This meant we would once again be split up from her, but she promised it would only be for a few days until she and my siblings could join us. The thought made my stomach turn. *I don't want to be away from her but I also know I can't take any more of this trip.* I was, after all, only seven years old.

My mother said she had made arrangements to have my brother-in-law pick us up and take us to our aunt's home where our older sister was staying. We would remain there until my mother could join us and find a place for us to live. I hated this plan but my exhaustion had overpowered my will to stay with her and I didn't protest. *I am ready for life to feel normal again. I am ready to be a kid without a care in the world.* Besides, I loved my brother-in-law and was happy he would be coming for us. Technically, he wasn't married to my sister, but he had been her longtime boyfriend and was the father of their newborn daughter, which made him family to us.

My mother entrusted him with us because in all the time he had been with my sister, he had always shown my twin and me a lot of brotherly love. He was a few years older than my sister, came from a good family, and was always kind and generous with us, taking us places or spoiling us with kind gestures; we loved him and were happy he was coming to take us home. I use the term "home" figuratively because in reality, we had no home to return to.

When my brother-in-law arrived, my mother handed him our bags and documents and prepared to send us off. She explained that we may be stopped at the border by officers needing to ask a few questions, but we were not to worry because all we had to do was tell them we were American and that our brother-in-law was actually our brother who was taking us home after visiting family. During our time in Guatemala, my twin and I had stopped speaking English, but my mother stressed the importance of answering all the questions only in English in order for the officers to see that we were telling the truth. In retrospect, I also realize that she had instructed us to say he was our brother because it probably would have looked quite suspicious that a single male who drove a glittery turquoise van with fuzzy dice on the rearview mirror was with two seven-year-olds unless there was a perfectly good explanation for it.

Although she had promised it would only be a few days, having to say goodbye to our mother once again was something that never got easier to do. Nevertheless, I put on a brave face for her, took my sister's hand, and off we went.

I wish I could tell you that we rode into the sunset with our mother meeting us soon after to live happily ever after. But that was far from what was to come. In the year that followed, we faced many hardships, including being separated once again because we were homeless and bouncing around different homes. We were depending on people's charity to help us get by, because not even family is always willing to take in a woman and her nine children. It was quite a difficult time, filled with a lot of uncertainty and instability, but we had made it this far and all we could do was keep moving forward.

8

My mother and siblings arrived in California several days after my twin and I had arrived. Because it had been weeks since my mother had visited my sister in the hospital, she was eager to pay her a visit immediately upon her arrival and asked my twin and me if anybody had taken us to visit her, but nobody had even so much as mentioned it. She was disappointed to hear this, but to be honest, there was nobody who could have prepared us for that visit better than our mother. This was a delicate situation that needed her gentle approach, especially because we were so young. It's no easy task having to explain to a seven-year-old that her sister, who was one of the most beautiful and strong beings she had ever known, was now unrecognizable and in such a fragile state.

My mother was eager to see my sister, so we prepared to go to the hospital the very next day. My sister had been moved out of intensive care and she shared a room with other patients, which meant that she could only receive a few visitors at a time. On this particular day, my mother decided she would only take the three youngest girls with her--myself, my twin, and my fourteen-year-old sister. This would be our first time seeing our sister in close to a year, since that day at the airport when we left for Guatemala. It was a weekday which meant that anybody who could drive us was working, and since my mother didn't drive, we took the bus. *I never liked public transportation because buses were always too cold and smelly. I didn't know how far we were going, but this bus ride felt like it would never end.* I could have dozed off, but instead, I daydreamed about reuniting with our sister. She had not only helped raise me but had always shown my twin and me tons of love and affection. *I couldn't wait to tell her that I finally got to sit up in the front seat of her boyfriend's van when he picked us up in Tijuana.* My mother's voice interrupted my daydream when she said we were almost there. I was nervously excited to finally get to see my sister and also really happy to be getting off that cold, smelly bus that made me nauseated.

As we walked toward the entrance of the enormous hospital, my mother stopped us. She wanted to have a talk with us about a few things before we went in. First, she reminded us that this was a hospital with many sick patients and not a playground, and we were to be on our best behavior. Many of the patients there were burned, and we were not to stare at them because staring is rude. Next, she warned that our sister looked very different from what we remembered, because the fire had changed her. She had lost both her hands and some facial features, and she was wearing something over her entire body to help keep her skin in place and heal her wounds. She said that even though our sister looked very different on the outside, she was exactly the same person we loved on the inside. Most importantly, we were not to cry in front of our sister at any time, no matter how badly we wanted to. Doing so would only hurt her feelings and we needed to be strong for her. There was nothing to be afraid of and we should go to her if she asked us to. Lastly, our mother said she would understand if we needed to step outside the room to cry. She never made us feel bad for not being okay but needed us to be strong for our sister's sake.

Recalling that difficult conversation my mother was forced to have with us is difficult for me to do without wanting to cry. I wished then, as I do now, that it had all been a bad dream we could have all woken up from. But it wasn't a dream at all. It was our reality. I couldn't understand how God could keep letting so many bad things happen to my family, but there we were, surviving the unimaginable. Perhaps that was the point of it all.

I would do as my mother asked; I would be a big girl and put my feelings aside for the sake of my sister who needed us to be strong for her. This was a defining moment in my life. It felt as though I had suddenly become an old soul trapped in a young girl's body; I was only seven years of age, but I had already lived a lifetime.

After her speech, my mother asked if we were ready to go in. We said yes and made our way into the big hospital room. On our way to my sister's bed, we passed a crib that looked like a metal cage. There were machines all around it. Inside was a boy who couldn't have been more than two years old. All I could see were his eyes, nose, lips, and swollen ears. He was wearing a compressor from head to toe to help keep his skin from expanding, but the parts that weren't covered revealed extensive injuries. Quietly, my mother explained in Spanish that he had been there for some time and had been burned in scalding bathwater. The sweet boy immediately recognized my mother, smiled at her, and greeted us with a soft hello. As we got closer to his crib, he stuck his hand out between the bars, reached out as if wanting to touch us, and excitedly continued to say hello. His voice was raspy, and I couldn't help but wonder if it was from the screams he must have let out in pain. My mother walked up to him with a warm smile on her face, gently reached for his hand, and in her broken English said, "Hi. How are you?" She looked over at us and asked us to come closer and join her in saying hello. We did, and the boy was visibly happy. This small act of kindness made him giggle with joy and melted our hearts. From that point forward, if he was awake whenever we walked by, we were sure to stop and say hello. No matter how bad things sometimes get, there are always others experiencing far greater suffering than our own.

When we reached my sister's bed, our mother walked ahead of us as if she were preparing to introduce us to somebody we had never met before. My sister appeared to be taking a nap. We stood briefly in silence. My sister must have felt our presence because she woke up and seemed happy to see our mother standing next to her. It had been several weeks since they had last seen each other. They embraced and my mother mentioned that she had brought us along to see her. While lying flat on her back, my sister turned to face us, said a happy hello and asked us to come closer. *She was right, my mother. My sister did look quite different, but somehow, I knew she was there.* She seemed so happy to see us. She said we had grown so much and asked if we remembered her. *Of course I remembered her. How could I not? The familiarity of her voice resonated in my heart. Her deep brown eyes were the same ones I had looked into hundreds of times before as she held me and nurtured me while my mother worked. As different as she now looked, all I saw was the sister I had always known: the one I loved and who loved me so.*

It wasn't the happy reunion I had been daydreaming about on the bus ride over, but it was still beautiful. My fourteen-year-old sister, my twin, and I had been so brave in that moment, never shedding a tear--at least not in front of our big sister. The first chance we got, we asked to be excused; we made our way to the restroom and the moment the door closed behind us, we began to cry. Just as we had done so many times in Guatemala, the three of us stood there in the middle of that beige, cold bathroom and consoled one other.

After we had shed enough tears to get us through the rest of the visit, we gathered ourselves and returned to the room with smiles on our faces. I realize now that as brave as I thought we were at the time, nobody had been braver than our big sister. After all, it was she who had endured all that emotional and physical pain and whose life had been altered. Not for a moment but forever. She not only had a long road of recovery ahead, but she had to learn to face the world, which could be so cruel because people would never let her forget that she was different. There were countless times we were out for a family outing, attempting to get through the day as normally as possible, when we would see people staring, pointing, or making comments like, "Must have been a bad accident." If we found those experiences difficult to endure, I cannot begin to imagine what it was like for my sister who had and has to live with that every day of her life for the rest of her life.

Since the day I came into the world, I have always known that I was surrounded by strong women, but none were stronger or braver than my mother and sister. What they each endured and had to overcome was more than most could even dare imagine. Witnessing their resilience and perseverance was awe-inspiring without them even realizing it. My sister's determination taught me valuable life lessons, like not focusing on my limitations but living beyond anyone's expectations, including my own. She may not have ever told me to believe in myself, but she certainly set an example of what believing in yourself looks like. I firmly believe that while the accident happened *to* my sister, it happened *for* my family to learn from her.

9

As my sister's health improved, our lives started to regain some normalcy. She was released from the hospital, and we were all able to come back together as a family. We moved into a small rental on the westside of Los Angeles. We didn't have much and were scraping by, but that didn't matter because we were all together again.

We started getting back to celebrating the good things in life: the holidays, my sister's fifteenth birthday with a traditional Latino celebration known as a Quinceañera, and my older sister's wedding engagement. Things were definitely looking up, and it was a nice change of pace to have those beautiful moments to celebrate and look forward to again.

This was around the time my sister's case that stemmed from the house fire settled. It was the best possible outcome that could have come from such a tragedy. Obviously, there was no amount of money in the world that could have brought my sister back the life she once knew. This would, at the very least, help her provide for her child and live a comfortable enough life. She could now move on with her life, begin focusing solely on her ongoing recovery as well as being a mother to her baby, who was also going to require special needs and attention.

My sister was gracious enough to invest some of her money toward the purchase of a home for all of us to live in. We had been renters all our lives, squeezing into small spaces, hoping our landlords would never discover how many of us there were. We were even homeless. Now, we would have a home to call our own. It was a happy feeling for us all. The best part was that she promised to buy a home large enough to accommodate our entire family. We were grateful because this meant we could finally put down roots and we would no longer have to move from place to place.

This was the most exciting thing that happened to our family in a very long time. It was like starting a new chapter. It was a fresh start. It didn't even matter that we were moving to white suburbia. Well, it's not suburbia anymore because today it's known as the city of Burbank, home to the largest Ikea in North America and several production studios. Today, it is a high-density, diverse city, but in the early eighties, this was a small town made up mostly of privileged white families. We had never lived anywhere so nice. It was a quiet neighborhood in the hills with tree-lined streets and nicely manicured homes. I laugh at the thought of our neighbors watching this huge brown family pull into the driveway. The old man across the street trying to discreetly peep through the blinds, his eyes widening and saying to his wife, "Well Marge, there goes the neighborhood!"

Frankly, we were not the least bit concerned with what the neighbors thought. Are you kidding? We finally had a home to call our own--big enough for us to have our own beds and with more than one bathroom! We had a backyard equipped with a swing set, a fig tree, and a seesaw. It was a palace. More than we could have ever asked for. We loved it! At last, my family who had endured tremendous loss could rejoice. It was all thanks to my sister who had paid a mighty big price for us to be able to afford to live here. At that moment, there was nobody on earth who could steal our joy. Besides, we were as worthy and deserving as anyone to live here.

Living in this neighborhood provided some of my favorite summertime memories, like playing baseball with the neighborhood kids, riding bikes or roller skating up and down the hill, and having neighborhood scavenger hunts where we knocked on different neighbors' houses to collect items on our lists and the first person to collect them all would win. I also really loved that our family would get creative on things we could do together. We went to the lake or the beach from sunup to sundown, went camping, bought junk food and baked treats to take to the drive-in, and played board games for hours at a time. We played everything from *Loteria* (Latino version of Bingo), Bingo, Rummikub, Uno, and Jacks. We didn't have a lot of money to travel far or take weeklong vacations, but my mother and older sisters always found creative ways for us to make amazing memories without having to spend a lot, and you know, they succeeded. To this day, the memories of our fun times still bring a smile to my face, and will forever hold a special place in my heart.

Certainly, life did not suddenly become perfect because we had a home. My mother worried a lot because my brothers worked graveyard shifts which meant they were often pulled over as they drove to or from work. A couple of brown guys driving through a nice neighborhood in the middle of the night was far too suspicious of an act. And if it was the holiday season, forget about it; the cops were definitely getting called to our house because our parties were too loud for this quiet neighborhood. But seriously, you can't kick people out when half the party already lives in the house. It may sound funny, but it's true! If you are a large Latino family and there's a holiday party going on, inevitably the music will get loud; some folks will get a little drunk; and dancing will go on well into the next morning, afternoon, or, if it's a really good party, well into the next evening. If you're Latino, you know what I'm talking about. If you're Latino and don't know what I'm talking about, though,

I'm sorry to say you missed out on a lot of fun times (minus the cops being called, of course)!

After my sister's accident, my mother never returned to work. She dedicated all her time and energy to caring for my sister, my niece, and our household. She had her hands full but seemed happy and at peace those days. More than a mother, she was the glue that held us together as a family and made our house a home, filling it with her love, her contagious laughter, the aroma of her amazing cooking, and the sound of her favorite music playing in the background. She had little downtime with a houseful, but the evenings were her time for *telenovelas* (Spanish soaps). We used to get caught up watching them alongside her, which was always dangerous. If you know anything about *telenovelas*, you know they are a serious time commitment because they run several months. It was not easy having to choose between a nail-biting story or playing outside with your friends. And back then, there was no On Demand, TiVo, or DVR. If you missed an episode, you were left behind and couldn't get in the *chisme* (gossip).

The holidays were an extra special time of year in our home, with our mother preparing all the traditional Guatemalan fixings, like *tamales* (corn-based dough with meat or veggies inside, wrapped in plantain leaves), *rellenitos de plátano* (ripe plantains filled with black beans and covered in sugar), *ponche de fruta* (hot punch made up of fresh and dried fruits), and *torrejas* (a Spanish dessert made with bread in a sweet custard). I can still smell the cinnamon and *piloncillo* (sugar cane) boiling which made the house smell spicy and sweet.

Every morning, my mother's beautiful voice echoed throughout the kitchen: she always sang and hummed while handling all the preparations. As exhausted as she would be doing all that work, she seemed to enjoy it a great deal. I learned to love *café con leche* (coffee with milk) at an early age because of her. Before school, she would set her coffee down on the dining room table and call us over to do our hair. While she brushed or braided, I would take sips of her coffee, which was mostly warm milk. Now, whenever I'm missing her, I make myself a cup of coffee just like she used to make. It amazes me that the mundane everyday things are often the treasures we hold on to the most.

I was a happy camper living in our own home, with friends to play with around my neighborhood and most of my family in one place. My siblings and I were enrolled in what was known as the best school in town. It was just outside our district which meant we had a long way to walk to and from school every day. But hey, after you've crossed a hot desert on foot, anything else is a walk in the park. Very soon after being enrolled, I began to flourish and excel in school. I was involved in everything that didn't require a fee my mother couldn't afford to pay. I was a flag monitor, a tutor, and I volunteered in the library. I took a religious studies class every Tuesday off-campus and also attended an after-school religious studies course at the church up the street from our house. I learned to type in the fourth grade on a vintage metal typewriter, which was really cool. Best of all, I learned to square dance. We would move the desks all around and my teacher would play records for us to dance to. And, if we were really good, we could pick out a troll from our teacher's china cabinet that we were allowed to keep for the entire week. The rule was the better we behaved, the bigger the troll we got to choose. This was exciting stuff, let me tell you. I was a nerd living her best life, and I cannot remember a time I had been happier.

Elementary school was my happy place. There, I felt like I mattered. My efforts were seen and celebrated. This made me feel purposeful. At home, however, things were beginning to unravel for me.

10

We have come to the part of my story I have been dreading to share with you. I have gone back and forth on what exactly it is I wish to say about it. In fact, I have even questioned whether it is important enough for me to share it at all. And then I realized that to not tell it would be an injustice to my story because it is part of me. So here it goes.

I was sexually abused. It is something I can no longer carry in silence or feel ashamed about. Telling you this part of my story is, in many ways, my radical act of self-love because it takes back all the power that had once been taken from me. It also restores the innocence I lost in the process of it all. But more importantly, this is how I get to heal the generational trauma that has plagued my family, and countless others, for far too long. This is me tearing the scarlet letter of my shame off my chest and shredding it into a million pieces because it was placed there by somebody else's doing and not my own.

As I have shared with you, my twin and I are the youngest of nine children. When you are one of many, it is easy to get lost in the shuffle. This is especially true if you have a single parent juggling many responsibilities. Even though it could sometimes get lonely, I never felt neglected in any way. In my household, we never heard the words *I love you*, but we definitely expressed love in other ways. For us, it was through physical affection, which is something that never lacked in our home. My mother was a loving and extremely nurturing person which naturally meant her children would grow to be the same. Hugging, kissing, and sitting on one another's laps or climbing over one another was nothing unusual in our household. Whenever my twin and I were out and about with our mother, we held hands, and that is something that carried over well into our adulthood when we would go out on the town. My brothers were not as affectionate as my sisters. In fact, they had a tendency to be a little rough with us girls and were always horseplaying and roughing us up, which upset our mother. She would constantly have to remind them that we were girls and that they needed to be more gentle with us. For the most part, they listened, but there were days I would go to school bruised up from the punches they would throw as they walked past me. At the very least, it toughened me up.

The eldest of my brothers was around nineteen years old during this chapter of my life. He had gotten into some trouble, which landed him in a detention home for young men. This was an alternative option for high-risk youth to avoid having them placed in jail. This is the same brother who had been straying and was the reason my mother had taken us to live in Guatemala a few years prior. Things had not improved much since our return. In fact, it seemed the older my brother got, the angrier he became, and the more destructive his behavior was. He was my mother's first-born son and she wanted the best for him--as she did all her children--but she worried about him more than the rest of us because it was obvious he was struggling; she just didn't know why. During his stay at the home for boys, my mother made him goodies and we'd visit him on the weekends. It was there where he really began showcasing his many talents, such as his artistry. On his room walls hung amazing murals he had drawn himself; it was plain to see he had tremendous potential--if only he'd chosen to stay out of trouble. My mother always gave him words of encouragement and wisdom and would ask him to take this opportunity to turn his life around. I loved my brother, too. Very much, in fact. I looked up to him. Whenever I saw him, I would jump into his arms, hug, and kiss him as I would my other brothers. That is, after all, how we showed love in my family.

Eventually, he was allowed to return home. My mother was excited to have him back and was hopeful that he had returned with a new outlook on life. On the outside he seemed perfectly fine. We all believed he had turned a corner. But he wasn't okay, and it became increasingly obvious over time.

One summer afternoon, not long after my brother had returned home, everyone had decided to go out for the day, except for my mother. It was unusual to see our house so empty, but it was also nice and quiet. I decided to stay home and keep my mother company. She was usually in the kitchen, which had an open floor plan combining the kitchen and dining area. Because she spent so much time in this part of the house, she had a television set installed there. We'd sometimes sit there to eat and watch her favorite Spanish *telenovelas* or classic black and white films.

Other than the house being quieter than usual, this was a day like any other. I was nine years old and was independent enough to look after myself. I woke up late that day, had breakfast with my mom, and got dressed in my usual summer attire: a t-shirt, shorts, and flip-flops. I had nobody to play with, so it was a lazy day of going back and forth between reading and going into the dining room to watch television with my mother. In one of those instances, I walked in and saw my eldest brother sitting on a dining room chair watching television while my mother prepared something for him to eat. I was happy to see him, and as usual, I greeted him with a great big hug. We played around, and then I jumped onto his lap. We sat for a long while watching whatever it was they were watching at the time. It was something boring, and, still sitting on my brother's lap, I began to doze off.

If only I could go back and change that moment. If only I had never sat on his lap or allowed myself to fall asleep. If only my mother would have woken me up and asked me to go to my room. But I did fall asleep and she didn't question anything that was happening because as far as we were concerned, there was no reason to be concerned. I was, after all, in my brother's arms. We both trusted him because he had done what many predators do. He groomed us. He very patiently built trust and waited for the perfect time to strike. I was so blinded by my love for my brother that I unknowingly and unwillingly became his compliant victim.

What comes next is anything but pleasant.

For what I think was a few minutes, I had actually fallen into a deep sleep on my brother's lap. That was until I was awakened by a strange sensation I had never felt before. *What is this strange feeling in my private area?* I was confused at first and then realized that what I was feeling was my brother's fingers running up and down my vagina, caressing it the way you would the top of someone's hand. My heart raced and I froze in absolute fear. I don't know how he was able to maneuver his hand and position it in such a way that he could touch me there at all, but he did and I didn't know what to do. *Does he know that what he is doing is wrong? That it makes me feel dirty and strange? Am I responsible for this? I mean, I'm the one who jumped onto his lap. Maybe my actions provoked him?* I didn't know. I was too scared and too confused, and nothing made any sense to me. *If this is somehow my fault, how can I get up and tell my mother? What if she blames me? I don't know what to do.* I sat there frozen. *Can he not feel my knees shaking or my heart pounding? I want to run but I can't. Why can't I run?*

Not being able to bear another second of the torture, I wiggled around to reposition myself and somehow got him to move his hand away from my private area. All I wanted to do was jump off his lap and run into my mother's arms. But, as soon as I moved, he got up with me still in his arms and told my mother I'd fallen asleep, and that he was going to put me to bed. I suppose that was as good a time as any to reveal I was awake and jump out of his arms, but my legs were mush and my mind was in a fog. Nobody ever warns you about such things. Nothing prepares you for a moment like this, and I simply didn't know what to do. My mother, also blinded by her love and trust, never questioned my brother. She made no attempt to stop him or wake me up. Still preoccupied with her cooking, she gave him the okay and off we went.

I went on pretending to be asleep, even though I could feel my heart in my throat and tears welling up in my eyes. I hoped my mother was somehow right behind us, following us into the bedroom. What a silly thing for me to think. She wasn't coming because she trusted him. With me still in his arms, he walked out of the kitchen, took a left turn into the hallway that led to the bedrooms, and walked until we came to the first bedroom on the right side at the end of the hall. This was the room I shared with my twin and our teenage sister. I could no longer hear the voices coming from the television in the dining room, and a deafening silence came over the house because everybody else was still out for the day. Hope began to fill my body because I was sure he would put me down and walk right back into the kitchen.

Our bedroom was covered in pink walls and there were three beds total: a set of bunk beds to the left and my big sister's twin bed directly across. Everybody knew that I slept on the top bunk and my twin on the bottom bunk. Just above my big sister's bed was a window that looked out onto the front yard of our house and let in the afternoon light. My brother could have woken me up at that point and asked me to go up to my bed, the top bunk. Instead, he proceeded to put me down on my big sister's twin bed in a very caring and gentle manner. Almost the way a loving father would his young sleepy daughter. I remained still and continued pretending to be asleep. In my head, I pleaded with him. *Please put me down and leave. I don't know why you did what you did, but I don't want you to do it ever again. I don't like the way it made me feel. You are my big brother and you're supposed to love me. You're not supposed to touch me there and do that thing you were doing in the kitchen. Why would you do that to me? I'm your little sister. Please leave so I can be alone.* My thoughts went unheard.

Instead, I could hear him breathing heavily over me and his nose making a kind of whistling sound. My eyes remained tightly shut because this was too awful a reality to face. I could feel myself becoming increasingly afraid of what would come next if he didn't leave. *Should I sit up? Should I say something? What if I screamed? What if he hurt me if I screamed? Would my mother come running? Would she believe me? Would she believe him? I have never been afraid of him but he is really scaring me.* Then I realized he was in no rush to leave at all. As he sat down next to me at the edge of my big sister's bed, I could feel the mattress sinking. *I wish the bed would swallow me whole.* In a very slow and calm manner, he leaned over and began running his fingers up and down my skinny legs, which were exposed because I was wearing shorts. Then suddenly, he took both his hands and tried to pry my legs open.

It was at that moment that I completely left my body. It was as though I was watching this nightmare unfold from the outside in, from over his shoulder. *This cannot be happening. I am a child. Why me? Did he hate me because we didn't have the same dad? Had he done this to my sisters? Where was my mother? Wasn't she wondering what was keeping him? If she saw what he was doing to me, what would she say? What would she do?*

I was suddenly back in my body again, and I knew I could not let him pull my legs apart any further. I was so afraid of what else he might do if I didn't stop this from happening. *I'd rather be dead.* I did the only thing I could think to do which was to stiffen my legs as hard as I could. I know with all my heart that in that moment he knew I was awake. He immediately stopped and sat quietly, as if waiting for me to open my eyes and say something to him. But I couldn't. What was there to say? I was also very afraid of him and he knew it. He had a violent streak and I didn't know what he would do to me if I said anything at all. After a moment of sitting immobile and in silence, he got up in the most unapologetic and nonchalant sort of way. I know he knew I was awake. Yet he still had the audacity to lean over and kiss my bare inner thighs before walking out of the bedroom. I could still feel the moisture of his slobber on my skin. I cringed and felt sick to my stomach.

Too afraid to open my eyes, I kept them shut tightly until I was absolutely sure he was gone. Very faintly, I heard his voice in the kitchen. He was talking with my mother. *How can he talk with her after what he just did to me? How can he pretend he is not a monster?* I began to cry and suddenly the bright day became dark and grey. I curled up into a ball. I was filled with shame, guilt, and disgust. I had never felt so helpless and so alone in my young life. When I finally opened my eyes, I looked around the room and found that everything looked the same, and yet, nothing would ever be the same. This room which had once been my safe haven was now a witness of a crime committed against my body, against my soul, against the spirit of my innocent self. That cloud that had just covered the sun was the same cloud that would follow me for many years to come. As I lay there and stared at the pink walls, a nauseating feeling came over me; they saw what I refused to let my eyes see, and they knew my dirty little secret.

This was a secret I vowed to keep from everyone, especially my mother. Not to protect him, of course, but to protect my mother who had already endured so much pain. The thought of being responsible for any more of her suffering was too unbearable for me to ever consider speaking up. It would not only tear her heart apart but could also possibly tear my family apart if I spoke up.

More than anything, I feared that nobody would believe me. After all, there was no physical proof. It was my word against his. I wasn't known to lie, but I knew my siblings would believe him and not me and would, without hesitation, take his side over mine. If my mother chose to believe me instead of him, it would drive a wedge between my siblings and her, and I couldn't be responsible for such a thing. I had everything to lose and I knew all too well that nothing good would come of me speaking up. I did what I thought was best for everyone. I buried my secret in the deepest parts of myself.

No child should ever have to carry such a heavy burden. Yet there I was. At only nine years old, I made one of the most grown-up decisions of my life; for as long as my mother was alive, my secret would remain in silence.

"...having to also navigate all my hurt feelings and trauma made it easy for me to take my anger out on the only person I could hurt: myself."

11

In the days and months that followed, I went through what I now describe as a mourning period. I mourned the carefree child I had been until then, the innocence of my indiscriminate eyes through which I had viewed the world, and the safety I had felt in the walls of my home and in the arms of my loved ones. I was in a constant state of vigilance, wondering if every male figure in my life was a predator wanting to hurt me or take something from me. Strangely, I also found myself mourning the loss of the brother I had once loved so dearly--the young man I thought I knew, trusted, and looked up to all those years. In an instant, all the love I had in my heart for him ceased to exist, and the only two emotions I felt toward him were absolute disgust and distrust. His sickness and perversion had not only robbed me of my innocence and many moments that could have been joyful but also robbed me of the brotherly love that had once made me feel safe and protected.

Being victimized at such a young age and never being able to vocalize my feelings about any of it caused me to develop unhealthy coping mechanisms. One of the most obvious has been my inability to control my temperament when I feel triggered. It is still something I continuously work through to this day. If it wasn't for prayer, meditation, and extensive shadow work I do each and every day, I don't know that I could be married and have a healthy relationship with my husband. My wounds are still healing, but my inner child can still sometimes show up when she feels unheard, afraid, or in any way threatened. When she feels this way, watch out because we go into the "red zone." This is when I get loud and raise my thundering voice until I feel heard and understood. It isn't something I've ever been proud of, but it is how my unhealed inner child coped with all those feelings she never got to express. My mother would sometimes tell me she couldn't understand how somebody as beautiful as I could be so temperamental. I wish I could have told her; perhaps then she'd understand.

The longer I continued silencing myself, the more my mind struggled and my body began to show signs of stress. I was in a constant state of self-loathing, self-blaming, self-shaming, and self-sabotaging. I hated myself for what I thought I had allowed to happen to me. I hated being his accomplice by not speaking up and possibly allowing him to hurt others. When he eventually fathered a little girl with wife number two, my family would praise him for being a great dad, yet all I could do was pray he'd never touch her. I hated that because of him I was angry and distrustful of everyone. I hated that I spent years perpetuating my own punishment. More than anything, I hated how disconnected I felt from my body--so much so that compliments often felt offensive.

All that hate and anger I was holding inside me was beginning to manifest physiologically to the point that I developed severe IBS (Irritable Bowel Syndrome). I would sometimes go weeks without being able to go to the bathroom. In desperation, my mother would take me from one doctor to the next, only to be told there was nothing physically wrong with me. They would prescribe laxatives which did little to nothing and there were days I was so ill, I could not physically make it to school because I'd barely be able to sit up or walk. My stomach was so bloated I looked like a pregnant child. What my poor mother and all the doctors could not see was that my body was holding space for so much negative energy that it literally made me physically constipated.

Without ever being able to address my issues, the brokenness I felt became my identity. The more I struggled with my health--mental, physical, and emotional--the more I searched for people who were as broken as I was, if not more. In them I saw myself because they reflected my pain back to me.

What made matters even worse, and what took my pain to a whole new level, was getting separated from my mother when I was only thirteen years old.

As I previously shared with you, after the house fire that left my family homeless, my sister bought a home for our family to live in. This living arrangement lasted for several years until my sister met a man she fell in love with. She had met him at the burn hospital where she would still occasionally go to adjust her prosthetics. Although he had also sustained injuries in a house fire, his injuries were not as significant as my sister's. The attraction between them grew quickly and their relationship blossomed almost immediately. Before we knew it, she had moved him in, they were engaged to be married, and they wanted to start a family of their own as soon as possible. I don't know why they were in such a rush, but everything moved rather quickly and she had no problem getting pregnant shortly after their wedding.

While we were all very happy for them, we started to see changes in my sister. She was so blinded by her love for her husband that she couldn't see how manipulative he was, and she did whatever he asked of her. After the birth of their first child, my sister's husband felt our home was overcrowded and he wanted more privacy, so he convinced my sister to move us out. The only two people who were permitted to stay were the youngest of my brothers, with whom my sister had a close bond, and my mother, so that she could help care for their children. Despite being the youngest, my twin and I were no exception, and my eldest sister, who was also married with two young sons of her own, was asked to take us in indefinitely.

I cannot even begin to imagine how my eldest sister and her husband must have felt to be put in that position of being asked to take us in when we were not their responsibility. We had a mother who had given everything up to help care for my sister after her accident, and it made no sense that we, the babies of the family, had to move out when my brother, who was older than us, got to stay. I was so confused. *How is it that my twin and I are always the ones being pushed aside and tossed around as though we don't matter? I get it, we are the half-sisters, but we don't deserve this. Nobody does.*

I remember the day my mother broke the news to me. She pulled me into the bathroom and sobbed, promising me that she had done everything she could to convince my sister to let us stay, but she was too influenced by her husband who didn't want us there. My heart was shattered, but despite hearing this news, I remained strong for my mother, gave her a consoling embrace, and told her everything would be alright. A child should never have to be the one to console its parents, yet it is a role I often played up until the very end of my mother's life.

Being a teenager is challenging enough, but having to also navigate around all my hurt feelings and trauma made it easy for me to take my anger out on the only person I could hurt: myself. Everything I had endured until now--my sexual abuse, my family's rejection, my lack of stability, and everything in between--played a role in making me feel like I was somehow to blame for all of it and I started to become resentful of my own existence.

The hardest thing for me to accept about myself was that my body was beginning to mature in a way that made me feel dirty. I didn't want to be subjected to any unwanted attention. I even failed Physical Education in ninth grade for refusing to change into the shorts and white t-shirt we were forced to wear and run around in. I hated being the subject of cackling and inappropriate gestures so much that I much preferred being sent to the dean's office or to detention. My grades began to suffer as a consequence, but I didn't care anymore.

    Over time, I started noticing that whenever I became stressed out, I would quickly lose weight, and I liked the way my body looked when I was at my thinnest: plain and too skinny for anyone to bother looking at. *Wait a minute, I'm on to something here. If I don't eat, I lose weight, and when I lose weight I appear less curvy. Perfect, I'll take that approach!* That is when my obsession with my weight began. I wanted to be as skinny as I could in order to be as unprovocative as possible, because in my self-blaming, I had convinced myself to believe that my nine-year-old self had somehow provoked my sexual abuse. Between school, dance class, and my part-time job, keeping the weight off was a practically effortless endeavor. Not that I cared, but I was so incredibly thin (weighing well under one hundred pounds) that I was surprised nobody in my family seemed to take notice or ever mentioned it. Perhaps they never noticed because it was the late eighties, when baggy clothes, shoulder pads, and big hair were in style, which made it very easy to conceal the things I didn't want others to see.

    Around this time, I also befriended a girl I met in detention (I'd been late to homeroom one too many times) and I didn't know it then, but she would go on to become a lifelong friend who is, to this day, like a sister to me. We had an instant connection from the moment we met and became inseparable, even passing long notes between classes because I wasn't allowed to talk on the phone when I got home from school. Even though I felt like I could tell her virtually anything, there were some things I was too ashamed to admit even to her. I can still remember the time she told me she hadn't realized how thin I actually was until she saw me in gym clothes. I could have told her then that I hated my body, but I didn't want her to think I was weird for saying that. So instead, I told her I had always been thin, which was true except now I was deliberately not eating to become as thin as possible. She didn't know it then, but that was the idea behind me wearing oversized clothes; I wanted to make everyone think I was healthy when I really wasn't. My life just felt so chaotic and out of control that my weight became the one thing I did have control over, and that made me feel empowered. Although I never identified as anorexic or bulimic, because I never made myself throw up or became emaciated, I did become dangerously thin to the point that I stopped menstruating at the age of fifteen. Believe me, the damage of stress and not eating would eventually catch up to me.

Looking back, I can see this was a time in my life when I was existing and surviving, but not fully living and thriving. I didn't have it in me to nurture any dreams for the future and I only lived in each moment. I couldn't see the bright future other kids my age talked about, like going to college, having a career, and traveling. I didn't even know college was an option for me because nobody ever told me it was--not my family, not my counselors, not anyone. Perhaps it was because they saw in me the same emptiness I saw in myself. I can only imagine what I would have been able to accomplish if someone had taken notice of my pain, had guided me in healing, or just told me they believed in me.

Throughout my various school years, I did have several teachers who seemed to take notice of my gifts and talents, and who would encourage me and tell me to push myself, but they were mostly male and I didn't allow myself to fully trust them. In eighth grade, I had a history teacher named Mr. Eberhard. He was so passionate about history and actually made it interesting to learn, which I appreciated a great deal. On the last day of school, he told me that he couldn't explain what it was about me, but he could see

I had something really special to offer the world. I wanted so much to believe him, but I couldn't allow myself to trust that he wasn't just saying that because he wanted something from me. *There it is again, my pain rearing its ugly head and sabotaging my self-worth. I want to feel worthy of praise, but I don't know how to accept it with an open heart because I fear I will have to give something in return.*

I knew I was smart, creative, talented, and capable of so much, but my lack of self-love and self-esteem didn't allow me to tap into those parts of myself. I began developing friendships and relationships with people who weren't the best influences. My mother would warn me about hanging out with the wrong crowd and would remind me that I was a reflection of the company I was keeping. I refused to believe that and I'd tell her she was being paranoid and that she had nothing to worry about. I could never admit to my mother that deep down inside I knew she was right. And, even though I never thought of myself as a follower, I knew I was lacking direction. That is why I gravitated toward people who were also broken and were doing nothing with their lives, because with them is where I felt most accepted.

What I did have going for me, and was ultimately my saving grace, was that I was never a troublemaker or a drug user. Even though my grades were not stellar (because I spent my first two years of high school doing a lot more partying than I should have been), I was doing enough to pass. If I had a test, I would either wait until after taking the test to join my friends at a party, or if the party was close enough, I would momentarily leave the party to return to school and do what I needed to do, then leave. This isn't anything I'm proud to admit, especially because I had once loved school so much, but this was the road I was on during those years of my life.

From ditching school to teenage drinking and being out in the streets all hours of the night, I was behaving recklessly and I recognize how fortunate I am that nothing bad ever happened to me. I hear of young women having drugs slipped into their drinks or being raped on dates, and with the destructive life I was leading that could have very well been me, especially because I was attracted to troubled boys. In particular, I liked those living the gang life. I didn't look the part of a girl who liked those types of boys. I liked dressing up, not down, and I looked like a preppy girl, not a homegirl. A boy I once dated asked me, "What is a schoolgirl like you doing dating a homeboy like me?" *I really don't know.* I just knew I liked smart guys, even if they were in a gang. Perhaps it was because, like me, they had tremendous potential. Yet just like me, they also lacked self-worth and self-love.

One particular afternoon when I was in ninth grade, I was on my way home from school and happened to walk past an alleyway. I noticed some commotion down the way and as I got closer, I realized it was my good friend who was being jumped and stabbed by a group of young boys carrying makeshift weapons consisting of taped up screwdrivers. I was horrified. All I could think to do was run. I know he survived, but I never did see much of him after that. I sometimes still think about him and wonder whether he ever made it to adulthood or if he ended up in the prison system. After all, the path he was on would only lead to one of those two destinations. A part of me felt like I had let him down, but I also knew I couldn't save him any more than I could save myself.

You would think that witnessing such a thing would have scared me off, but it didn't. I continued dating "bad" boys and making friends with some kids who were up to no good. Come to think of it, I was kind of living a double life because I had two sets of completely different friends. The friends I had in school came from hardworking families, got good grades, and were disciplined even when they were ditching, while my other friends, the ones who would never show up to school, came from broken homes, had little to no parental guidance, and eventually just dropped out. Each set of friendships provided me with something I was lacking, love and acceptance.

When I was a sophomore in high school, my world was rocked once again by the news that my mother had been diagnosed with cervical cancer. She had a benign tumor the size of a grapefruit in her cervix that needed to be removed. Unfortunately, because the tumor was obstructed by vital organs, surgery to remove it was not a viable option. Foregoing surgery meant that my mother would have to undergo intensive treatment to shrink the tumor. Being the fighter that she was, she went all in and submitted herself to a clinical trial through UCLA, which consisted of chemotherapy and radiation therapy and offered a promising prognosis. My mother, who was always a pillar of strength for everyone, was suddenly the one in need. I was scared for her, and for us, but I couldn't let my mind think about what would happen if my mother did not survive this. It was then that I decided to part ways with those friendships my mother did not approve of; it was time to start taking life a lot more seriously.

During this time, I became friends with a young man who was a year ahead of me. He was incredibly sweet, thoughtful, outgoing, and super funny, and I leaned on him for much needed moral support. We didn't have any classes together, so we used to write long letters to each other and exchange them in the hallway between class periods. He was quite the ladies' man, which made me some enemies. I couldn't understand what girls liked about him because I did not find him the least bit attractive. We were both dating other people, but we enjoyed our friendship. We actually found it incredibly annoying that everyone thought we were more than just friends.

I guess everyone could see what was happening. We were two kids and the best of friends falling in love, and we didn't even realize it. This young man would soon become my first everything and my worst nightmare.

"Despite having been raised and surrounded by strong women, sex was an untouchable subject in my family."

12

All my life I have been a hopeless romantic. I have always been in love with love. As a young girl, I enjoyed watching my sisters be courted, fall in love, and get married. It was all so beautiful. I knew my Prince Charming was somewhere out in the world, and that one day he would dance his way into my life, sweep me off my feet, and we'd live happily ever after. Like Patrick Swayze and Jennifer Grey in the film *Dirty Dancing*. My sister even gifted me a life-size poster of Patrick Swayze to hang on our bedroom door. He was dreamy.

In a million years, I would have never guessed my first love would turn out to be a skinny, pale kid from the hood with two left feet and no rhythm. Go figure.

Because we had been best friends for some time, our love was not one of fireworks but rather something that happened subtly and quietly and took us by total surprise. I think what really did it for me was that he had a way of making light of things (perhaps as a coping mechanism to deal with his own family troubles) and being around him helped me forget about everything that wasn't perfect in my life. From the moment we confessed our feelings to each other, we became inseparable and he quite literally became my everything. On paper, we had absolutely nothing in common. He was a total jock with the signature look of a baseball cap, jeans, and a t-shirt, while I was a preppy girl, with my hair and makeup done nicely every day, and my outfits planned out days in advance. Some thought we were quite the odd couple and others thought I could do better. Looking back, I know they were right, but at that time he was my Prince Charming.

He was adventurous, funny, caring and always surprised me with romantic gestures. That was one of my favorite things about him. We lived a block away from each other, down the street from our high school, but he would pick me up and drive me to and from school and work. He always made sure I'd have something to eat, and because he didn't really know how to cook, he would make me peanut butter and jelly sandwiches with chocolate milk. One of my favorite memories is of the time we saved up enough money to buy matching bikes so that we could ride them to the park and have picnics. My most favorite of all is the time he pulled into the parking lot at a strip mall and asked me to wait in the car, his baby blue Volkswagen bug. When he returned, he had a dozen red roses in his hand. For a girl who had never been on the receiving end of such gestures, his thoughtfulness and generosity meant everything to me and falling in love was easy. Before I knew it, I was proudly wearing his letterman jacket and a promise ring with two hearts which represented each one of us. He may not have been the dreamiest guy to some, but to me, he was a dream come true and I loved him in a way I had never loved anyone else.

Sadly, as the novelty of our new relationship began to wear off, our immaturity and insecurities began to surface, and we would argue about just about anything. Mostly, we argued because he was an extremely jealous guy and didn't like that I had male friends, even though he knew them or of them. His jealousy consumed our relationship because he was temperamental, and trying to have constructive conversations with him when he was upset was impossible. He also had a lot of insecurities when it came to my family because he thought we were "white-washed" and snobby, which could not have been further from the truth. I always felt like he was trying to pin me against my family and it caused me tremendous anxiety because he wouldn't drop it. The more we argued, the more heated and intense our fights became.

What I was refusing to accept was that he was so much more broken than I was. His father had died when he was a child and his mother had given him up to her parents, who raised him as their own. He had two sisters he never got to see because they lived in Texas and were being raised by his paternal grandmother, who he hardly knew. He carried a lot of pain and anger because even though his grandparents gave him everything he could possibly want, he didn't have the one thing he really wanted: the love of his mother. Somehow I thought I could give him all the love he hadn't received from her, but I failed to realize that I couldn't give him something I couldn't even give myself. After our fights, which resulted in yelling at each other, he would express sorrow and would endlessly apologize, often with sweet gifts like an ice cream cake with the words "I'm sorry" on it. I'd forgive him, but it would only last a while because eventually the fights would start back up again.

The arguing and fighting got so bad that I felt the only solution was to break up. I couldn't deal with his jealousy and temperament, but I still loved him. Our breakup didn't last very long and, against my better judgment, we soon got back together. At this point, everything intensified: the love, the fighting, and my constant need to prove my love to him so that he would feel secure. It was then that I decided the time had come to show him how much I loved him, and I gave him full access to my body. He was my first sexual partner and while this may be hard to believe, I had absolutely no idea what I was getting myself into. Despite having been raised and surrounded by strong women, sex was an untouchable subject in my family. To go to them and ask about birth control was absolutely out of the question. Being as naive as I was about sex, I asked him what he thought our best birth control option was, and he suggested we use the pull-out method. Trusting and loving him as I did, along with his promises to be responsible, I agreed to it. I figured that between his efforts and my body's inability to menstruate, we would be fine.

Then, during the Christmas break of my senior year in high school, I began experiencing something I'd never experienced before. I felt the constant need to urinate. When I consulted with my sister and friend, they said I probably had a urinary tract infection which is not uncommon when you're sexually active. I was certain they were right. I made an appointment to see a doctor right away. I figured it would be a quick fix.

A couple days prior to my appointment, my family had come over to visit. One of my brothers pulled me aside and asked me if I was pregnant. Appalled by his question, I quickly and angrily said no. He seemed relieved to hear this and, as he walked away, he warned that I'd better not be pregnant. Overhearing the conversation, my mother quickly jumped to my defense and told him to leave me alone because I hadn't been feeling well and had a pending doctor appointment. I loved how she always had my back.

On the day of my appointment, my boyfriend drove me to the clinic and waited for me in the lobby while I went in to see the doctor. She was a Filipino woman who was incredibly gentle and kind with me from the moment I stepped foot in her office; she was almost maternal. During the consultation, she asked me a series of questions, such as whether I was sexually active, what birth control methods I was using, and whether I could recall the date of my last menstrual cycle (which I couldn't because it had been too long). Based on my answers, she asked whether it would be okay for her to run a quick test using a monitor to listen to my womb. I agreed. She asked me to lie down, she moved my top over just enough, poured a blue gel onto my stomach, and began scanning over it with the small apparatus.

The doctor said that based on the look and feel of my belly, she suspected I may be several weeks pregnant. If she was correct, the machine would detect a heartbeat. A million thoughts began racing through my mind and I drifted away. The first thought I had was of my mother. She had high hopes for me and did not entirely approve of my relationship with this young man. She not only thought I could do better but was concerned that he was too controlling of me. The second thought I had was of school. Girls who became pregnant were automatically transferred to a neighboring continuation school. I was a few months away from graduating and I couldn't imagine not getting to walk with my classmates. The third thought was of my boyfriend. I cared for him very much, but I knew our relationship was volatile and I couldn't fathom the thought of raising a child with him. Then suddenly, I was back in the examination room, because the quietness was interrupted by the thumps of a tiny heartbeat. I was, in fact, pregnant.

13

It was a cold winter day in January of 1992. I lay on that examination table attempting to process the much unanticipated news of my pregnancy and I couldn't help but feel ashamed. I had just turned eighteen, I was living under my eldest sister's roof, I was still in high school with only a part-time job and no car of my own; I had absolutely nothing to offer this baby. I was overwhelmed with emotion.

The doctor looked into my eyes, which were overflowing with tears that ran down the sides of my cheeks. With a concerned tone in her voice, she went on to explain that this heartbeat was that of a baby who was a lot farther along than I appeared to be. She estimated I was about four or five months along and would be due in a few month's time. I couldn't understand. I had not experienced even the slightest morning sickness, and here I was being told I was several months into my pregnancy?

Without proper prenatal care and being as underweight as I was, for as far along as I was, I had a lot of catching up to do. She gave me several prescriptions to fill and advised me to get my weight up to ensure that I would deliver a healthy baby.

A sadness fell over me because I realized I had been so disconnected from my body that I had been carrying a child in my womb for months and I didn't even know it. My poor baby had gone unnoticed and unattended all that time, just as I had felt for most of my life. *How could this be?* I walked out of my doctor's office determined to do whatever was necessary to ensure that my baby would be born as healthy as possible.

When we got in the car, I broke the news to my boyfriend; I told him we were expecting a baby. Without pause or hesitation, he expressed his joy and said we'd have to get married. *Married? Wow, take it easy.* First of all, I wasn't even sure I wanted to raise my baby with him, much less marry him. In fact, sitting there, I gave him an out and told him I'd rather he leave now rather than later, because in my opinion, having no father at all was better than having an absentee father. Something told me he wasn't ready for this but he insisted he was. He said he wasn't going anywhere and he wanted to get married right away. Then it dawned on me that he didn't seem the least bit surprised or shocked by the news of my pregnancy. *Why wasn't he surprised?* I looked him squarely in the eye and asked him how it was that he didn't seem the least bit surprised. What did he know that I did not? With a hint of humor in his voice and a smirk on his face, he admitted that he had been trying to get me pregnant for some time and that he was actually surprised it had taken as long as it had.

How is this even possible? I couldn't believe what I was hearing. I reminded him of his promise to take care of us and do his part in ensuring that we wouldn't get pregnant because we weren't ready. We were barely managing to hold on to our relationship and now he wanted us to be a family? He didn't care about any of that. All he talked about was our future, as though I had no say in it. He said he would be enlisting in the military and we would have to get married right away. *I don't want to marry him! I'm not ready for that! I'm not even ready to be a parent yet, much less a wife!* I felt incredibly betrayed and disappointed. The feeling that came over me felt all too familiar, and suddenly I was nine years old and back in that pink room again. I felt violated. Except this time, I wouldn't take it lying down in silence.

I raged! *How dare he make such a decision without ever so much as consulting with me?! This was my body and my life, and all of it would now be altered forever; it was reckless and irresponsible, and I was angry!* I let him have a piece of my mind and it was not a very nice conversation.

This isn't how it was supposed to be. I wasn't supposed to be forced into something I hadn't consented to. And for what? To be trapped into marriage? How could he do that to me? How could he do that to this baby who deserved better than that? Then, as though somebody had poured a glass of cold water over my face, I had a moment of clarity--*I have to accept my role in this. I was partly responsible for being in this position because I could have done more to protect myself and advocate for my body. I could have done what many girls my age were doing and went to Planned Parenthood to get on birth control. Instead, I took the easy way out and opted to believe and trust in him. How could I have been so foolish?* I felt as though once again I had become a compliant victim to a male I loved and trusted with my life.

I sat there in total disbelief, anger, and betrayal. He tried talking his way out of it, but there was no justifiable explanation for what he had deliberately done without my full consent; absolutely nothing he said could right this wrong.

I couldn't look at him. I asked him to take me home immediately because I couldn't bear being anywhere near him. I didn't know it then, but this moment, in the parking lot outside my doctor's office, would be the first of his many betrayals--to my body, to my soul, to all of me.

14

It was only midday when I arrived home from the doctor's office. I was drained, emotional, and extremely confused. What should have been one of the happiest days of my life felt more like the longest roller coaster ride I couldn't seem to get off of. All I could do was touch my tiny belly and pray that despite the uncertainty, my baby and I would be okay.

The first person I saw upon arriving home was my twin. I told her everything that had transpired throughout my morning and admitted how scared I was to tell our family because I didn't want to feel judged. And I especially didn't want my baby to be rejected as we had often felt. She said that no matter what happened, she would support me and stand by my side every step of the way. Her words uplifted and encouraged me, but the good feeling quickly drifted as I heard our eldest sister enter the front door of our home.

As I prepared to break the news to her, I couldn't help but think about the fact that she had made many sacrifices taking my twin and me in all those years prior. I didn't want her to think my situation was a poor reflection on her, much less have her thinking that my child would be an additional financial burden for her and her husband to carry. I was determined to do whatever was necessary to ensure that my child would not be anyone else's financial burden.

Upon entering the house, she walked straight to my bedroom and stood in the doorway. She asked how my appointment had gone and I broke the news to her with a crack in my voice. She didn't scold me or express disappointment, nor did she make me feel ashamed. On the contrary, she looked at me gently and promised everything would be okay. Her only piece of advice was that I tell our mother immediately. She offered to drive me the next morning and be there with me if I wanted her to. I confirmed that I did. I was grateful to my two sisters for their love and support throughout this incredibly overwhelming time.

The anticipation of having to face my mother the next morning was too much to bear and I hardly slept at all. I was afraid, not of her reaction but of breaking her heart. Under different circumstances--like if I had been older, financially stable, and with a boyfriend she approved of--I know she would have been happy for me and accepting of my situation. But this was different and I knew it would not go over very well.

My mother had been expecting us when we arrived. Except this morning, we were not greeted with the usual warm welcome filled with loving hugs and kisses. She must have suspected our reason for being there because she sat facing the opposite direction and refused to look my way. Sitting next to her was my second eldest sister, whom I'd never really been close to because I always felt she was resentful of my existence. She had always treated my twin and me differently, and seeing her there made me feel incredibly anxious because I knew she would express her judgmental disappointment. My mother's reaction riddled me with guilt and shame, but I mustered the courage to sit with my head up high and face them. Unlike my other secret I had been carrying all those years to protect my mother out of love for her, I could not hide this one much longer.

My eldest sister asked our mother to look at me because I had something important to tell her. My mother refused and said that she was listening and whatever it was I needed to say, I could just come out and say it. This was the first time my mother had ever rejected me this way. I was saddened by her indifference but I couldn't blame her for feeling angry and immensely disappointed in me. *Heck, I am disappointed in myself!*

I sat there at a loss for words. My mother was the only person whose approval mattered, yet she couldn't even look at me. The room was silent until my eldest sister spoke up. She informed my mother that we had come there to tell her that I was expecting a baby and to ask for her blessing. Still looking away, my mother agreed to accept my situation but there was one caveat: I would have to marry my boyfriend before the baby was born.

Hearing this, I could not remain quiet. I immediately said I was not interested in getting married, much less having a shotgun wedding. I knew people would talk but I didn't care. The only thing I wanted was to know my family would stand by my side. Her response was that unlike me, she did care about people's opinions of her children, and they would be far more respectful of me if I later chose to divorce than if I simply had a child out of wedlock. There was no compromise; I would either marry him or she would never speak to me again. I'm guessing that at that moment, she was projecting her feelings from her personal experience with my father.

Knowing what I know now, I realize my mother would have eventually come around, but I was desperate for her approval and was willing to do whatever was necessary to get it at that moment. Betraying myself once again, I consented to do something I wish I hadn't done. I agreed to marry my baby's father.

Immediately after agreeing to go through with the wedding, the energy shifted. With the exception of the youngest of my brothers, who stopped speaking to me after the news of my pregnancy broke, my entire family lent their moral support. I had a small civil ceremony on a rainy Friday afternoon in March and an intimate family reception the following day. There is not much to say about this occasion other than it didn't feel like much of a celebration to me. It was awkward and uncomfortable because our families were polar opposites, but I put on a happy face and expressed my gratitude to everyone for their love and support. There was no honeymoon or anything romantic about my wedding.

My now husband moved in with me at my sister's place. He had enlisted in the military and was awaiting his deployment for training, which meant he would be gone for several weeks immediately after our baby was born. I disliked everything about our living arrangement, but I knew it was temporary and therefore tried to make the best of it.

In the meantime, I had school to finish. Afraid that I would be asked to transfer to a continuation school and not get to finish my last semester with my classmates or graduate on stage, I concealed my pregnancy by wearing oversized t-shirts and sweats. It helped that by the time I was a senior I only went to school for half the day because I was ahead in credits. I would stay long enough to have lunch with my twin and friends, and then I'd leave.

Had my life as a newlywed been happier, I would have been rushing to get home every day, but it was quite the opposite. My husband was miserable living with me at my sister's place and he was making my life impossible. He worked, but the minute he'd get home, he would make his discontentment known. He didn't even like to have dinner with my family in the dining room and instead would make me bring his dinner to our bedroom. That not only put me in an awkward position with my family but made me feel isolated from them. His attitude became increasingly aggressive, and what was once only verbal aggression--yelling and screaming--evolved into physical aggression, grabbing my wrists or arms and leaving marks on me. I had never been in a relationship with anyone who was verbally or physically abusive, and I didn't really understand that abuse comes in varying degrees. A person doesn't have to leave permanent marks or bruises for it to be considered abuse.

I was in denial and kept making excuses for him because I wanted to believe that he was just feeling the stress of all the recent changes in our lives. My pregnant state did not make him gentler with me, either. If anything, I feel like it only aggravated the situation, and it wasn't long before the physical violence escalated to more than just arm grabbing and pulling.

The first time it happened was one afternoon when we were home alone. He was sitting on our bed, visibly agitated. Seeing him like this made me sad and I asked what was wrong. He began to cry and said he missed his grandparents and hated living in someone else's home. I reminded him that this was only temporary and that soon we'd have a place of our own. I suggested that in the meantime, he visit his grandparents as often as he liked, even if it meant having dinner at their place. They were, after all, just over the hill. He said it wouldn't be enough for him. He was too homesick and unhappy.

I was so confused by him. It was he who had wanted to impregnate me. It was he who had wanted to get married. So here we were doing everything he had wanted and now he was going to complain about it? I expressed my frustration which led to an argument that quickly escalated. He got his keys, packed his belongings in a bag, and started to walk out the door. I followed him and pleaded with him to be rational and think about the consequences of his actions. My family was already unhappy about how everything had transpired with the pregnancy, and they would be extremely disappointed to learn that he was essentially abandoning me and our child. As we approached his car and I attempted to calm him down, he turned to me and punched me in the stomach.

Stunned, with the wind knocked out of me, I began to cry and walk away from him. He tried grabbing me as though to apologize, but the damage was done. I pulled myself away, ran inside the house, and locked the door. He had hit me, closed fist, in my pregnant belly. *How could he?* As he violently banged on the door, I went around to the window and asked him to leave and threatened to call the police if he didn't. I was only bluffing because the last thing I wanted to do was to call the police and risk having my sister or her husband come home to find them there. But he wouldn't leave. He said he wasn't going anywhere and started banging on the windows. Afraid of what he would do next, I felt I had no choice but to call for help and dialed 911.

After taking down all the information, the 911 operator assured me officers were on their way and advised that I keep the windows closed and refrain from engaging with him any further to avoid making things worse. I crawled onto the floor and sobbed until the police came. By the time they arrived, he had already left. They searched the premises just to be safe, but he was gone. They asked if I knew where he'd gone and whether I would like to press charges. Against my better judgment, I said no. I told them this was the first time it had ever escalated to this degree and that I didn't think it would happen again. One of the officers handed me his business card and asked me to call if my husband returned. I promised I would but he never did come back.

It was wrong of me to not press charges and hold him accountable for his actions. His grandparents had always enabled his bad behavior, which I hated, and now here I was doing exactly the same thing. Except I was worse, because I would also make excuses for him and allow him to weasel his way back into my life.

The worst part is that I couldn't tell my family. I had only been married a few months, and my marriage was not only falling apart at the seams but I was being physically hurt. I was too ashamed to admit this to myself, much less anyone else.

I thought that by protecting him, I was somehow also protecting myself from the judgment of others, and I decided the best thing to do was to lie to my family. I told them he had become homesick and asked me to move into his grandparents' home, which I declined, and we'd decided it was best for him to move back home until it was time for us to get our own place. I'm pretty certain they didn't believe my story, but they didn't question me. The only one who spoke up was my brother-in-law who expressed his immense disappointment in my husband's lack of maturity, but I said nothing. What was there to say? He was right.

Upon moving out, my husband distanced himself and acted as though I was to blame for our problems and our circumstances. He would go back and forth between apologizing and pushing me away. This is not at all how I envisioned my life as a newlywed, but I also blamed myself for having put myself in this situation in the first place. I felt as though I deserved what was coming to me. Sadly, because my life had not been easy, I was used to the self-blaming game. After all, I was the common denominator, which made me feel like I somehow provoked others to want to hurt me. I had spent most of my existence in a constant state of fight or flight, and this was no different.

By the time my baby was born in mid-June, just days before my high school graduation, my husband and I were hardly on speaking terms at all, and he was pretty much living the single life, going out partying and doing God knows what with God knows who.

I went into labor on a Friday afternoon. It was a very warm day out and I was thankful that classes were officially over. That week consisted solely of enjoying our final senior activities, and on this particular day, we had our senior picnic. It was a day of getting yearbooks signed and hanging out with the entire senior class and our teachers one final time before our graduation the following week. The students got to take a vote on which local eatery would cater our lunch, and we all decided on a local favorite known as Original Tommy's World Famous Hamburgers. If you are from L.A., or have ever visited, you have probably seen or heard of this eatery known for their chili cheese burgers and fries. Even though they were located in a rival high school's territory in the next city over, it was our hangout after every football game and we were going to memorialize this day with those signature burgers.

It was such a fun day, and for a moment, I forgot about all my marital troubles. *I can't believe I'm even saying this. I haven't graduated high school, yet I'm sitting here expecting a baby any day now (hopefully after graduation) and having marital problems with my estranged husband. Whose life am I living, anyway? It certainly doesn't feel like my own. I'm just a kid! What was I thinking?*

The only symptom I ever encountered during my pregnancy was heartburn. Everything caused me serious heartburn. The cheeseburger and fries I had just taken down gave me the worst heartburn I'd felt yet. Or so I thought. As soon as the picnic was over, I told my twin I wasn't feeling my best and asked if we could head home. We lived down the street from school, just a couple blocks away, and I slowly wobbled my way home. My sister mentioned needing to go back to school to return some books she had forgotten about and asked if I'd walk back with her later, but I told her I didn't think I could. I needed to take it easy because I thought perhaps I was having indigestion from the chilli.

When we arrived home, I started to feel funny, and the pain had now moved to my lower back. I wondered whether I was going into labor and thought I needed to get myself ready just in case. I called my cousin who was also very pregnant and due a couple months after me, and I asked if she wouldn't mind picking me up and taking me to my doctor's office to get my paperwork from her. When I arrived, I asked if I could see the doctor so that she could check to see and confirm whether I was in labor, but she had already left for the day. I had no choice but to wait and let my body guide me. If I was in labor, my body would let me know soon enough, so off we went.

It had gotten quite hot by now and my cousin and I decided to pull over at a local ice cream shop to buy ourselves something sweet and cold to enjoy. As we sat there, I admitted to her that I was very nervous about giving birth but that I had reached the point of no return and had to prepare for whatever would come. The pain was progressively getting stronger and I knew nobody would be home for a few more hours, so I asked my cousin to drop me off at my other sister's house because my mother was there. Being there with my mother who'd birthed nine children would help me feel less afraid. When I arrived at my sister's place, both she and my mother thought it would be best for me to call the hospital and speak with my doctor.

I proceeded to call the hospital and spoke with my doctor who could not believe I was actively in labor because I was holding the conversation down so well. I was eighteen years young; my body was resilient and strong, and even though I was pretty certain I was in labor, I was taking the pain like a champ. The doctor said that had I actually been in labor, I would probably not be able to have a conversation from the pain I'd be in, and suggested that I might be having bad indigestion. He recommended I lay on my left side and drink lots of water, but that if there was any change, I should come right over to the hospital. *This is the problem with being a young mom, or in my case, a young mother-to-be. Nobody takes me seriously because they think I am too young and too dumb to have a clue about what my body is feeling. But fine, you're the doctor and I'll do as you say, even though my instincts are telling me I am in labor.*

After the conversation with my doctor, I suddenly felt incredibly vulnerable and sad, because I had no idea where my husband was and he never so much as called to check in on me or our baby. I knew he was off work by now, so I decided to page him, hoping that he would offer to pick me up and take me home to prepare my bags in case I needed to go to the hospital. When he returned my call, I told him what the doctor had said, to which he responded that he was not home but that I could page him if anything changed, and he would come right over. *I can't believe he isn't dropping everything to come be with me and lend me the support I need. Isn't this what HE wanted? A baby? Well here we are and he's nowhere to be seen--wait, I cannot tell my mother and sister that he's refusing to come. I'll tell them he's working late but on standby in case I am in labor, which I am, because my body is telling me I am, even if my doctor refuses to believe me! Ugh, I'm so frustrated, but I have to take it easy.*

After a couple hours of resting and the pain continuing to worsen, I asked my sister to take me home so that I could shower in hopes that it would help ease my pain. When I arrived, my eldest sister and brother-in-law were home, and I informed them that I was in labor and I was going to shower and finish packing mine and the baby's bags to be ready to go. They were more excited to hear this news than my own husband, and they assured me they'd be with me every step of the way. I was so thankful to have their support, yet I couldn't help but feel sad that my baby's father wasn't here as he had promised he would be. I cried in the shower, not from the physical pain in my body but the emotional pain in my heart. *How did you get here, Karen? No, don't bother answering that question because you know how you got here and none of that matters right now. You've got a baby on the way. This baby is all that matters.*

I had been timing my contractions all evening, and by the time I got out of the shower, they were two minutes apart. I changed as quickly as my pain allowed and wobbled into the living room to tell my family it was time to go. Before I could even grab my bags from my bedroom, my brother-in-law was already in the car waiting for me, which I found so sweet and endearing. *When my twin and I first moved in with them four years prior, he wasn't all that nice to us because I think a part of him resented having to take us in, but since learning of my pregnancy, he's been like a father to me and I love and appreciate him so much for that.*

The hospital, which was in Glendale, was about twenty minutes away by freeway, but my brother-in-law felt it was best to take surface streets, which took twice as long. By the time we arrived at the hospital, I was in absolute agony. The pain I had taken like a champ all day was now knocking me to the ground and I could hardly stand. I was so grateful when the nurse arrived with a wheelchair and wheeled me away. *I've seen this happen in movies, except in my case there isn't a husband nervously running next to me, reminding me how much he loves me and how much I've got this. It's just me and this stranger wheeling me down this funny-smelling grey corridor with linoleum floors. I hope they give me something for the pain. I'm in so much pain.*

Once I was admitted and resting uncomfortably in my private room, equipped with a couch and television, the nurse brought in my sister, who'd been waiting down in the lobby. She asked if I wanted her to stay so that she could send my brother-in-law home. I did want her to stay and I thanked her for doing so. At this point, somebody must have paged my husband because she told me he was on his way. *I'm happy to hear this, but I'm still mad at him for choosing to be out there instead of here with me. It isn't my sister's job to be here, it's yours, you selfish asshole! What lame excuse will you give me for not being here? My God, how can I still feel love for you even after everything you've put me through?*

It took hours for my husband to arrive. He had been drinking, which was unusual for him, and he said he'd been dropped off because he couldn't drive. *What the hell is wrong with you? I wanted you here, but not like this.* He sat on the couch and said he was tired from the long day and was going to take a nap. He asked that we wake him up if we needed him. *Are you serious right now? Why did you bother coming at all if you aren't going to give me so much as a word of comfort? Ugh, I'm so mad at you! But I'm too tired and in too much pain to focus on you right now. Where's the nurse? I'm ready for that epidural.*

After the anesthesiologist administered the epidural, I was on cloud nine. It felt as though my body was floating in the clouds and I was light as a feather. *Even my drunken sleeping husband can't get to me now! What an amazing feeling!* Too bad the fun couldn't last as long as I'd hope it would. A couple hours after I'd been pain free, I started to shiver and had cold sweats. I buzzed the nurse to get me another blanket but she noticed I was running a fever and immediately called the doctor. When the doctor came in, he confirmed that I had a fever and said they needed to get my temperature down immediately to avoid any complications. Also, it seemed the epidural was preventing me from having strong enough contractions that would help me dilate. Unfortunately, they needed to remove the epidural and break my water bag in order for my body to catch up and prepare for delivery; if I wasn't dilated enough by early morning, I'd have to go in for an emergency c-section. *C-section? No, please now, that wasn't part of the plan. Take the epidural and let my body do what it must, but please don't cut me open. I'm not prepared for that. Besides, I have my high school graduation to attend in a few days. It's important to me. I want to prove to myself and everyone else that I can still graduate on stage despite having a baby. I need this. Please don't take that from me.*

By early next morning, after a sleepless, long, and excruciating night, and all that uncertainty of not knowing whether I would deliver my baby naturally, I was finally dilated enough to deliver.

For what seemed like forever, my sister stood holding my right leg and my husband my left, and every time a contraction would come, they would have to bring each leg up to my chest to help me push and push and push to get the baby head crowning and ready to deliver. With each push, I prayed and waited. Then finally, my baby was crowning and everyone cheered as the nurse prepared to wheel my bed into the delivery room across the hall. I was so scared but so ready to do this.

My sister had been by my side the entire night and I really wanted it to be her who stood there next to me as I welcomed my baby into the world, but she reminded me that it was my husband's right to be there and witness the birth of our child. Reluctantly, I agreed. This moment was about so much more than my hurt feelings and I had to put that all aside in order for our baby to come into the world knowing she or he was loved.

As the doctors and nurses prepared and hooked me up to monitors, I asked them how long the delivery would take because I was ready to be out of pain. They all laughed at my question and said that it was entirely up to me; I would decide how hard to push and that would determine how quickly the baby would come. The most painful part would be getting the baby's head out, but after that, the rest of the body would easily come through with a slight push. I was relieved to hear that but suddenly felt a burning sensation. The doctor was running his finger around the baby's crown and it felt as though he was taking a knife to my skin and cutting me up. *Please God, let this be over soon.*

After all the pushing I'd already done, I had little energy left in me, but it was now or never and I was ready to rumble. I took a few deep breaths and started to get really nervous. *This is the long awaited moment of truth, Karen! Will it be a girl or a boy? I already love this baby so much. Does she or he love me too? Do they feel love yet? I cannot believe this is actually happening!* The doctors had instructed me to push as hard as I could with each contraction, so I pushed once, twice, and by the third push my baby girl emerged from my womb and made her grand entrance into the world. She was born on Saturday morning, on the 13th of June. *Thirteen, what a lucky number.*

We named her *Samantha* because we liked the idea of being able to call her *Sam* or *Sammy*. My sweet girl was such a good baby from the moment she was born. Despite all the chaos and trauma in the months leading up to her birth, she managed to be born perfectly healthy and she hardly let out a cry. She simply laid there next to me cool, calm, and collected. I cried as she opened her eyes and looked straight into mine as though to say, *Don't worry Momma, I'm here now.*

In that magical moment, when everything seemed so perfect, I could have never guessed or prepared for the trauma that awaited her and me. So much that it would threaten to break us but would ultimately make our bond unbreakable.

"Feeling financially unstable was triggering for me because it reminded me of the scarcity I grew up in…"

15

The birth of our daughter felt like a new beginning for us, and in some ways it was. Something about her birth seemed to affect my husband in a way that brought out a sweet side of him, reminiscent of the early days of our relationship. Although we were still living apart, we were committed to trying to make our marriage work for our baby's sake. As he prepared to leave for military training, he was even more committed to spending time bonding with her and making plans with me for the future. He promised he would never lay a hand on me ever again. I wanted so badly to believe him and decided to give him the benefit of the doubt. It was nice seeing him this way again and I really held onto hope for a future as bright as the one he promised.

Over the course of the next year, my husband would go off to training, be deployed overseas for a six-month period, and in the process would miss many of our daughter's firsts. We purchased a video recorder to capture the many special moments of her early life, but I know how much it would have meant to him to have seen them first-hand. He wrote me letters regularly to share about the different places and things he saw and what it was like to be so far from home for the first time. I was always happy to receive his letters because I got to see the world through his eyes.

In his absence, I was determined to gain my independence. I had a car, I was working, and with a strong support system around me, I was able to manage with relative ease. This was the first time in a long time I felt like myself and I was really enjoying it. I never admitted this to him (or to myself until now), but I hardly missed him at all and actually felt liberated from the tight hold he had on me. I was able to see my friends again, to be around my family without hearing his criticisms, and I wanted to be selfish, which was something I had never allowed myself to do.

While his letters were frequent, sweet, and loving, I hardly responded, and when I did, they were just reiterations of things I had already shared before, like how work was going and how our daughter was growing so fast. If there was any mention of me longing for him and missing him, it was mostly to reciprocate his feelings. I did later come to regret not being more consistent and intentional about writing to him because at the time, I did not fully comprehend the importance of those letters. He later explained to me that during deployment periods, the letters soldiers receive from loved ones are extremely important because they are their only lifeline to the world they left behind; it is how they feel connected no matter where they are. I think a part of him always resented me because my letters were the only ones he received while he was gone and my lack of effort made him feel rejected and alone.

As his date to return home neared, we received word that he would be stationed in a small town in central California, about three hours northeast of Los Angeles. Because he was married and had a family, he qualified for family housing on base, which was welcome news because it meant we would live rent-free and we could afford for me to stay home with our daughter. I was, however, feeling anxious about moving so far from home and away from my support system, particularly because this would be the first time my husband and I would be living under the same roof after having been apart for some time. Nevertheless, I was all in, and by the time he arrived home, I had gotten us all settled into our new place.

Military housing is unique because while there are civilians living there, it is, above all else, a military base. Because of this, there is a strict protocol to access anything within the confines of the base. There is a strong military police presence and upon reaching the front entrance, one must go through a clearing process. My military identification had to be on me any time I left the base for purposes of reentry, and anytime I shopped within the base. I was also provided a sticker to place on my windshield which identified me as a resident. If we had family or friends visiting, we would have to provide their information to the front office, and they would have to go through the clearance process as well. It was all very official and, for the most part, I felt quite safe.

Once inside the base, it didn't look much different than a middle-class gated suburban community. There were barracks, which is apartment style living for single soldiers; the Commissary, which is the grocery store on base, along with other government sponsored shops; and there is the family housing area which looks a lot like cookie-cutter housing developments, sprinkled with small playgrounds and schools around the neighborhood. Because housing is free of cost to families, there are strict rules about the maintenance and upkeep of the homes. There are officials whose job it is to drive around and give warnings or fines to anyone not following the maintenance rules. Just our luck, we got a house with giant fruit trees in front and back, which required a lot of work but eventually became something I enjoyed maintaining.

Over time, we made friends with other young couples and slowly began creating our own little community, helping each other out whenever anyone was in need. My husband would sometimes bring his single friends over for a home-cooked meal, and while I wasn't the best cook, I was happy to help them feel a little less homesick.

I was only twenty years old and living the life of a full-blown homemaker, which was not something I ever thought I'd do. While I was grateful for being home with Samantha, I was growing increasingly anxious about our financial situation, because we never seemed to be able to get our heads above water, and often had to seek assistance from his grandparents, which I absolutely hated doing. The hardest thing for me was not financially contributing to our household; because of this, I did not feel it was my place to question him on where our money was going, so I didn't.

Feeling financially unstable was triggering for me because it reminded me of the scarcity I grew up in, which is everything I didn't want for our daughter. To not be able to buy her things was incredibly disheartening for me, and I didn't want to depend on anyone for help. As checks started bouncing and he was getting into trouble because of it at work, my frustrations grew and our arguments started back up again.

I didn't know how to properly communicate my fears around money because at the time I wasn't aware I had any, but I couldn't stand by and do nothing about our situation when we were obviously in over our heads and in dire need of a second income. I think my husband interpreted this as my lack of faith in him, but that wasn't the case at all. I just knew that he wasn't accustomed to budgeting and having to work for the things he wanted because he'd always been handed everything without ever having to work for it. He couldn't understand that being the sole provider meant that he was responsible for providing financial support, all on his own, for our daughter, me, and himself. In my determination to solve our financial trouble, I decided it was time to look for a job. I figured that at the very least, we could pay our bills on time and have a little extra money for fun, which we never had anymore.

The town we lived in barely had a few fast food restaurants, which meant I would have to work in the next town over, about 20-30 minutes away. Since I had experience working in retail, and because they offered flexible enough hours, I applied at the town department store and was happy to have been offered a position almost immediately. I arranged it so that I worked evenings and weekends to avoid having our daughter in daycare. My husband reluctantly supported my endeavor to work, but as far as I was concerned, he didn't have any other choice but to accept it.

Of course, I missed being home with Samantha, but I was also secretly happy to return to work and regain some independence. For starters, I have always enjoyed dressing up, doing my hair and makeup, and having an excuse to do these things gave me a boost of confidence I seriously needed. It was nice seeing myself in something other than jeans and a t-shirt and with my hair in a bun. Although I wasn't making a ton of money, I was happy to have something to call my own and also welcomed the second stream of income.

It was also nice to be able to make new friends, and for the first time since our move, I really started to feel at home. This was especially the case because I became instant friends with one particular co-worker who was also living on base with her sister and brother-in-law. As we got to know each other over lunch or breaks, she mentioned that her sister ran a daycare from their home, so they always had a house full of kids. Her brother-in-law was preparing to be deployed, which meant she would have to pitch in and help her sister from time to time. I mentioned to her that now that I could afford it, I had been considering putting Samantha in daycare at least a couple days a week to help her develop social skills because she was an only child. It would also really help my husband and I because we were having difficulties aligning our schedules. She went on to say that her sister had a couple openings if I was interested, which I absolutely was, and upon meeting her sister, we enrolled Samantha in her daycare. I was even more excited when I came to learn that because my husband was a government employee, both he and I could go to school at no cost to us, and they would help me pay for daycare expenses. I couldn't pass up this opportunity, and much to my surprise, neither could he. We both enrolled in college as soon as a new semester started.

This period of time in my marriage felt incredibly promising. We created a plan that worked for us: he was able to attend school during work hours, and I attended school a few nights a week while he watched our daughter. Like my job, my classes were also off campus which made it a little more challenging for me, but I didn't care. We were going to be stationed at this base for at least two years, which would give me sufficient time to either get my Associate degree or earn enough credits to transfer wherever we moved to next. *I can't believe this is actually happening. I'm so excited to finally get myself enrolled in college!*

For a time, we fell into a nice routine and we were both happy with our classes. I was laser focused, and I had to be in order to juggle family, school, and work. He, on the other hand, wasn't taking school as seriously as I was. Frankly, I think he was just doing it to prove he could go to school too, but there was no competition. Me wanting to go to school was not about anyone but myself. I wanted to prove that I could do it. Especially because I was aware that my family totally thought that because I had gotten pregnant with Samantha, more kids would soon follow. But as they say, "Fool me once, shame on you. Fool me twice, shame on me." Believe me, after Samantha was born, I knew better than to relinquish control to my husband, and I was taking full care of myself to ensure I wouldn't get pregnant again unless I intentionally planned to do so.

Despite my husband's disinterest in his coursework, he seemed to enjoy his classes and was even making friends. He had also told me about a girl he had become friends with who was the only other Latina in class and who, like him, was originally from Texas. He said that she was also a military wife with a young daughter, and they also lived on base just a couple blocks over from our place. He suggested that I meet her sometime in the near future, which I agreed would be nice because I was always open to making new friends. *I am ecstatic that he's happy and we are in a good place.*

There was one lingering issue I couldn't seem to get under control no matter how hard I tried: our finances. This was still a sore subject we would find ourselves going in circles over, because I couldn't understand how despite us both working, having no rent to pay, and having our school and daycare covered, we continued to be short on money. I knew he wasn't being forthcoming about his spending and that made me distrust him. Especially because he knew I would have preferred to not have to work and just focus on our daughter and school. He would always promise to get better, but money just seemed to disappear, and I didn't know where it was going.

The more we argued, and the more independent I became, the more his insecurities began to resurface. He started becoming jealous of everyone, even my gay co-worker, whom he swore was in love with me. I was continuously having to remind him that I would never be unfaithful and that I wanted him to support me having friends as much as I supported him having friends.

His insecurities, his constant need for attention, and his wanting to control me was exhausting and, frankly, frustrating, because I had so many things I was already juggling that I hardly even had time for myself. Perhaps if we had gone to marriage counseling or therapy, I would have understood that his insecurities had nothing to do with me but rather his mother's abandonment of him as a child. This was something that was never talked about and that I knew he had been struggling with. As long as he wasn't addressing his pain, he was going to continue projecting it on me. I was too young and not at all equipped to handle this sort of conflict, which made us navigate our troubles in an unhealthy manner. Our household often felt unsafe to me because we were always at war over something. What's worse is that I couldn't protect Samantha from it, and even though she was very young, she witnessed a lot of our arguments, which had to be traumatizing for her.

    I wanted so badly for us to be good to each other for the sake of Samantha, who had been the sole reason we married. But unfortunately, the more independent of him I became, the worse things continued to get and the more unbearable our marriage was.

"… I knew love was supposed to bring out the best in people, yet somehow it seemed to only bring out the worst in us."

16

As my husband's insecurities worsened and his accusations of infidelity grew, our communication reached a point of total breakdown. We were no longer the best friends we had once been. In fact, there was not a trace of that friendship left. In public, we maintained a loving relationship to the point that people often referred to us as *The Perfect Couple*, but behind closed doors we were rivals at war. Even though I avoided using any type of negative or foul language with him, particularly because our daughter was now a toddler and would often repeat what she heard, he did not care and, over time, became relentlessly abusive both verbally and emotionally.

It started with name-calling. His favorite name for me became *fat bitch*. Sure, I had put on a little weight in the months I was home with our daughter, but while I was not entirely happy with my body, I still looked great. I found it strange that the few extra pounds I had put on had never been an issue for him before, but suddenly it was all he could focus on. For Christmas, he even filled my stocking with workout videos, which would not have been insulting if it were not for the fact that he had been making offensive remarks about my body on a consistent basis. He took every opportunity he had to make me feel awful about myself. He also made sure to remind me that he was actually doing me a favor by sticking around even though he was growing increasingly tired of me and my nagging. I was so confused because my husband made me feel ugly while everyone else always complimented me and told me I was beautiful. *Why doesn't he think I'm beautiful?* I would often cry to him and ask him how he could be so cruel and say such mean things to me, but he would express no emotion and just tell me I was overly sensitive. He would never dare apologize for treating me as badly as he did and I know he knew it hurt me.

A person can only take this sort of verbal abuse so long, and before I knew it, he had broken me down; my self-esteem was shattered. Anything which might have been left flew out the window as the verbal abuse continued worsening. Things got so bad that I actually believed all the horrible things he would say to me and about me. I started to believe I was unlovable, fat, and used up with nowhere to go, which is why I stayed. People on the outside think it is so easy to leave when you find yourself in a situation of this kind, but it is actually quite hard. In my case, my abusive husband chipped away at my spirit by taking information about me and using it as a weapon to break me down emotionally and mentally. He knew my whole history; he knew I had been raised without a father and that I'd been sent to live with my eldest sister against my will. And he used that information to constantly remind me that nobody loved me, not even my so-called family. Since he was the one on the outside looking in, I figured he could see what I could not, and I took it to heart. The more I believed I was unloved by my own family--my everything--the more I clung to him to be my lifeline and the more he used that to his advantage. I don't even think he was conscious of his actions; he just started figuring out what my weaknesses were and used them toward my destruction.

He had worn me down so much that it became easy for the verbal abuse to escalate to physical abuse. It happened when I least expected: early one fall morning as we drove into town to have what was supposed to be a family fun day. It was the first day in a while that we both had a day off from school and work and, with the tension building at home, we thought perhaps a change of scenery would be nice. We decided to spend the day in one of my favorite towns called Visalia. It is a small city about an hour south of the town we lived in and something about that place always brought me joy. I think it was the tree-lined streets and small town feel that was reminiscent of olden days when families gathered for potlucks, parades, and whatever else families do in the towns they grow up in. I had always wanted that and I hoped to give that to Samantha as well, but the way things were going, I wasn't so sure I could.

I had been running late that morning because I was responsible for getting Samantha and myself ready. I was hungry and hadn't had time to eat breakfast, so I decided to pour myself a cup of cereal to eat in the car. It was chilly and cloudy outside, so I made sure we packed a few warm layers in case it got colder throughout the day. *God, please let this be a good day. Our little family could really use a good day.*

Much to my surprise, the drive started out quite pleasant. My husband was driving and listening to '90s R&B on the radio, our daughter was happily sitting in her carseat, and I was sitting in the passenger seat, staring out the window and watching the clouds and fields of cows as I took bites of my cereal. I was getting excited about the day ahead. I continued to pray for a good day. *Please God, let this be an amazing day. We really need this right now. I want Samantha to have a memorable day with her mom and dad. We can do this; I know we can.*

Before continuing, we had to make a quick stop at the bank to get money. My husband ran inside while Samantha and I waited in the car. Even though she was only two years old, she was very wise for her age and I loved talking with her. I was telling her we were going to see really pretty trees and hopefully get her some ice cream too. As my husband approached the car, I noticed he looked irritable. *I wonder what happened in the bank? Were we short on money? I hope not because we've been extra good lately.* When he got in the car, he questioned me about our spending and I told him I hadn't spent any money other than for bills and groceries. I wasn't a spender like that and he knew it, but I think he was trying to cover up for himself because he was the financially irresponsible one. Patiently, I asked him what had happened and he said that he had taken out the last of our cash, but that would mean we'd have no money for the week. *Wait, how is that even possible? I just received money from financial aid; I just got paid at work, and so did he. How were we in the negative?* I told him I didn't understand how this could be possible and asked what we were supposed to do now. He said I shouldn't worry and that he would call his grandparents and ask them for a loan to get us through the week. I told him I was tired of borrowing money, which wasn't even really borrowed because my husband never bothered to pay anyone back; it was humiliating. I told him that based on what we were bringing home, we should have been living very comfortably and the fact that we weren't made me very concerned. He didn't like hearing me say this and became very upset.

 He raised his voice and told me it was my fault because I wasn't budgeting our money properly and I needed to be better about it. As he got louder, I reminded him that our daughter was in the backseat, but he didn't care. I wanted us to have a good day despite this hurdle and told him we would figure it out when we got home. To show him that I wanted us to have a peaceful day, I reached out to put my hand on his arm, and the next thing I knew, I had been punched in the face. I was stunned and it actually took me a minute to realize what had just happened. My face was throbbing and my cereal had gone flying everywhere with milk running down my window. My husband wasn't the slapping type; he went straight for closed-fist blows, as though I was some kid from the hood he'd grown up in, and as though our child was not in the backseat witnessing this violation of her mother's body and spirit.

 Not being able to fully grasp what had just happened, I began to sob uncontrollably. My mind went numb, time seemed to stop, and everything went silent for a moment as I tried making sense of what had just happened. You know that feeling when you're in the shower or the pool and you get water in your ear, how everything goes silent and all you hear is mush? That is how I felt at that moment.

The mushy silence in my head was broken by the sounds of my screaming child. When I turned around to look at her, I could see fear and confusion in her little face. Not knowing what to do, I gathered myself, unstrapped my seatbelt, and jumped into the backseat to console her and assure her that everything was fine. Silent tears streamed down my face as I assured her that mommy was fine. I had no words and very faintly asked him to please turn the car around and take us home. As he sped off the highway and onto the dirt off-ramp, all he could do was defend his actions by saying that it was my fault because I had come at him and provoked him, and that I should have never done that. I said nothing.

When we got home, I locked Samantha and myself in our bedroom. She eventually got bored and asked to go with her daddy. As angry as I was with him, I wasn't going to hold her hostage, and I opened the door for her to go with him. As I sat there all alone, I felt a sense of total despair and sadness. *How did we come to this? How was violence the first resort instead of the one thing you never did? Where had the love we once felt gone and when did it turn so sour that all that seemed to be left was anger and resentment?* I didn't know a whole lot about relationships, but I knew love was supposed to bring out the best in people, yet somehow it seemed to only bring out the worst in us. That realization made me sad and I wondered whether I was the problem. *Why is it that the people I love most are the ones who hurt me most? Perhaps I am to blame. I am, after all, the common denominator.*

My abuse destroyed my perception of reality and half the time I wasn't sure whether I was going crazy and imagining things, or whether they were really happening. My logical brain refused to believe that someone I loved, who was supposed to love me, could treat me in such a way. Then I got to thinking, *Wait, I chose this person, so what does that say about me?*

The days that followed this incident were dark. We were not on speaking terms and although he seemed remorseful, he never expressed it. I missed work and school the first couple days, but eventually had to return and hide the bruising with my hair and make up. I remember sitting in class listening to a lecture one evening and all I could think about was how bright the lights were and how afraid I was that someone would notice my bruising and ask what happened.

In my desperation to talk with someone who may have some words of encouragement, I reached out to my childhood best friend and shared with her how sad I was that my marriage was falling apart and that my husband had not only become verbally abusive, but also physically. It was so hard for me to admit it to myself, let alone anyone else, but this was my best friend, the person who knew many of my deepest secrets, and I thought she would have something meaningful to offer. Unfortunately what I got was the complete opposite. After I told her that he had not only become abusive but that it wasn't the first time, she didn't seem the least bit concerned or worried or even angry--nothing. In fact, she was so nonchalant about it that I wasn't even sure whether she had actually heard me. I mean, if she had called me and told me her boyfriend was abusing her, I would have been devastated and would have wanted to help her in whatever way I could, but that was not at all how she reacted. It never occurred to me that maybe she just didn't know what to say or how to support me at that moment, so she said nothing at all. I interpreted her reaction, or lack thereof, to mean that perhaps I was blowing things out of proportion and making the situation bigger than it actually was. If she didn't seem the least bit concerned about me, upset for me, or even willing to encourage me to leave, then perhaps my situation wasn't so bad and I should just suck it up. And if she felt this way, perhaps everyone else would too, so there was no point in telling anyone else. I had been so hopeful that I would feel better getting things off my chest, but instead I felt let down, confused and more alone than ever.

I began experiencing depression like I had never experienced before, not even in my worst days growing up. The winters in central California can be quite cold, gloomy and foggy, and they would magnify my feelings of hopelessness and despair. Intrusive thoughts began crossing my mind--thoughts I didn't want to have but which were becoming more frequent over time. As I thought about my life, I'd wonder whether it was worth living if it meant that my entire existence was going to feel this heavy, this miserable, this isolating. I couldn't seem to find the light at the end of this very long and dark tunnel, and sometimes during my late-night drives back home from school, I would contemplate closing my eyes and steering the wheel toward the center divider. I'm sad to admit that this was just one of the many thoughts I had, and it was easy for my mind to go down that dark rabbit hole in which I'd often get lost.

Then, as if to throw me a lifeline, my mind would race back to Samantha. *My beautiful, sweet girl who hadn't asked for any of this. What fault was it of hers? Why would she have to pay the price growing up motherless because her father and I couldn't seem to get it together and do right by her? She deserved to know a happy home. She deserved to have a mother and father who not only loved her but who could be good and decent to each other, even if the love between them was gone. I brought my child into the world and I couldn't leave her motherless. I couldn't allow her to grow up wondering if my absence was her fault, or if she could have done something to save me, or worse, to forget about me altogether and only know me through photos and stories she'd hear about me. No! I couldn't allow that to be my story, or hers. I had to be strong and shake this darkness away.* I promised myself at that moment that

I would never again allow my mind to go back to that dark place, and it never did.

I always say that I may have been the one who brought Samantha into the world, but she is quite literally the one who saved me.

"This was my moment to take back all my power; this was the blessing in disguise I didn't know I had been waiting for …"

17

You would think that the verbal and physical abuse I was enduring was enough for me to call it quits and run back to my family. But it wasn't. I was lost in the murky waters of my toxic relationship where I had started to believe that without him, I would drown. I couldn't see it then, but the more I thrived at work and excelled in school, the more my husband attempted to control and isolate me by making me feel guilty about everything I did, from how I looked when I went to work, to the friends I was making there. I don't know what else I could have done to make him happy. My routine was pretty straight forward: I went to work, school, and back home to be with him and Samantha. I was tending to everything and everyone but myself, yet nothing I did seemed to meet his expectations.

He would diminish the abuse by saying that it wasn't like he was coming home and beating me up every day. He was right in that he wasn't beating me every day, but even just once was too many times. Abuse is abuse, no matter how infrequently you do it. What he didn't realize is that while his occasional hits left visible bruises that diminished over time, his daily doses of verbal and emotional abuse cut deeper and more profoundly than any punch he'd ever thrown my way.

With each one of his hurtful words, like calling me a *fat bitch* or telling me I was used up and nobody would want me, he took a piece of my self-esteem and self-worth. The physical bruises healed quickly, but the scars of the verbal and emotional abuse remained for many years. As hurtful as his words were, I believed them and took them so deeply to heart that I was actually the one begging him to stay with me and was willing to do whatever he wanted in order to keep us together. He had succeeded in breaking my spirit and gained full and total control over me, and I was a willing participant at his mercy.

Around this time, I started to notice he was spending quite a bit of time on the phone. This was long before cell phones became available, and every home was equipped with phone jacks to connect landlines. We had two telephones in our house; one was mounted on the kitchen wall and the other was on the nightstand in our bedroom. He always chose to talk on the kitchen phone. He would pull up a chair, make himself comfortable, and proceed to speak in a low voice as though he didn't want me to hear his conversations. If I walked into the kitchen, he'd say he was talking with a childhood friend from back home or he'd quickly say his goodbyes and hang up. I found his secretive behavior odd, but for the sake of keeping the peace, I'd pretend I hadn't noticed and would keep it to myself. I found myself doing a lot of that these days--dimming my voice just as he was dimming my light.

In the years we'd been together, my husband had never really been one for going out partying or hanging out and drinking at bars. He made it abundantly clear that he did not approve of me doing such things. But as of late, he had gotten in the habit of going out drinking with colleagues after work. I hated his double standards, but I figured it was healthy for us to have independence from each other, and as long as he was being responsible, it was alright by me. It wasn't like he was going far. Since we lived in a remote area in the middle of nowhere, he and his friends were just at the bar on base, which was a few blocks away from our place.

One day he came home from work and said there was a party happening that weekend and asked if I was okay with him going. I didn't tell him this, but we were spending such little time together as a family these days that it made no difference to me if he went or not. All I said was that if it was something he really wanted to do, he should do it.

On the evening of the party, he got ready to go and as he left, he said he would not be out too late. By the time I went to bed around two in the morning, he still had not arrived home nor had he called to check in and say he was okay. I worried and thought about paging him, but I wasn't sure if he would get upset and decided not to. I laid in bed awake, waiting for him to arrive, but he never did. The next morning came and still nothing. The only way I could reach him was by paging him. I even put in a 911 prompt letting him know it was urgent, but I received no response. I was becoming increasingly worried. Then finally, he called. It was now late morning the day after he'd left for a party he was only supposed to be at for a few hours. Sounding embarrassed and concerned, he apologized for not calling me sooner. He said the party had gotten a little out of control, that he'd gotten drunk and had passed out on his friend's bed.

Fine, he had gotten drunk and passed out, but it was now the next day and rather than being home with his family, he was on the phone calling me from God knows where. He went on to say that he was nervous about coming home because his friends had played a joke on him which he knew would upset me. I thought, *What could they possibly have done to him that would upset me?* I was growing impatient and asked him to just come out with it and say whatever it was he had to say! He said that while he was passed out, his friends had gotten one of the girls at the party to give him hickeys on his neck.

What? No, he was lying to me because nobody in their right mind would do such a thing. Especially not to a married man with a family at home. When I told him I thought he was lying, he swore up and down he wasn't and said that this was exactly why he had been avoiding coming home, because he knew I wouldn't believe him. *Are you kidding me? He was the one who had been out all night without so much as a phone call, and now he was telling me his neck was full of hickeys. But he was somehow turning this around trying to play the victim?* I couldn't understand how it was that no matter how guilty he may have been, he somehow always flipped the script to make me feel like I was the one in the wrong.

I asked him where he was now and he said he was still at his friend's place. I was having a hard time wrapping my head around this and I didn't want to argue, so I asked him to just come home because our daughter was asking for him. I figured it was best to continue this conversation in person anyway.

As I stood in our kitchen waiting for him to pull into our driveway, I felt a sinking feeling in my stomach. Was I actually naive, gullible, or stupid enough to believe this story? I felt as though I was losing my mind.

As he opened the door to enter our house, I saw his neck. He didn't just have a few scattered markings; this was a deliberate chain of hickies that went across the entire front side of his neck. I stared into his eyes in total disbelief, feeling disgusted, humiliated, and embarrassed, for me and for him. He immediately hugged me, said he was sorry, and asked me to forgive him for being irresponsible. He promised he was telling the truth and promised it would never happen again. I felt numb and just stood there not knowing what to do next. I couldn't and didn't want to believe that in addition to enduring domestic violence, I would now also have to endure infidelity. So, instead of accepting my reality, I did what I had been taught to do so many times before: I pretended to be okay and I swept his indiscretion under the rug.

A few weeks later, as he sat in the living room watching television while I pressed his uniforms on the ironing board, he decided to drop a bomb on me. He said he was thinking about going to El Paso, Texas to visit his sisters for a few days. I was confused. Why was he thinking about taking a trip without Samantha and me? I asked him what the purpose of this trip was and why he wasn't including us in the plans. Without making eye contact with me, he said he needed space and time to clear his head. I couldn't understand what he needed to clear his head about, so I asked him why he couldn't just invite his sisters to come visit us instead. I said it would be nice to see his sisters and have them spend time with our daughter. Still refusing to make eye contact and looking straight at the television set, he said it wasn't up for discussion. He wanted to get away from me for a few days to think about our relationship. *Am I just supposed to accept this?* I began to cry and begged him to reconsider, but he said his mind was made up.

I reminded him that he wasn't a single man who could just come and go as he pleased. I also reminded him that we couldn't afford to just drop money on a roundtrip ticket like that because we had responsibilities. He said I didn't have to worry because his grandparents had given him money to go and he had already purchased a non-refundable ticket. In fact, he would be leaving in a couple days. *What? How could he do this to us?* In my desperation to get him to change his mind, I told him I'd be happy to call his sisters and ask them to fly out to us, and even offered to pay for their flights. He was unwilling to meet me halfway or come to any compromise. All he said was that I needed to stop insisting because I was only making this worse; I was the reason he needed to get away and my behavior was proving him right.

I was devastated. I told him it was incredibly unfair for him to notify me after he'd already decided, and selfish of him to not give me enough notice for me to make plans to go to Los Angeles and visit my family while he was away. It's the least he could have done, but I know now that this was all part of his plan. He enjoyed keeping me isolated from the people I loved. It was how he was able to coerce and manipulate me. Besides, he knew that if I went to Los Angeles, I'd pay his grandparents a visit and would discover that he had been lying to me.

I was angry, sad, and disappointed in him for leaving us and in me for choosing to stay despite everything he was putting me through. Instead of standing up for myself, I gave him my blessing and told him that if space and time is what he needed, I would give him that.

In the months leading up to this, I had become close with my co-worker friend and her sister, who was also Samantha's daycare provider. I had mentioned being sad about the news of my husband's imminent trip. They thought it would be a good idea to get my mind off things and said we should have a potluck that evening. I could definitely use the distraction, so we agreed to have some adult fun in the living room while our kids enjoyed a playdate in the playroom. I had been perfecting a recipe for an enchilada casserole my brother-in-law taught me to make and decided to bring that as my dish. I was hoping to see my husband before heading out for the evening, but he didn't make it home in time. I grabbed our daughter and my casserole dish, and off we went.

Although my friends were Latinas, they had been born and raised in the midwest, Indiana to be exact, and didn't speak a lick of Spanish. My co-worker friend was in her late twenties, single, and on a diet to lose weight because she had gained a few extra pounds after her most recent breakup. Perhaps it was because we worked in retail, but I always thought she dressed very well and I admired how she always completed her look with the perfect accessories and her beautiful makeup. Her older sister was the complete opposite. Her daily attire was that of the typical '90s stay-at-home mom: oversized t-shirts, baggy shorts, running shoes with scrunched up socks, a messy high ponytail held by a scrunchie, and not a drop of makeup or a single accessory other than her wedding ring. Their house looked like something out of a *Country Living* magazine, with plaid scattered throughout the house, wooden decorations everywhere, and roosters all throughout the kitchen. It was a busy house, but everyone who entered was always welcomed with much love and met with my friends' big personalities, which I loved being around.

    When I arrived at their place, I was greeted with the usual warm welcome. As I made my way into the kitchen to drop off the casserole, my friend told me that she hoped I didn't mind, but she had invited one of the new mommies whose daughter was also in her daycare. It so happened that both their husbands were in the same squadron and were currently deployed on the same ship. I didn't mind at all. *If anything*, I thought, *the more the merrier.* When the guest arrived, we were introduced and she seemed like a nice person. Like me, she was petite, had darker skin and long dark hair. My friend actually pointed out how much she thought the new mommy and I had in common; besides having similar features, we were about the same age, we were both Latinas, and our daughters were both named Samatha. I agreed that we seemed to have some things in common, but something about her was giving me a weird vibe. I had only just met this girl, but she was sizing me up, checking me out, and just staring at me with such intent that she was making me a little anxious. *Whatever, I wasn't there for her and I really needed this night with my friends.*

The evening progressed and after dinner, we sat around the dining room table chatting, laughing, and enjoying some dessert. I couldn't help but notice that the new mommy wouldn't take her eyes off me and seemed to be asking a lot of questions--of me in particular. I shared a little about myself, then asked her to tell me about herself. She said that she was originally from Texas. She said in fact, she was flying home for the weekend because it was her birthday and her dad was throwing her a big party. With her husband being gone, she was feeling especially homesick and was really looking forward to much needed family time. I sympathized with her because being a military wife could be quite lonely, especially when living so far away from the people you love.

Overall, the evening turned out to be everything I needed. I was glad I went and made the best of it, despite my husband's trip weighing heavily on my mind. After helping clean up a little, I decided it was time for me to head home so that Samantha could spend time with her father before bedtime. With her in tow, I thanked my friends for a lovely evening, wished the new mommy a happy birthday weekend, and headed home.

When Friday morning arrived, and my husband prepared to leave, I could feel myself becoming emotional. He had made arrangements to get to the airport on his own because I had to work and couldn't take him myself. I figured it was probably for the best because I was not in the right frame of mind. I just wanted the weekend to be over quickly so that we could move past whatever this was. We said our goodbyes and went our separate ways. It was such a strange feeling, knowing that my husband was leaving solely for the purpose of clearing his mind and figuring out the future of our relationship, as though I had committed a crime and was awaiting my sentence.

As I sit here typing these words, I cannot believe how absolutely naive and blinded I was. Could I really not see the writing on the wall? Had I really not pieced the puzzle together yet? I guess I needed to have somebody spell it out for me.

After we parted ways, an unshakable heaviness set over my heart. I was extremely emotional but tried distracting myself with work, and later, with homework and Samantha. It was all in vain because I couldn't focus and my mind kept coming back to him. I wondered whether he arrived safely and what he might be doing or even thinking about. I felt a desperate need to call him, but how would I reach him? I didn't have his sisters' numbers and I wasn't close to them like that anyway. Over the five-and-a-half years my husband and I had been together, I had only met his sisters a handful of times.

As Samantha and I prepared to turn in for the night, I thought it would be nice to have her sleep in my bed rather than her crib. Keeping her close to me always made me feel better, especially when her dad was away or working late. I always left a nightlight on for us and loved staring at her beautiful porcelain face as she closed her eyes and her long dark lashes draped over her lids. She liked having the tips of my fingernails gently scratch her tiny arms or caress her sweet face, which is what I would do until she fell asleep.

It had been a long day and an even longer night, but as heavy as my eyes felt, I was too restless to get them to close or my mind to quiet down. I hadn't heard from my husband at all since he'd left that morning and I wondered why he hadn't checked in, not even to wish our daughter a good night. I couldn't help but feel angry at him, but my mother had always said to never go to sleep with anger in my heart, so instead, I prayed. I prayed that he had arrived safely, I asked God to soften his heart and help him come to his senses, and I hoped he would call first thing in the morning. With that thought, I finally got my eyes to close.

I was deep asleep when I heard our home phone ringing from a distance. *Am I dreaming of it or is it really ringing?* As I opened my eyes, I looked over at the alarm clock and saw that it was close to four in the morning. *Who could possibly be calling this late? Wait, maybe it's my husband. Oh my gosh, what if something happened?* I panicked because nobody gets a middle-of-the-night call for any good reason. I quickly picked up and said, "Hello?" I was met with silence. *Perhaps my voice was too low and he didn't hear me.* Giving it a second try, this time sounding more alert, I repeated, "Hello?" A familiar voice suddenly came over the line, except it wasn't my husband's. This voice was that of a young woman.

I let out a sigh of relief when I realized it wasn't either of my sisters-in-law because this girl had a southern twang and they didn't. If it wasn't them, that means my husband was okay. Listening with intent, I heard the woman say, "Is this Karen?" I was trying to remember where I'd heard this voice before and wondered what this voice was doing, calling me in the middle of the night. But my brain was still half asleep and nothing was registering.

I responded, "Yes, this is Karen. Who's this?"

She said, "My name isn't important. I'm actually just calling to tell you that I'm fucking your husband."

Is this some kind of sick joke? Who would put this girl up to do such a thing? Before I could even respond she said, "Hello, are you there? Did you hear me? I'm calling to tell you I'm fucking your husband. He came to Texas to be with me. He's here with me now and even wants to have one last quickie before he flies back home to you." *Oh. He is in Texas, just not with his sisters. Okay.* Then it dawned on me: this was the girl I met over dinner at my friends' place. I knew because she had an unmistakable southern accent I'd never heard before. *But wait, how did she know my husband? How did she know my friends?* I was so confused. *Did they know? Did my friends know my husband was having an affair with the girl I'd met at their place? Did they set me up by inviting us both for dinner to see if I could piece it all together when she said she was going to Texas for her birthday the same weekend as my husband was going to Texas to see his sisters? No, it couldn't be. They loved me and they adored Samantha. They wouldn't be so cruel. No. There had to be another explanation for this coincidence.*

As Samantha slept just inches away from me, I looked over at her and tears slid down my face. It was one thing for me to be dragged through the mud, but she didn't deserve this. Besides... *Wait, wait a minute! How did this girl have my home number? How did she... ah yes, of course, this was the girl my husband must have been on the phone with all those evenings he sat in the kitchen talking quietly; it was never his friends he was talking to, it was her. This was the girl he befriended in school.* It all made sense now. A few months prior he had asked whether our daycare provider had any openings because his classmate was looking for a job but didn't know anyone on base who could watch her daughter. He must have given her our provider's number and that is how our daughters ended up in the same daycare. *The hickies. The chain of hickies he'd come home with a few weeks prior, they were from her and not some random girl his friends had coerced at a party. The writing on the wall was now clear as day. All those months of enduring his lies, I thought I was losing my mind, but now I could see I wasn't crazy at all.*

As I lay there trembling, speechless, with a million thoughts running through my head, I felt like I had just been sucker punched. But I couldn't let this girl get the best of me. Together with my husband, she had taken enough from me, and I wasn't about to let her take my dignity too. I wouldn't give her the satisfaction of thinking she had broken me. This was my moment to take back all my power; this was the blessing in disguise I didn't know I had been waiting for, and it was the final straw I needed to break free from the ties that had been binding me to this miserable, God forsaken marriage.

It felt as though hours had passed, yet it had only been seconds. I came back to the call and calmly asked, "Who is this? Why are you the one calling me if he's there with you? If you are brave enough to call, be brave enough to tell me your name."

Angrily, she said, "Are you stupid or what? I'm telling you I'm fucking your husband and that he's here with me in Texas, and all you care about is what my name is?" Before I could respond, she continued, "He's in the bathroom and he doesn't know I'm calling you, but I wanted you to know."

"No. I'm not stupid at all because I know exactly who this is and honestly, I thank you for calling me because you've actually done me a great favor." My response was not to her liking.

She became so angry you would have thought I was the one sleeping with her husband. "So what are you going to do about it? Now that you know he's sleeping with me and wants a quickie before going home to you, what are you going to do?"

Let's be honest, what could I do? At that moment, there was literally nothing I could do other than scream, cry, curse at her, and him! But even if I wanted to, I wasn't going to allow myself to stoop to their level or shed another tear for him. As I pictured them together, laughing at me for being naive and foolish and for getting away with their secret affair, I could feel whatever love I had left for him drain out of me. If it didn't hurt so much to be put in this position by the man who called himself my husband and the woman who looked me squarely in the eyes while eating my delicious enchilada casserole just a couple of nights earlier, I swear I would have burst into laughter. This was truly a comedic tragedy.

That's what this was. And frankly, I was done playing the role of the fool in this sorry-ass, low budget film.

As calmly as I could, I said, "I'm not going to do anything about it because he's not even worth it. I don't want him. I haven't for a very long time and the two of you deserve each other, so have at it."

Exasperated, she abruptly said, "Hold on!" and I could hear the phone getting passed or tossed around.

Then suddenly the sound of his voice, my husband's voice, the cheating bastard's voice, came over the line. Sounding very confused and obviously having no idea I was on the other end, he said, "Hello?" If there had been even an ounce of doubt in my mind that what this woman had said was true, hearing his voice cleared it all. He had in fact flown to Texas to be with her while our daughter and I lay all alone in the middle of nowhere waiting and praying for him to return home to us. It was everything I needed to hear to regain the strength I thought I'd lost when he dimmed my light.

To keep my voice from cracking, I quietly called his name and said, "By the time you get home tomorrow evening, we will be gone." I hung up, and just like that, my marriage was over.

18

I can write several more chapters on the aftermath of my separation from my ex-husband. However, and I hope you can understand why, I have chosen not to. I simply cannot justify giving him another ounce of energy in my story. What I will say is that the days, weeks, and months that followed were some of the most trying and challenging times in my life, not because I was sad it was over, but because he was determined to make leaving impossible. He wasn't used to not getting his way, especially not with me; the more I resisted his begging and pleading, the angrier he became. His anger led to stalking me, terrorizing me, and even threatening to kill me. As afraid for my life as I was, I couldn't and wouldn't allow myself to be paralyzed by my fear. I had to keep living and trust that God had my back because my story was only just beginning. After two restraining orders, numerous court hearings, and close to two years of looking over my shoulder, he finally came to accept that it was over, and I was finally free of him.

I was twenty-one years old, divorced, with no formal education or money, no furniture or place to call my own, and a two-and-a-half-year-old toddler in tow. We went from sleeping on my sister's couch to starting from scratch and moving into an empty apartment with not even a bed for Samantha and me to sleep on. Sleeping on the floor with only a sleeping bag and some covers caused her to develop a series of painful ear infections. We spent a lot of time in emergency rooms those days, and while I was losing sleep and so much weight that my family became concerned, I felt more alive and determined than ever before.

Ironically, seeing me in such a desperate situation, my mother and older sister encouraged me to return to my ex-husband, for the sake and welfare of my child, they said. They encouraged this despite having learned of the domestic abuse and infidelity I endured. It was hard for me to believe that the people who were supposed to want the best for me were also encouraging me to go back into the lion's den. I couldn't really judge them, though, for they were of a different place and time--one which encouraged women to stay in unhappy and unhealthy marriages for the sake of keeping the family together. I was not of that mindset.

I knew that had I stayed, or gone back, I would not only be risking my mental and emotional wellbeing, but also my physical health. Because while my ex-husband claimed to have had protected sex with his mistress, I later discovered she had not been the only one. Upon learning of his other conquests, I feared the worst because my divorce was final in 1995, the same year that AIDS was at an all time high in the United States. I spent months after our divorce running tests to ensure I had not contracted any disease during our marriage. *The fact that I was put in that position at all sickens me to no end. If he was unhappy, why not be man enough to leave? How could he have played Russian roulette with his health and, by extension, mine? What about Samantha? How could he be so selfish that he didn't stop to think about what would happen to her if we weren't around to care for her? Did he really never consider the consequences of his actions? No, I would never so much as consider going back to that man.*

I understand and don't judge anyone who has ever chosen to stay or return to their abusive relationships, but for me, going back would have made me lose all self-respect. Frankly, it would not have been the example I wanted to set for Samantha, who deserved to know what a gentle, respectful, loyal, and loving relationship feels like. If I went back, I could never tell her not to date the kind of person who would hurt her, put their hands on her, or betray her, when I was married to that person. So while my mother and sister were encouraging me to go back for the sake of my child, it was, in part, for her sake that I chose not to, and I'm so thankful that I didn't.

The first year after the divorce was the hardest for Samantha because she was too young to understand the why. This made things more emotionally difficult for me because I felt a lot of guilt and sometimes even shame for having put her through the ringer. Until then, she had never really been a temperamental child, but I understood that it was part of the painful processing she had to go through. Although for the most part she was still a happy little girl, the divorce profoundly changed her, and she became an anxious and highly sensitive child. How could she not be when she witnessed and heard violence in her formative years, the most important years in a child's development? How could she not be anxious when her life was suddenly, and without warning, uprooted and changed forever? I have had to work exceptionally hard to forgive myself and rid myself of the guilt I have carried over the years for not having been able to protect her and give her a more beautiful childhood experience. Yet, no matter how hard things sometimes got for us, she was and has always been my rock, my motivation, and my biggest cheerleader. This may sound strange, but her love for me was so unconditional that I sometimes felt unworthy of it. I will forever wonder how I came to be lucky enough to have a child who could somehow see past every single one of my flaws and still think I was amazing.

I have her to thank for encouraging me to return to school and finish what I had started years prior. I always knew that someday, when time and money permitted, I would return to school and make my dream of earning my degree a reality. Although I had accepted that I needed to put my dreams on hold until she could stand on her own two feet, she insisted that I not wait. She asked and pushed until I gave in and enrolled in college.

Financially, it was going to be tough to do because Samantha was in private school and I received no financial assistance from her father. But as they say, "Where there is a will, there is a way," and I found my way. I became the first and only one of my mother's nine children to graduate from a university--with honors. It is something I am not only proud of myself for doing but grateful to Samantha for. She encouraged me to believe in myself as much as she believed in me. Exactly eighteen years to the day of my high school graduation, which she had attended, Samantha also watched me graduate college. I not only dedicated my achievement to Samantha and to my immigrant Guatemalan mother but also to my inner child who had never been told she could do anything she ever wanted if she simply allowed herself to believe she could.

"… the sweet and soft spoken lady who so bravely crossed the border illegally to give her children a better life, was now officially a U.S. citizen!"

19

When I was twenty-five years old, and my life was quietly stable, the sister my mother was living with to help care for her children decided she wanted to be more independent. At this point, my mother was not yet at retirement age but had not worked in so long that finding employment would have been impossible for her to do. My sister felt that because I was single and financially stable, perhaps it would be a good idea for our mother to come live with me.

I worked very hard to reach professional goals and was doing relatively well for myself, but people drew their own conclusions about my financial status with absolutely no idea of the sacrifices I made just to be able to make ends meet. I was on my own and without the financial support of my former spouse. Regardless, I was happy to have my mother come live with me and Samantha. I cannot think of a greater gift I could have been given.

I will admit that the thought of living with my mother was also nerve-wracking. Not only had I not lived under the same roof as her for over a decade, I was also still somewhat resentful of her for pressuring me into marrying my ex-husband and for trying to convince me to go back to him despite all the pain and suffering. But, I figured this would help us reconnect and provide an opportunity for us to heal that past. I was especially grateful to my twin because she stepped in by offering to also move in with us in order to lend her financial support. We got a place big enough for all of us to live comfortably and it was one of the best chapters in my life.

Samantha was incredibly fortunate to literally have three mothers under one roof: her grandmother, her godmother, and her biological mother. It was such a special time, even in those imperfect moments when we would get on one another's nerves. What I loved most was that we created traditions that were our very own. Traditions like taking my mother, who was a very picky eater, to The Cheesecake Factory on her birthday, which she surprisingly loved. And, because we are foodies, all our outings were centered around food; we would go to our favorite spots where we became regulars and all the staff knew us.

My mother was very talented and became a pretty amazing entrepreneur late in life. She would make arts and crafts, or she would buy silver jewelry from a woman she befriended at the jewelry mart and sell it to family and friends. My twin and I would promote her business and help her sell her jewelry at our respective workplaces. It was nice seeing my mother gain some independence and feel like she could contribute in her own way.

Most of all, I was incredibly proud of her for working as hard as she did to become a U.S. citizen. She had been a U.S. resident for many years, but becoming a citizen was a dream she never gave up on. She had been hesitant to pursue citizenship because before being a senior citizen, she would have been required to take the oral exam in English and without an interpreter, which made her extremely uncomfortable. She never gave herself enough credit for understanding the English language. She knew it better than she admitted to herself, but she didn't even feel confident enough to speak English around her children for practice. Instead, she waited patiently to reach an age where she could take the oral exam with a Spanish interpreter present.

Through my aunt, my mother met an American nun who taught free citizenship classes for anyone preparing to take the exam. My mother was very taken by this nun and became incredibly fond of her and her classmates. They would have potlucks and parties to celebrate those who'd passed the exam, and my mother poured her heart and soul into her studies. I can still remember the day of her appointment. I took the day off from work because she asked me to be her interpreter. I had no idea what I was getting myself into, but there was no way I would say no to her.

Immediately upon arriving at the immigration offices, I noticed a visible change in my mother; she was nervously shaking, flushed and sweaty. I hadn't realized until that moment how much pressure my mother put on herself, and I wondered whether it was a trait she had passed on to me, because I have always been my worst critic and put a tremendous amount of pressure on myself. I wanted to ease her mind and give her the same encouraging words I often gave myself, *you don't need luck when you show up prepared*. As we sat in the waiting area with the other nervous test takers, I could sense the nervous tension in the air. I took a few deep breaths, gently grabbed my mother's left hand, and quietly reminded her how hard she had worked and that she had this in the bag; this was her moment to shine and nothing was going to get in the way of that. My calming presence and confidence in her seemed to help.

When my mother's name was called, we immediately got up and walked toward the door to enter the interviewing office. *This is it. This is the moment my mother has spent the last several months preparing for. My heart is pounding but I can't let her know that.* Because I had come as her interpreter, I was allowed to enter the interview room with her. We were greeted by a middle-aged American woman with bleach blonde hair wearing a white suit; she looked serious and somewhat intimidating. With barely a smile on her face, she introduced herself, said she would be conducting my mother's oral exam, and asked us to follow her down into her office. As nervous as my mother was, I could see that she was ready to get this over with. I, on the other hand, did not feel ready at all. I had not spent enough time going over the questions with my mother and I didn't know the direct translation for most of the terminology used for these types of exams. O*h my gosh, what have I gotten myself into? I cannot have my mother fail because of me! I could never live with myself if I let her down.*

The interviewer must have noticed my nervousness because she told me to relax, take a deep breath, and just do the best I could. She instructed me not to coach my mother on what to say and asked that I slowly relay the randomly chosen questions to her as best as I could translate them. Then, I was to listen for the response, which I would translate into English and provide to her.

One by one, the interviewer asked the questions printed on the white pages of her thick notebook. I translated some half-assed version of whatever she asked, but thankfully, my mother took whatever she could make of what I was saying and answered each and every question beautifully. She was asked about ten to a dozen random questions and when it was over, the interviewer gave us the great news that my mother had passed with flying colors! While we were not surprised at all, we were beyond thrilled and we looked over at each other, hugged, and cried tears of joy. My mother even made the serious lady tear up because, in her very broken English, my mother couldn't stop thanking her with tears streaming down her face. *I* felt like such a proud momma at that moment. That look on her face, when the lady said she had passed, is embedded in my brain for the rest of my days. We couldn't stop smiling as we walked out, and ironically, some of the staff even suggested I should apply for a position at their offices. *Thanks, but no thanks,* I thought. This was all the translating I could handle.

When we made it to the car, I called my family to let them know that our mother, the sweet and soft spoken lady who so bravely crossed the border illegally to give her children a better life, was now officially a U.S. citizen! We were all immensely proud of her.

20

When a person becomes a U.S. citizen, they are given the option to legally change their name before the swearing in ceremony. My mother, who had stopped using her deceased husband's name years prior, decided she wanted to take his name back. She indicated that when the day she passed came, she wanted her married name to be reflected on her tombstone. I was surprised to hear her say this as I didn't know she gave her mortality much thought at all. For one, death was a subject she was never open to discussing unless it was in reference to somebody who had already died, and two, she thought of it as a taboo subject, both tasteless and unnecessary to bring up in conversation.

Obviously, death isn't the most cheerful subject to bring up in conversation, but I do believe it is a subject worth discussing with loved ones because it is guaranteed that if you come to exist, you too will come to pass. Yet, so many of us choose to ignore this fact. I encourage people to normalize having these conversations because they are rituals which allow us to honor our loved ones after they've departed. I, for one, have no problem talking about death and what I envision my services to look like. In fact, I often remind my family that I want my life to be celebrated with a huge party and live music, and if any tears are going to be shed, I want them to be tears of joy because I have lived an amazing life and I know I'm simply returning home to my rightful destination.

Needless to say, I was pleasantly surprised and grateful that my mother opened the door to that conversation because it allowed me to inquire about details I felt were important to know. In that conversation, I learned that she preferred to be cremated because she didn't want worms crawling all over her dead body. She also said she wanted her ashes buried under two trees to give her plenty of shade in the hot summer months. I lovingly giggled at her requests and assured her I would do everything possible to grant her those wishes.

As I look back on that conversation, I'm overcome with a bittersweet mixture of emotions because I was happy to know what it was my mother wanted, but sadly, I also know it was a conversation preparing me for what was to come sooner than I ever expected it would. A few short years after this conversation took place, my mother was diagnosed with terminal ovarian cancer, also referred to as *the silent killer*.

As we came to learn, ovarian cancer is one of the deadliest cancers a woman can develop because there are little to no symptoms, which makes it difficult for doctors to detect despite all the advanced technology available today. For most women diagnosed with this type of cancer, by the time it is actually detected, it is already in its late stages or has metastasized to other vital organs, which leaves little to no chance of survival. Of course, doctors will always offer treatments such as chemotherapy, but it is only to prolong one's life without necessarily offering one a good quality of life.

We aren't quite sure how long the cancer had been present in my mother's body, but it was becoming increasingly apparent that something was terribly wrong. Her once youthful looks were slowly getting lost in her sunken face as she inexplicably began losing weight and energy. The walks she had so loved to take with Samantha when she picked her up from school were becoming more difficult for her to endure, and she would have to make several stops to rest in between. She went to different specialists who ran a series of different tests, but nobody could seem to find the source of her ailments. I worked and went to school full-time, which made dedicating time for my mother's doctors' visits impossible. Thankfully, one of my sisters was a stay-at-home mom and had enough flexibility to take our mother to her appointments.

After exhausting all viable options, the doctors felt the only thing left to do was to perform a biopsy. It was the only way of knowing for certain whether there was any illness present that was not detectable through tests. I wish I would have been able to be more proactive in my mother's care and taken the time to get a second and third opinion, but all I could do was hope and trust that my mother was in good hands and that the doctors were guiding my family in the right direction. Her biopsy, an invasive surgery which would take hours to complete, was scheduled for early one Monday morning in late January of 2007. It was a sunny day, too warm for winter, and my entire family was there. We were such a big group that we occupied about half the space in the hospital lobby, where we patiently, anxiously, and nervously waited.

With every passing hour, you could feel the air in the room filling up with tension and fear, making it increasingly difficult to breathe. We sat around, sometimes in silence, sometimes quietly talking, and sometimes even cracking jokes to lighten the mood, but it was almost as though we were all holding our breath in anticipation.

Then finally, the surgeon in his light blue scrubs, white lab coat, and salt-and-pepper hair came out to speak with my family. I immediately stood up and walked ahead, ready and prepared to hear whatever news he had to share. By the look on his face and the energy around him, I knew right away that it was not going to be good news and I braced myself for whatever would come. I could feel my entire family standing near and around me, but my eyes were fixated on the doctor who had just performed my mother's biopsy and hopefully had all the answers we had been waiting for.

He started by saying that my mother's heart had briefly stopped during surgery. They had successfully resuscitated her but her heart was weak. She was now in stable condition and they would continue monitoring her closely. *Okay.* I let out a sigh of relief. *It wasn't news I was expecting to hear, but she is stable and that is a good thing. Is that it or is there more?* I searched his face and I could see there was more. *Okay, there's more. Brace yourself, Karen.* He continued by saying that much to his and the other surgeon's shock and surprise, my mother had what appeared to be ovarian cancer, which had already significantly spread to her vital organs; it was everywhere. He was sorry to inform us that there was absolutely nothing they could do for her and had no choice but to simply close her up.

Just as he finished speaking, I began to hear crying and sobbing all around me, but I didn't cry. I wanted to, but first I needed to know. I needed him to tell me how much time we had, and I asked the question nobody wanted the answer to. He said that based on his professional experience, my mother had roughly three to six months to live. *Three to six months? Okay, let me wrap my head around this. It's late January, which means that in the worst case scenario, she might barely make it to Mother's Day. Best case scenario, she would make it past her seventy-first birthday in late May and Samantha's fifteenth birthday in June. But she will be gone long before the holidays.*

It was strange to think that life, or that we, would have to carry on without her. I didn't even want to think about that right now. As I stood there, doing this God forsaken math in my head, tears began welling up in my eyes and there was a lump in my throat so big I could hardly speak to thank the doctor for informing us. He expressed his deep sorrow and said he wished he had better news for us. For now, he would be submitting his initial findings to the lab and once we had confirmation, they would provide options for a plan moving forward. In the meantime, the nurses would notify us when it was okay to go in to see our mother.

As the doctor walked away, I turned around to face my family, and all I could see was everyone I loved falling to pieces and sobbing in one another's arms. I was in such disbelief that I didn't know whether to sit, stand, run outside to catch my breath, thank God for saving my mother's life, or curse at him for threatening to take her from me. I thought about my mother's heart, which the doctor had just described as weak. He didn't know my mother well enough to know that it was actually stronger, braver, and more resilient than it appeared. *If her heart was weak at all, it was only because she has spent her entire life giving pieces of it away to the world, which has not always given very much back to her.* She was, after all, the woman who survived the loss of both her parents and her husband before the age of thirty-five, the woman who single-handedly crossed the U.S. border with her seven children to give them a better life than the one they were destined for in Guatemala, the woman who had been left at the abortion clinic by my father with nobody to fend for her but herself, the woman who endured countless hardships but never used any one of them as a crutch. Laying there in that surgery room, she may have needed to take a little break to recharge, but make no mistake, there was absolutely nothing weak about my mother's heart.

As my mind raced, I thought about Samantha who had been in school all day and had been picked up by her father. She must have been worried because I hadn't reached out to her. Not because I didn't want to, but because I didn't know what I would say to her. *How can I tell her that my mother, her beloved mama (because my mother didn't like being called anything other than that) who'd played such an important role in her raising and upbringing, would soon be leaving us? How do you explain something which you can hardly comprehend or accept yourself* to somebody else? My head hurt from all the crying I'd been doing and I couldn't think straight. I would have to talk with her when I felt strong enough to do so.

As the day turned night, and we continued waiting in the hospital lobby to see our mother, I was growing restless. And frankly, I had grown tired of looking around that cold, bland hospital lobby with those dirty beige walls and fake plants, and at the sliding glass door opening every few seconds from people walking in and out. *How is this space supposed to provide any comfort to the families sitting around worrying about their loved ones? Why do these poorly upholstered chairs have to hurt so much to sit on? Why didn't I go buy myself some water before the gift shop closed? And can somebody please, for the love of God, turn the channel to something other than the news? What do I care about the weather forecast or sports updates when my world is crashing down around me?!* I wanted to leave so badly but I wouldn't until I had a chance to see my mother. I needed to see for myself that she was really okay.

As we continued waiting, we slowly began to find the strength to talk with one another. We had so many questions, like where do we go from here? What were we going to tell our mother? Would we tell her she was dying? If so, how would we break this news to her? Who will be the one to tell her? Did we need to make funeral arrangements? My brother, the middle of the three boys, abruptly objected and said it was too soon for that. He wanted us to wait until we knew for sure. We agreed that we would wait.

It dawned on me in that moment that it often takes something of this magnitude to happen in one's life to realize how absolutely precious time is. We live our lives thinking we have plenty of it and put off doing or saying the things we want, while at the same time wishing we had more of it because it never feels like enough.

The universe had set the time clock into motion and my family became instantly aware that time would soon begin to run out, not just for our precious mother, but for our family as a whole. Because the truth is that she was the foundation that made our family indestructible and was keeping us together despite all our differences. Whether we were willing to admit it or not, we all knew that without her, we would come crashing down as any structure without its foundation eventually does.

Our mother had been given three to six months to live and we, her children, were given that same amount of time to do whatever was necessary to keep the clock from running out of time.

21

It came as no surprise that the lab work supported the surgeon's initial findings and confirmed what we had been praying was not true: our mother was, in fact, terminally ill. This is the kind of news that doesn't get easier to hear no matter how many times you hear it. It feels a lot like experiencing a series of earth shattering quakes and having no time to grab hold and prepare for the next one.

By now, my mother had been released from the hospital and was comfortably resting in our home. On the day she was released, a few of us had gone to pick her up. On our way out of the hospital, my sister who'd come in from San Francisco said she wanted to stop in at the gift shop because she had seen some nice nightgowns and wanted our mother to pick one out for herself. Of course, my mother being the fancy lady that she was, picked out the fanciest and most expensive one in the shop, which was a beautiful ivory silk nightgown with lace trimming. We all laughed and told our sister she should have known what she was getting herself into when she offered.

My siblings and I were more united than ever during this time. We wanted to make our mother's journey ahead as smooth and non-disruptive to her wellness as possible, and we began holding family meetings to discuss how we could best support and care for her. As we considered the immediate future, I realized it would be difficult to be fully present if I continued working and going to school full-time while also attempting to juggle my personal life and my mother's care. I needed to take some things off my plate, which included distractions and commitments of lesser priority. We all did what we had to and for me, that included walking away from a relationship with someone I really cared for. I wasn't emotionally available or strong enough to keep us together, and the relationship was suffering as a result. We made every attempt to remain friends, but my heart wasn't in it and he grew tired. In addition, I reluctantly made the difficult decision to once again put my dreams of finishing school on hold and I took an indefinite leave of absence, because I knew that if I didn't, I would come to regret it later. I was grateful when my workplace accommodated me in transferring to an office that was minutes away from my home. I wasn't alone, because my entire family made their fair share of sacrifices, but it was the least we could do for the one person who had sacrificed everything for us.

As we suspected, my mother's treating doctors provided a plan to move with recommendations which included she undergo chemotherapy. It actually felt more like we were being pressured into convincing her to undergo chemo, but it wasn't up to us because the only person who was going to decide her fate was my mother. We asked all the necessary questions, including whether chemotherapy was a life-saving option, but the doctors said that it wasn't because her cancer was just too advanced. The only thing chemo might possibly do was prolong her life; however, they could not guarantee her a good quality of life in the process.

Upon hearing this, my siblings and I agreed that chemotherapy did not seem to be a viable option for our mother. What would be the point of having her alive if it meant she would be in pain or suffering because of all the side effects? But, because it wasn't up for us to decide, we provided our mother with all the information she would need to make an informed decision. Regardless of our personal opinions, we would offer her our support in whatever decision she made.

We did, however, decide that for the time being, it was best to withhold one piece of information: we would not tell her that she was terminal. This may sound selfish, but we really wanted our mother to fight for her life and we feared that if she knew she was terminal, she would give up prematurely and choose not to fight at all.

Based on my mother's reaction to the news of her diagnosis, it seemed as though she had already been mentally preparing herself because she showed no emotions whatsoever. She did not express any sadness, fear, anger--nothing--she didn't even cry. I think a part of her was relieved to finally have the answers she had been desperately seeking all those months of visiting different doctors and running countless tests. I also think she was just tired. In many ways, my mother had lived a beautiful life, but it had also been quite a hard life. I honestly feel that she held on as long as she did for the sake of her children more than for herself.

From the beginning, my mother was adamant about not wanting to undergo chemotherapy; she had already done it before to treat her cervical cancer and she swore she would never do it again. Against the doctor's recommendations, we supported our mother's decision to decline any traditional medical treatment and instead, we offered her some alternatives to consider.

My mother agreed to give the holistic approach a try because it was less invasive and would not have the same side effects as traditional medicine treatments. We had researched and found a holistic treatment center in El Grullo, Jalisco, Mexico, which offered a variation of plant medicine treatments and had a high rate of success. To avoid having her go alone, my sister and brother-in-law put their lives on hold and offered to accompany her for the duration of the treatment. This was a huge sacrifice for them to make because they had three teenage kids at home, but they were more than willing to do it for our mother. The fact that my brother-in-law was willing to uproot his life for the sake of my mother's is a testament of the profound love everyone in her life felt for her.

Although my siblings and I were all financially established, seeking holistic treatment in a different country is a huge financial undertaking because none of it is covered by medical insurance. We decided to pool our resources together to make it possible for our mother to have a fighting chance. With no time to waste, we made all the necessary arrangements to get our mother to Mexico and get her started on her treatment.

Upon her arrival at the treatment center, the doctors laid out a plan for my mother to adhere to in order to see results. We knew from the beginning that the treatment plan was going to be challenging for her because it required an entire lifestyle change, including a strict plant-based diet. My mother had never been a serious carnivore, but she was used to eating whatever she wanted and the dietary restrictions were not to her liking. She hated not being able to have her morning *cafe con leche* and *pan dulce* (coffee with milk and sweet bread). As she put it, her least favorite thing of all was having to wake up before dawn to bathe in ice cold water. I didn't blame her for hating these rules she wasn't used to, but it was certainly better than how awful chemotherapy would have made her feel.

Although my mother had taken several books to read and music to listen to, and could spend as much time as she wanted outdoors with my sister and brother-in-law, she quickly began showing signs of mild depression, which she had struggled with in years past. We thought that having family around would help keep her spirits up, but she was withdrawing and opting to isolate herself in her room. My sister would sometimes find her sitting in total darkness, which began to concern us a great deal, but we were hopeful that she would hang in there long enough to at least finish her first round of treatment. Much to our disappointment, she didn't.

Just a few short weeks into her treatment, our mother asked to be discharged and return home. While I was happy to be able to see her again, hearing that she had given up on her treatment was a blow to our spirit because we knew that without that, her cancer would only continue advancing. But, we had promised to support her unconditionally and that meant accepting whatever decision she felt was best for her.

Upon returning home, one of my other sisters, who lives in Northern California, suggested trying Chinese medicine. She had done some research on it and thought it was worth giving a try; and, our mother would not have to stay in a clinic because she would stay with my sister who would facilitate the treatments as directed by the Chinese medicine doctor. My mother agreed to give it a shot and headed to San Francisco. My sister had also put her life on hold in efforts to support our mother in this endeavor, and we were all very grateful to her. Also, we were hopeful that our mother would respond well enough to the treatment to stick with it.

A few weeks went by and we were all relieved to hear that my mother seemed to be responding well to treatment. We figured that being in the comfort of my sister's home and having her grandchildren there was helping keep our mother's spirits high. Although it was comforting knowing that our mother was closer to home, I was missing her a great deal and our place felt less like a home without her presence. It was now May, four months since her diagnosis, and between her leaving for Mexico and then San Francisco, it felt as though she had been gone forever.

As Mother's Day approached, I decided to forego my own celebration with Samantha and instead pay my mother and sister a surprise visit in San Francisco. Samantha was in her final weeks of school and stayed behind, which made me feel a little better because I didn't know what state my mother would be in upon my arrival. Also, I figured it would be a good opportunity to give my sister a little break if there was anything she had been needing or wanting to do for herself. My twin sister wanted to go, and we extended the invitation to my other sisters, but only the eldest could join us.

Our flight from Burbank to Oakland was quick and convenient, and we arrived in just under an hour. As soon as we landed, I called my sister to let her know we had arrived. She indicated that my mother had a doctor's visit that morning but they would arrive home shortly, which was perfect because it gave us plenty of time to pick up the rental car and drive across the Oakland bridge into San Francisco. *I don't know why, but I am beginning to feel nervous. Perhaps it's all the excitement of surprising our mother. I can't wait to see the look on her face!* Just as we arrived at my sister's place, she and our mother were also arriving home. I didn't know what to expect upon seeing my mother, but I can tell you I absolutely didn't expect (nor was I prepared) to find her in the physical state she was in.

As my mother slowly got out of the car, I could hardly believe my eyes. She was unrecognizable. There was a tired and vacant look in her once lively, bright eyes; she was so thin her clothes draped over her tiny frame, and the hair she had always taken such pride in keeping up was now gray. I had no words. As I leaned in to hug her, I got a whiff of her sweet familiar scent that brought me to tears because I knew my beautiful mother was still there, holding on for us. *Don't cry, Karen. Today is a happy day. Don't you dare let her see you cry.*

All I wanted to do at that moment was fly my mother back home with me, cuddle up next to her and never leave her side again. But she wasn't only my mother, she was all of ours, and I had to accept that we were all equally invested in doing everything we could to keep her alive. I know it meant a lot to my sister to have our mother under her care. She was, after all, the sister who had been injured in the house fire, and I believe she was as determined to give our mother the best care she could as our mother had been for her all those years prior. Looking over at my sister, I could see her spirit was weary and that caring for our mother on her own was taking a toll on her. But as usual, she put on the same brave face she always did, and assured us she had everything under control.

We were there for a one-night stay and wanted to make the most of our time with our mother. We hung out, relaxed and talked, and enjoyed a nice lunch together. While in the kitchen preparing the food, we checked in with our sister to see how she was holding up. We listened to her talk about how things had been going for her while she cared for our mother and all the challenges they were having because my mother didn't like the teas she was given. I could see my sister was tired and discouraged because our mother's health was not improving. I think my sister did not want to accept defeat and admit that the treatment wasn't helping our mother get any better. My mother also complained about the teas and said she wished my sister would stop encouraging her to drink them because they didn't make her feel better. All my mother wanted was to be home in Los Angeles, but she didn't have the heart to tell my sister. It was such a frustrating situation because I wanted to advocate for my mother and tell my sister she wanted to go home, but I also knew that in doing so, it would create tension between my sister and me, and I wanted to avoid any conflict because we needed to be united in our endeavor to help our mother. *I'll call a family meeting when I return home. Together we will decide what to do.*

The next morning, my mother woke up with enough energy to suggest going to breakfast at a local Guatemalan eatery nearby, which we all agreed was the perfect idea. It was a beautiful sunny day with clear skies, but the wind coming in off the coast was so chilly that I spent the day regretting not wearing more layers. When we arrived at the restaurant, we all ordered our favorite Guatemalan breakfasts. I had eggs with weenies, black refried beans, and *platanos fritos* (fried plantains). The food was delicious, and while we did our best to keep the conversation light and fun by sharing old stories, there was a sadness looming over us because we knew our time to return home was nearing, and this would be the last Mother's Day we would get to spend with our mother.

After brunch, my mother mustered the strength to walk over to a couple nearby shops, but it was obvious she was struggling to keep up. We cut our shopping adventure short and decided it was best for us to head back to my sister's place. Besides, we were only able to stay a little longer because we had our return flight to catch and still had to make our way back over the Oakland bridge. It had been a perfect couple days and I wished this time could have lasted forever, but it couldn't. We were all dreading having to say goodbye.

My mother had been comfortably relaxing on a reclining chair in the living room when I walked over to her. My first instinct was to sit on her lap as I had done countless times throughout my life, but instead, I knelt down next to her. *I know I said I wouldn't cry, but I don't know how much longer I can be brave. I feel the tears rising up in my throat. Take a deep breath, Karen. Hold it together for just a few more minutes.* I wrapped my arms around my mother and as I attempted to tell her how much I loved her, every tear I had been holding back throughout the entire trip came rushing out of me. I sobbed uncontrollably in my mother's arms and I didn't want to let her go. I could hear my mother and sisters crying, which only made me cry more. As much as it hurt to leave my mother on such a sad note, I could no longer hide the pain of seeing her so fragile and of having to leave without her next to me. It took everything I had to get up off my knees and walk out of my sister's house not knowing whether I would get to see my mother alive ever again.

The trip back home was gut-wrenching and I was inconsolable. I knew my sisters were deeply hurting as well, but I was so consumed by my own pain that it was impossible for me to lend them any emotional support at all. Silence would have to be our travel companion as we headed home. Upon arriving at my place, I thought a good night's rest would do me some good and I'd wake up in better spirits, but that was hardly the case. Instead, I lay there in the darkness of my bedroom, feeling the emptiness of my mother's absence, remembering the look on her face as we said goodbye and missing her more than ever. I felt powerless at the thought of my mother's precious life slipping through our fingers with nothing to do except wait. *When my mother's time on earth comes to an end, will that make me an orphan? No, that can't be. I will always have a mother, even if she is only with me in spirit.* It was in the midst of my painfully sleepless night that it dawned on me--as much as I loved and appreciated what my sister was doing for our mother, it was time to get her back home to Los Angeles; she needed to spend her final moments surrounded by all her children and grandchildren. It was the right thing to do, not just for our mother but for all of us who loved and missed her so much.

The next morning, I contacted my siblings who had not been able to go on the trip with us. I explained to them that despite the treatments she was undergoing, our mother's health was clearly declining and I didn't think there was much time left for us to get her home. I proposed that we have a family meeting to discuss making the necessary arrangements for our mother to return home, and that we set up hospice care as the doctors had suggested we do when the time came.

The next evening, while we were gathered to discuss a plan to move forward, we received word from our sister in San Francisco that our mother had been rushed to the hospital. This was the sort of dreadful news we hoped to never receive, especially not with our mother being hundreds of miles away. But there it was, my mother's impending death, daring us to make the next move. Except we had run out of moves and our mother had no more fight left in her. She appeased us by trying the alternative options we offered her and they didn't work.

How does one begin to prepare for an inevitable departure? We all had to accept it was coming, but we knew our mother would never return from it. This was not like the many vacations she had taken over the course of her life from which she would return with little gifts for each one of us. This was a one-way trip with a nonrefundable ticket to a destination unknown, booked and waiting to be redeemed by our mother alone.

"At that moment, I had the profound realization that we had come full circle; my mother was now our child and we were the parents."

22

When my sister notified us that my mother had been rushed to the hospital, my head began to spin. This was everything I had hoped to avoid and why I was so adamant about getting our mother back home. There was no reason our one sister should have to navigate our mother's health issues all alone when the rest of us were more than willing to help. I had already decided I'd take the next flight out because I could not sit by and do nothing. I knew my mother was in good hands at the hospital, but I wanted to be there in case things took a turn and to let my mother and sister know they were not alone. The middle of my three brothers, who had been in total denial about the severity of my mother's illness until now, said he wanted to go and offered to drive anyone who wanted to accompany him. I was all in but said I needed to go home to pack a bag and make arrangements for Samantha to go with her father. My twin and three older sisters also said they would go and we decided to meet back at my place a couple hours later. It was late, but we wanted to make it to San Francisco by early the next morning.

This was the first time in years that we were in the same car together. Throughout my life, my family had been big fans of going on family camping trips, but there were so many of us that we would have to take several cars and caravan to our destination. Only my mother had the power to bring us together like this, and it was really nice.

I don't know whether it was the late night drive or the adrenaline wearing off, but I was suddenly exhausted and could no longer keep my eyes open. *It has been a long day and we still have a long day ahead. It is probably best that I try to get a couple hours of sleep.* As I closed my eyes, I thought about all the guilt I had been feeling the last couple days for wanting to bring my mother home, which meant removing her from my sister's care. I know how much my sister had sacrificed her time, finances, and energy in order to help our mother get better, but this was in no way about my sister or her ability to care for our mother. We needed to focus on our mother's wellness and even though she wasn't getting better, I knew that being surrounded by all her children and grandchildren is what made her happiest. My mother deserved to live the rest of her days filled with as much joy and love as humanly possible, and I wanted to ensure we could give her that, especially with her seventy-first birthday just a few days away. As hard as it was to accept it, this would be her last birthday with us. All I could do was hope we had enough time to celebrate her life one last time.

It felt as though I had just closed my eyes when my brother announced that we had arrived. I was so grateful to him for making the drive; I really don't know how he did it. We were all exhausted, running on fumes, and decided we'd stop and get some coffee to get us through the morning. My sister had called us with an update from the doctors who confirmed that our mother's left lung had collapsed, which is why she had been having trouble breathing. She was now on a ventilator. There were several decisions that needed to be made about our mother's care, but she would wait for us to discuss and decide.

My mother had been a relatively healthy woman her entire life, and until her diagnosis a few months prior, I had never seen her laying in a hospital or hooked up to any machines. This was uncharted territory for me and it was not going to be easy to see her like that. I know my siblings were also struggling and preparing themselves to see her, but we all knew we had to be strong for our mother.

It was early morning but the hospital seemed very busy. There were nurses, doctors, patients, and families in the lobby, elevators, and hallways as though it were the middle of the day. I don't know if it was the lack of sleep or that my emotions were running high, but seeing so many people made me feel overwhelmed and claustrophobic. The elevator going up to see our mother was at capacity and I felt a panic attack coming on. I didn't know what to do, so I looked up at the elevator ceiling and took deep breaths. *Relax, Karen. Everything is going to be alright. Mom needs you right now, so be strong.*

In the large open room where our mother was staying, there were two beds across from each other; my mother's bed was to the left. I was glad to see she was currently the only one occupying the room, and the noise we had just left behind us was now silenced. We all paused for a second, as if to catch our breaths and gather ourselves. My mother was awake and looking out the window next to her bed; she seemed to be a million miles away. Almost in unison, we all walked over to her bedside together, and as we got closer, our mother turned and realized we were all standing there. She looked as though she was trying to figure out whether this was real or a figment of her imagination. When we said hello, she began to cry and called out to us, *"Mis hijos!"* (my children). This was the first time since my mother's diagnosis that I had seen her cry, and we all cried with her. She said she had just been praying and asking God for us to come to her. Her prayers were answered, and one way or another, we would find a way to make sure she got to leave with us.

Our mother couldn't move her left arm because it was extensively swollen as a result of her left lung collapsing. She told us that she had been feeling fine the day before when suddenly upon laying down to rest that evening, she couldn't breathe and almost felt like she was drowning. I'm so glad my sister was there to call the ambulance. I don't even want to imagine what might have happened if she hadn't been.

We had only been there a short while when a nurse walked in and said she was going to take our mother for a few hours because they needed to do another procedure to remove the excess fluid building in her lung. My mother wasn't very happy to hear this because the first procedure had been excruciating for her. As it turns out, the procedure was not only painful but also risky, because the area which the doctors must open in order to access the lung and drain it could easily become infected. An infection would only compromise our mother's already fragile state, but it was necessary for them to do the procedure if we were going to try to get her home. To make her feel better, the nurse said one of us could go with our mother if we wanted but warned it would take several hours. One of my sisters offered to go with her and the rest of us decided we would step out for a bite and to catch a breath of fresh air. It was still morning, but the day had already felt long and emotionally exhausting.

When we stepped outside, I was pleasantly surprised to find beautiful sunny skies and a relatively warm day. Something about this beautiful weather filled me up with hope. We decided we'd go to Fisherman's Wharf while we waited and grab some lunch. We were all enjoying a nice meal when my brother suggested we order drinks to help us relax. I didn't really want to drink, but everyone else was drinking, so I gave in. It was nice being there with my crazy family, laughing and forgetting, for that one moment, all the heaviness of the last five months.

We walked around and enjoyed the scenery until it was time to go back to the hospital. My mother's nurse said one of us could spend the night with our mother, and I volunteered to stay. I thought it would be really nice to pamper my mother and give her a pedicure, so I had my brother drive me to the local drugstore to pick up a few items I would need. When we arrived at the hospital, my mother was in high spirits and cracking jokes like she used to. It was so nice seeing her like this and I know it was because we were there.

    After my siblings left for the night, I showed my mother the bag of goodies I'd bought and told her I was going to pamper her with a little foot massage and pedicure. She was like a giddy child at a candy store; it was so sweet. But first, because I didn't want my mother to smell the alcohol on my breath, I excused myself to brush my teeth. My mother would not have judged me for drinking, but I didn't want her to think we were out there trying to have fun while she was enduring all that pain. At that moment, all I wanted was for my mother to forget about her pain, the hospital, the smell, the machines--everything.

    My mother made room for me on her bed and asked me to sit next to her instead of the chair, which was my bed for the night. We talked and laughed for a while, as though we had forgotten about everything going on around us, and then she asked if I could put on her *telenovela* because she missed the previous night's episode. As she watched, I massaged her hands, then her feet, and gave her the best pedicure of her life. I had picked out the prettiest nail polish I could find at the store, a burnt orange color that looked really pretty up against her olive skin. When I was done, I reminded her that we needed to give her toenails some time to dry, so she had to keep her blanket above her ankles. She was so happy with her freshly polished toes that she wouldn't stop wiggling her feet and staring down at them with a big smile on her face. At that moment, I had the profound realization that we had come full circle; my mother was now our child and we were the parents.

23

Early the next morning, my siblings arrived and we prepared to speak with the doctor about our mother's health and what the next steps were. I was now on two nights of minimal sleep and delirium seemed to be setting in. I was surviving on more coffee than I care to admit, but there was no time to focus on my exhaustion. We were on a mission to get our mother home and at that moment, that is all that mattered.

Seeing our mother visibly better since our arrival gave us hope that she would not only be released that day but also that we would be given the green light to take her back home to Los Angeles. We had discussed all of this with our sister, who agreed this was the best option; now that our mother would need around-the-clock care, she could not do it on her own. Assuming our mother would be released and clear to travel home, my sister would stay behind to tie up some loose ends and join us in a few days. I'm guessing she probably also needed some time to decompress because she had been single handedly doing all the work of caring for our mother. We all understood how draining that must have been for her, especially because she's a handicapped person herself. We all gave her so much credit for doing all that she could, and now it was our turn.

As we waited to speak with the doctor, I couldn't help but feel a little nervous about whether our mother would be able to travel in her condition. The thought of possibly leaving San Francisco without her was unbearable, but I remained hopeful that it would all work out for the best.

When the doctor arrived, we got right to it. We informed her that should we get the green light, our intention was to take our mother home to Los Angeles immediately upon being released from the hospital. We were all relieved when the doctor said this would not be a problem at all; however, considering our mother's delicate condition, there were some things to keep in mind. Firstly, she wanted us to know that they had removed enough fluid from our mother's lung that she would be okay. But for the duration of her life, our mother would require help with her breathing and would need to have an oxygen tank with her at all times. With this in mind, she would not be able to fly home and could only be transported by vehicle. She then explained that we could hire a private ambulance service or medical van to transport her, but this would be costly to do, considering the distance.

Although we appreciated the options, we weren't interested in having our mother transported by anyone other than ourselves. She wouldn't have wanted that and we also felt she was best off in our care. It was interesting to see how overprotective of our mother we had all become when she was no longer able to care for herself. She was the matriarch and queen of our family and we were all determined to make sure that everything regarding her wellbeing was handled with utmost respect and gentle care. *If we had always been this attentive to her needs, perhaps she wouldn't be sick and none of this would be necessary. Don't dwell on what you can't change; we are here for her now that she needs us most, and that is all that matters.*

We decided our mother would be transported in my brother's SUV, which was large and comfortable enough for her to travel lying down and still have plenty of room for the oxygen tank to be next to her. My brother-in-law had driven up from Los Angeles and arrived a couple hours prior, which was perfect because he was able to take my two eldest sisters back home in his car. The rest of us--myself, my twin, and one older sister--would drive back with our brother and mother. *I'm so grateful everything is working out as we hoped it would.*

Before letting us go, the doctor advised us that our mother's health was declining rapidly and she did not foresee her living beyond three month's time at most. Her recommendation was that we place our mother under hospice care to ensure that she would be kept as comfortable and pain-free as possible. *We were prepared for this news, and three months is actually better than I expected. All I want is for my mother to have the best life she can have in however much time she will be with us. It's obvious we've all been avoiding the end-of-life conversation, but it's time we start making plans. It's been a heavy couple days, though. Perhaps waiting a few more days would be best.* We knew right off the bat that we did not want any nurses caring for our mother, but we did agree that it would be good for us to have a professional come and check in on her regularly and provide us guidance on how to properly administer any medications we would need to give her. We let the doctor know that we would like to proceed with this plan, and we were incredibly grateful that she offered to have the hospital staff make all the necessary arrangements so that we wouldn't have to.

A few hours later, with the help of the hospital staff, our mother was carefully placed in my brother's car and we got on our way. This trip had started out with us feeling so scared, helpless, and even hopeless, but having our mother with us now made us feel so full of hope and gratitude. It was a long drive home because we were all emotionally, mentally, and physically drained, but it was all worth it. By the time we arrived at my place, a local hospice facility had already been contacted and they had delivered our mother's oxygen tanks and medications. The efficiency was beyond any expectation we had, and I let out a sigh of relief knowing we were in good hands. I use the term *we* because this journey wasn't only about my mother, it was also about all of us who loved her so much and who, whether we knew it or not, were also losing a piece of ourselves with every last breath she took.

After getting our mother upstairs to her bedroom and making sure she had everything she needed, my family left and it was just the two of us in our quiet place. Samantha would join us the following day, so tonight I would soak in the stillness and embrace this moment of having my mother all to myself.

Just weeks before my mother had been diagnosed, I noticed she had started sleeping with a light on and closing her bedroom door, which she had never done until then. When I asked her why, she said she had experienced some things which made her feel afraid. It started with her falling off her bed one night, which had never before happened, and soon after, she began feeling a presence around her, particularly near or at her bedroom doorway. She couldn't explain why, but it made her fearful, and that's why she preferred to sleep with the light on and the door closed. After she was diagnosed and we learned that she was terminal, I thought about that conversation and I knew the spirits of her loved ones were coming to help her transition. But I couldn't tell her that because she didn't know she was dying.

After I freshened up and put on my pajamas, I crawled in bed next to my mother and just stared into her loving eyes as she told me that she was happy to be home, surrounded by all her things. Her presence was immensely peaceful and I was happy to see her so at peace. Her left arm was still swollen and we had it propped up on a pillow to relieve some of the pressure. I grabbed her right hand, told her how much I loved her and promised her that from that day forward, she would never sleep alone or in darkness; I would make sure of that. In her tired and sleepy voice, she told me she loved me too and closed her eyes.

There is not a single word in my vocabulary that can describe the immensity of my love and appreciation for this amazing woman. I can only hope that through my loving words and actions, she knows how profoundly loved she is, by all of us who've benefited from her generous and kind heart.

24

In the days that followed our mother's return from San Francisco, my siblings and I came together for family meetings to discuss everything from our mother's care to funeral arrangements. For obvious reasons, these conversations are difficult to have, but when there are people still living in denial, it makes them so much more challenging; this is what was happening in our case. Our middle brother, who had been with us in San Francisco and had personally heard the doctor say our mother only had a few months to live, seemed unwilling and unable to accept our mother's fate. Whenever we discussed anything relating to her passing, he would become upset and ask us to stop talking about it. These were times when we were all walking on eggshells, but I also knew it would benefit us all to have these conversations now rather than later. My brother and I had always been close, but the constant tug-of-war was creating tension between us. I wanted us to talk openly about our mother's situation to have an opportunity to take her wishes into consideration, rather than avoid the subject altogether and play guessing games afterwards.

As a family, we didn't want to make arrangements without our brother on board, but we had to start moving forward with plans because time was of the essence, and he knew that. After pleading with him, our brother finally accepted--or at least agreed to go along with--moving forward, which we knew was hard for him but important. Much to my surprise, he and my other two brothers said they would agree with whatever the sisters wanted, because we knew our mother best. It was true and I was relieved to hear this; the fewer hands in the pot the smoother things would go.

Before we proceeded, however, we needed to talk with our mother. We felt that for her sake, the time had come for us to tell her she was terminal. We wanted to give her the opportunity to tend to any pending business she may have had or any last wishes to see anyone or any place she'd been longing to see. My mother was such a private person that we didn't know what she would say, but we wanted to at least give her the opportunity. Whatever it was she wanted, we were prepared to give to her if it was within our power to do so. *The only question now is "Who will tell her?" Which one of us has the courage and strength to tell our mother she is dying?*

As I have said before, I grew up in a household full of strong women, and by that I mean strong-willed women with very strong personalities, yet not a single one of them felt they could be the one to break this difficult news to our mother, and I understand why. We all knew how incredibly painful that would be. How could anyone break such news to their one parent without having a total meltdown? Well, I would soon find out for myself, because for whatever reason, my siblings all felt that I was the right person to do it and asked me how I felt about it. How I felt about it was irrelevant, because we couldn't let our mother hear this news from a doctor. If she was going to receive what would possibly be the most heartbreaking news of her life, it would have to come from one of her children. We are the ones who knew her best and we loved her so much that we would find a way to gently break the news to her.

I don't know why my siblings chose me, but I knew there was nothing to think about. If, for whatever reason, they felt I was the right person to be the messenger of this news, then I was going to have to be, no matter how much it broke me. Preparing myself for this conversation was one of the hardest things I have ever done in my life. My only ask to my siblings was that they please be there with me for moral support. Much to my surprise, some of them declined, and of my mother's nine children, only four of us girls entered the room.

On this particular day, my mother happened to be in my bedroom where there was a trundle which sat low enough for her to easily get up if she wanted to. At that point, she was hardly walking at all, but she would occasionally still want to stand up for short periods of time. My twin, my sister who lived in San Francisco, my sister who'd been in Guatemala with us as children, and I walked into the room. My mother must have had an inclination that we were about to have a serious conversation with her because we sat around her with serious expressions. We attempted to keep our faces emotionless, but one can only fake-smile so long before the person staring at their face realizes it's just an act. I sat to her right and cupped her hand with mine. *Where do I begin? There is no manual for this type of conversation and I don't know where to begin. Breathe, Karen, breathe. Just start and the rest will follow. And whatever you do, don't cry! You know how much mom hates it when we cry around her.*

Making my very best attempt to remain as strong as possible, the conversation went something like this:

Me: Hi mom. How are you? How are you feeling?

Mom: Hi. I'm okay. What's going on?

Me: Nothing. We just wanted to come to check in on you and talk a little is all. How are you feeling? Are you comfortable? Do you need anything?

Mom: I'm okay, thank you. What's going on?

Me: Well, actually, we did want to talk with you about something important.

Mom: Okay, what is it?

Me (clearing the lump in my throat) *Hold it together, Karen.*: Well, I want to begin by saying that you have been the most amazing mother any one of us could have ever asked for. (As the words came out of my mouth, I looked around at each one of my sisters who were nodding in agreement with sad looks on their faces and I paused--*Ugh, I don't know if I can do this!!*)

Mom (confused): Okay, thank you.

Me: I'm telling you this because we all want you to know that there is absolutely nothing in this world we wouldn't do for you because we love you very much.

Mom (even more confused): Okay? What's going on?

Me: Well, we spoke with the doctors and they have confirmed that there is really nothing left for us to do, unless you have changed your mind and are somehow interested in chemotherapy to see if that might help turn things around a little.

Mom (very matter of factly while intently looking into my eyes): Okay. Am I going to die?

Me (trying not to look away or cry, but failing miserably): Yes, you are.

Mom (a little annoyed with me): Please don't cry.

Me (annoyed with myself) *I told you not to cry. Now you've annoyed her. Stop it!*: Okay. I won't cry. I promise.

Mom: If I do chemotherapy, is it going to cure me?

Me: No, it will not. It may only prolong your life but the doctors cannot say what quality of life you will have in the process. We want you to know that we support whatever decision you make because this is your body and your life. So you tell us what it is you want and we will make it happen.

Mom: Then no. I don't want chemotherapy if it isn't going to cure me.

Me: Okay, we understand. If you don't want chemotherapy, then we will do everything we can to keep you as comfortable as you can be here with us. The nurse will continue to come and give us whatever medications she can to keep you as pain free and comfortable as possible. Okay?

Mom: Okay.

Me: We will all be here taking turns to care for you. If there is absolutely anybody you would like to see or anything you would like to do, or eat, or whatever, you just tell us and we will make it happen. Whatever it is, you just tell us. Okay?

Mom (with a solemn tone looking down toward her feet): Okay, thank you.

Me: Is there something you would like to do or somebody you would like to see that you want us to contact?

Mom: No. But if anyone should come to visit me, whoever it may be, don't turn them away. Be sure to be hospitable and let them come in to see me. Okay?

Me (glancing over at my sisters because we knew she was referring to our distant relatives we preferred not to have to see): Yes, of course. We can do that. Don't worry. Anyone who comes to see you, no matter who it is, will get to see you.

Mom: Thank you.

Me: I love you very much.

Mom: Me too. I love you too.

And just like that, the conversation was over. With our hearts shattered in a million pieces, we all somehow managed to remain strong and (mostly) hold back our tears. I sat back and took a deep breath as my sisters took turns telling our mother how much they loved her and reminded her that if there was anything she wanted at all, all she had to do was ask.

I don't know what my mother's mindset was upon hearing her fate because she didn't express herself, much less show any emotion, but she handled it with absolute grace and courage, seemingly the secret weapons she had relied on throughout her life. My mother's body was deteriorating but her spirit remained strong, and it was her strength that carried us through the remainder of her days.

Now that our mother had learned the truth of her fate, we were able to ask her questions relating to any specific final wishes she had. It seemed as though she had been giving this much thought because she did have some minor but very specific requests. First, she had a few envelopes with money stashed around her bedroom and wanted us to use that money to entertain and feed the guests who came to any of her services. Also, she wanted to be cremated and buried under two trees, just as she had told me a few years prior. Finally, she had a few items she specifically wanted to give to each one of us, but she would do that another time.

With this information in hand, my siblings and I arranged to meet with the staff at Forest Lawn Mortuary in Hollywood Hills to make the necessary arrangements. First, we found the perfect burial location where our mother would be laid to rest and we were certain she would be very happy. It is in a section of the cemetery that looks like a hiking trail with large trees; the ashes are placed in a hollow cement square just under a large stone which is bolted into place and bears a small plaque with a dedication.

Our mother also wanted her family and friends to be able to pay her final respects before being cremated, and we thought it would be nice to have her body lie in repose for a full day of viewing. This meant that in addition to choosing an urn, where her ashes would be placed before burying them, we also needed to choose a casket. We made sure to choose something soft and feminine, befitting of our mother.

The final step was to give the funeral director a photograph of our mother, along with anything we wanted placed on her person during the viewing. We decided she would wear the ivory silk nightgown our sister had gifted her from the hospital gift shop a few months prior.

After everything was decided and we started to wrap things up, the funeral director stopped to pay us a compliment on how well we had all worked together in making the decisions based on what our mother wanted rather than what we wanted for her. She said she had never served a family of our size who'd shown such unity and intention, and she thanked us for not only making her job easy but also pleasant. This was something I not only felt very proud to hear but also made me appreciate my family so much more. There was no denying our emotions were running high, but we entered that space with such peace in our hearts that we managed to put our feelings and egos aside for the sake of our mother. For once in our lives, all nine of us agreed on every last detail and it was all to give our mother a send-off deserving of a woman such as herself.

The final weeks of my mother's life were intense. Her pain was worsening and we had a few scares; we even called in a priest on two separate occasions. But our mother was holding on to dear life with everything she had. Over time, her medications increased from Vicodin to Morphine.

I appreciated our hospice nurse so much because she really took her time in educating us and explaining the process of dying. The way she explained it made it all feel less scary and more like a beautiful transition from one dimension to another. She explained things like the physical signs we could look out for and gave me booklets about what to expect and healthy ways of navigating grief. She also explained that typically, the person who is transitioning knows which ones of her loved ones could handle being present at the time they transition; anyone they felt was in denial or would not be able to handle the situation would not be present. It amazed me to learn how intuitive we are even up to the end, and I wondered which ones of us my mother would determine were strong enough and which were not. Finally, the nurse advised that when a person begins their transition they sometimes stop speaking, but that should this be the case with our mother, we should continue talking with her because hearing is the last sense to go when a person dies.

Having this wealth of knowledge put my mind and soul at ease. Death had never hit this close to home for me, but between the nurse's teachings and a Death and Dying course I had just completed the semester before taking the leave of absence to be with my mother, I stopped thinking of death as a frightful end and I realized how profoundly beautiful it can be if we choose to see it as such. Death is a spirit's return home, and my mother was going home.

"This was it, the final moment I would get to say anything and everything I wanted to my mother."

25

The night before my mother passed away was one of those nights I will never forget. It started out quietly, as every night had for several weeks leading up to this evening. By now, we were buddying up and taking turns being by our mother's side around the clock. On this particular evening, it was myself and my brother, the middle of the boys who had until just recently been in denial. Samantha was also home that evening and we had stayed up talking with her. With everyone wanting to spend time with my mother, Samantha and I had lost all privacy, and I had not had any time to sit down and actually talk with her. I missed her, and I'm sure she missed me, but for the time being everything and everyone, including myself, took a backseat to my mother's care.

Before the nurse left that evening, she asked us to mentally prepare because it was only a matter of time now as my mother's body was starting to shut down. After she left, my brother told Samantha that because she had previously experienced death on her father's side, she would have to help the grandkids navigate through this loss as they had never been through this before. I felt it was a big responsibility to put on her because she was one of the youngest grandkids at only fifteen, but I also knew she would be up for it because she was a lot like my mother, strong and resilient.

It was a Tuesday night and both my brother and I had to work the next morning, and Samantha had summer school, so we decided to turn in early. Samantha went to bed, I slept in my mother's bed with her, and my brother slept on the reclining chair in the corner of her bedroom.

Over the course of the night, my mother began to do something she'd never done before. After starting to fall into a deep sleep, she would wake up as though she had been startled and let out a yelp. Then, from out of nowhere, she started calling out names I'd never heard before. When I asked my brother if he'd heard those names before, he said he didn't know all of them, but some were the names of people who had passed away many years ago. I had read this could happen, but I wasn't sure it was true until then. The spirits of my mother's loved ones were there, welcoming her home as she prepared to transition, except she wasn't ready to go and she fought it the entire night. *What or whom could she possibly be waiting for?* I didn't know what to do other than comfort her with my words and touch. I gently caressed her arm and I told her to not be afraid if she wanted to let go. She wouldn't let go and it went on like this for the duration of the night until it was time for another dose of medication, at which point she fell asleep.

By morning, my brother and I were exhausted and I encouraged him to go on and head to work early and try sleeping in his car for a bit. I figured I'd wait for my two sisters to arrive because they were taking over while I went to work. Samantha's classes ended at noon, and I figured we'd return home for lunch after I picked her up, to check in on my mother. When my sisters arrived, I explained everything that had transpired throughout the night and they immediately confirmed what my brother had said: those were in fact the names of people who had passed away long ago.

As difficult as it was to admit the end was near, we didn't want our mother to suffer and I reached out to the nurse to see what she could do to help her relax. The nurse said she had a couple other patients to see before our mother, but that upon arriving she would administer a palliative sedation (a cocktail of medications given to terminally ill patients intended to induce unconsciousness and reduce or eliminate suffering). She suggested our family come together once the sedation was administered because it was unlikely our mother would regain consciousness.

I didn't want to leave my mother's side and go to work, but my supervisor had been giving me a hard time about taking so much time off that I had to go into the office, even if it meant leaving early. Besides, I knew that with my sisters by her side, my mother was in the best care and they would immediately call if anything changed. I was useless at work that morning, but I think it's safe to say I had been useless a lot in the months leading up to my mother's passing. Later, after I picked up Samantha from school and was headed home to drop her off, I received a call from my sister. She said it would be best for me to notify work that I would not be returning, as our mother had been given the sedation and was beginning to transition. She had already called all our siblings who were on their way. Although I had been mentally preparing for that call, it still shook me so much I barely managed to get out of the car.

When I walked into my mother's bedroom, she was no longer conscious. Her breathing was labored and she was no longer fighting to stay awake. I remembered the nurse telling me that hearing was the last thing to go, and I told my sisters that we should all start saying our goodbyes, one at a time. My mother had specifically asked that the grandchildren not see her that way, so I called Samantha's father and asked him to pick her up. She was very upset to have to leave without saying a proper goodbye to her grandmother, and while I could empathize, I reminded her those were my mother's last wishes and that she would always be with us in spirit.

One by one my siblings began to arrive, and as they did, each one went into our mother's bedroom to say their private goodbyes. My brother who had stayed the night with us had not yet arrived and I was afraid we were losing time. I called him and he said he was on his way but he was stuck in traffic and would arrive as soon as he could.

When my turn came, my heart was pounding and I didn't know what I would say. *How do you say goodbye when you know it is forever? At least in human form, anyway.* You would think that having had six months to gather my thoughts and plan out what I'd like to say, I would have walked in with an essay to read to her, but I didn't. Instead, I went in prepared to speak from my heart, raw and unrehearsed.

This was it, the final moment I would get to say anything and everything I wanted to my mother. *How can I fit the last thirty-three years of my life into one brief conversation?* All I could think to do was to express my utmost gratitude for everything. I thanked her for giving me life, for having showered me with her unconditional love and support, and most of all, for having been the best grandmother to Samantha, who was so much like her. As much as I didn't want her to go, I gave her my blessing to let go without any fear about what would happen after she was gone because we would be okay; she had done her best and we would make her proud. Now it was time for her to reunite with all those people she'd lost too soon, whom she'd lived missing for so long, and were all waiting for her with open arms, ready to welcome her home. I told her that I looked forward to seeing her again someday, whenever my time should come, and that knowing she would be there with her arms wide open made me less afraid. I asked her to send me a good man from wherever she was, because I knew how much she really wanted me to settle down. Above all, I reminded her how proud I was to be her daughter and how grateful I was to God for her. I must have told her I loved her a couple dozen times, which didn't seem like enough, but I know she knew that my love was too wide and too deep to fit into words.

To put a lifetime of words into one conversation is impossible to do. My mother is more than just a parent, she is my partner who helped me raise Samantha, a companion who never stops offering me support, my friend, my rival, and everything that strong-willed mothers and daughters grow to become over the years. I am only thirty-three years old, with so much life yet to live, and I don't know how to even begin to live in a world in which she does not exist. Is that even possible to do?

As I made my way downstairs, my twin was preparing to go in. I was hurting, but even then my heart hurt for each one of my siblings who were also losing their mother. When you are one of many, you can easily get lost in the shuffle, but I wanted to acknowledge their pain as much as mine because even though I have a sibling or two who would like to believe that their love and pain was somehow greater than everyone else's, I know this to be untrue. Love looks different for all of us; and how can anyone measure love anyway?

When I reached the bottom of the staircase, I asked my sisters whether our brother had arrived yet, but they said he had not. Everyone was there except for him and I was beginning to worry he would not make it in time.

Just as that thought entered my mind, the door to my mother's bedroom opened and my twin emerged. *She just walked in a couple minutes ago. That was too fast. Something must be wrong.* With fear and confusion in her voice, she yelled out for us to come up and check on our mother because it appeared as though she had stopped breathing. In a panic, we all ran upstairs. In an attempt to keep my cool, I took a deep breath and approached my mother's side while all my siblings stood around her in agonizing suspense.

As I scanned her body, I noticed her chest was no longer expanding and contracting, that the sound of her labored breathing was now silent, and there was fluid coming out of her nose. I wiped her nose clean and proceeded to check her pulse. There was nothing. Our beautiful mother was gone.

My mother left us one hot summer afternoon in July of 2007. Standing there surrounding her lifeless body, we turned off the ventilator and the silence that suddenly filled the room was quickly overtaken by mournful cries. I wanted to comfort my family and take their pain away but I couldn't because I needed comforting too. I looked around hoping to see my mother's spirit floating around us, but instead, I could only feel the emptiness of her absence. One of my sisters asked us to look over at the wall next to our mother's bed, where the sun was hitting it and forming the shape of a heart. She was there, telling us without words that she loved us and her heart would be with us forever. Seeing that made an immense sense of peace wash over me and the tears of sorrow I had been crying suddenly became tears of acceptance because my mother was no longer in any pain.

Unfortunately, the nurse had been right: the only one of my mother's children who did not make it in time to say goodbye was the middle of the three boys. He showed up just minutes after she passed. He was inconsolable and there was nothing we could do except comfort him and cry alongside him. I truly believe that is something he will never fully recover from. That was a painful reminder that we always think we have plenty of time, yet the truth is that there is simply never enough.

I stepped outside the room to call the nurse and give her the news so that she could make the necessary arrangements. She wanted to give us more time with our mother and arranged for the mortuary to send for her a couple hours later, which was a good idea because we were not ready to say goodbye.

As we stood around the room allowing our new reality to sink in, we decided to commemorate this moment with a toast to our mother. My brother-in-law ran out to buy a nice bottle of cognac, which my mother would drink every once in a blue moon. We each took a glass, went around the room and said a few heartfelt words, and gave one final toast in her honor. It was such a touching moment and I knew our mother was there toasting her life with us.

The best word I can use to describe the days following my mother's passing is bittersweet. We were all holding it together as best as we could for everyone else, as people from near and far, who had known or loved our mother, came to the various services we held for her throughout the week. Whether it was the vigil, Catholic mass, or her burial, there were so many people who showed up for her and we were grateful to everyone for the outpouring of love and support our mother and family received.

The most beautiful gift we gave our mother as we bid her a final farewell was the release of seventy-one white doves to represent each year of her life. As I looked up and watched the doves flying above us in unison, tears streamed down my face because I knew my mother's spirit had finally broken free, and I could only hope that she was dancing and singing as she liked to do when she was happy. I hoped she was spreading her wings as wide as the sky and soaring over the world she had made a little more magical because she came to be. *Gracias mamita linda, por su presencia y su amor que vivirá eternamente dentro de mi ser.* (Thank you, beautiful mommy, for your presence and love which will live eternally within my being.)

26

Loss, sorrow, and mourning are all part of a long and painful process that comes with no manual or instructions. I had spent the last six months of my life running myself ragged, having a house full of people and a noisy ventilator keeping my mother breathing, but as the dust began to settle and all the noise became a deafening silence impossible to ignore, the pain of my mother's absence grew stronger. This is the part nobody had warned me about, the aftermath, which can be so much more agonizing than being in a constant and numbing state of fight or flight.

It wasn't until after we laid my mother to rest that I began to assess the extent of the damage caused by months of personal neglect. I had hardly been able to hold down any food all those months, so I was skin on bones. I had become so anemic that my skin turned grey. Some in my family were concerned about my health and urged me to see my doctor. One of the first things I did after my mother's diagnosis was get myself into the doctor's office. I asked him to run every test possible to ensure that I was not genetically inclined to develop cancer. *I have a young daughter, I can't leave her motherless, too.* Fortunately, I wasn't as sick as I appeared, and how I looked on the outside was simply a reflection of how I felt on the inside: fragile, emotionally exhausted, and fighting to regain consciousness from everything we'd just endured. I had spent so many sleepless nights worrying myself sick that my once dark brown hair had turned grey; dyeing my hair was no longer an option but a necessity. There was also the fact that I had spent such little time with Samantha that she now appeared to be a young woman who felt like a complete stranger to me; my little girl had grown up and I had missed it all. Let's not even get started on my finances, which had also taken quite a hit.

Something else nobody had warned me about was that when you collectively lose the matriarch of your family, everyone is knee-deep in mourning, which means you have little support to lean on. I couldn't be there for my family any more than they could be there for me. I needed them and I'm sure they needed me too, but we were all mending our broken hearts, and attempting to be there for each other would have been a lot like the blind leading the blind. I depended a great deal on my friends during these times, especially my best friend who had lost her stepfather just four months before I lost my mother. She was there holding my hand as much as I had been there holding hers a few months prior. But, my friend had a home, a career, and a life of her own to tend to, and the last thing I wanted was to become a burden to anyone, so I attempted to cope on my own, which only made me feel worse.

Over time, my sadness morphed into rage and I became angry, so very angry. I couldn't walk or drive past an elderly person without wondering why they got to live and my mother didn't. *What made them so Goddamn special?* Then, instead of encouraging Samantha and myself to lean on each other, I unconsciously took my frustrations out on her and pushed her farther away. We began arguing about anything and everything--from her grades, what she wore, the friends she had, to the tone she took with me when I questioned or tried to engage with her. The less in control of her I felt, the bigger our problems became, and our arguments would escalate to full-blown yelling matches. This wasn't at all how I envisioned our relationship would be, especially not now, but I couldn't seem to grab hold of anything good long enough to last and my mental health was spiraling. I didn't even know that's what it was, but in hindsight, I can see it plain as day.

I was in such a state of darkness that I could not see Samantha's pain; she was hurting too. She lived with my mother and me, after all. She had been right there, witnessing my mother's painful transformation from an untouchable warrior to a wounded soldier fighting for her life. She was angry that after being so close to her grandmother, she was the only one of the grandkids whom my mother never came to in dreams, and she wondered why not her. She was sad for herself and for me, but she cried in silence to avoid burdening me with her pain; she knew I was carrying enough for both of us. All those months I had spent trying to keep my mother alive were months Samantha had no moral support from me to help her process any of it. I was physically present but emotionally unavailable, and frankly, unequipped to manage all that pain for both of us. She was feeling as empty and lost as I was, but I couldn't see it.

Instead of providing Samantha a safe space to talk about and release her pain, I shut her out and she began acting out. As her cries for help went unheard, her grades slipped, the friendships she kept were not with people I approved of, she stopped sharing things with me (which made me feel like she was keeping secrets), and I began to distrust her. I interpreted her cries for help as rebellion and an offense against me because I was the one who'd lost her mother and I wasn't emotionally strong enough to deal with her hormonal teenage rage. I would ask her, "How can you do this to me when I'm in so much pain?" And I never bothered to ask her how she was doing or how I could help support her in her grieving. I begged her to give me time to heal and asked that she please behave herself until then because if things continued to worsen, I would be left with no choice but to send her to live with her father. I didn't want this, and I know this is not what my mother would have wanted either, but I didn't know what else to do. I felt so lost.

I tried my best to make things at our place feel as normal as possible, but there was too much pain there. Everywhere I turned, I was reminded of my mother. The kitchen no longer smelled like her delicious cooking. The plant she kept next to the kitchen sink had died, which broke me even more. The living room where her laughter could once be heard was now lifeless space. Her bedroom had been painted and filled with Samantha's things, but nothing could help me forget that my mother had taken her final breath in that room.

I returned to school hoping it would help, and in a way it did, because it served as a distraction, but in reality, it was just a bandaid. On my first day back, I received a call from my twin who wanted to check in on me and see how I was doing. I told her how strange it felt to be back; I had left school because our mother was dying and now I had returned to school because she was dead. *How does one reconcile such a thing?*

With my mother gone, I became the foundation of my home, but without being able to get my footing on solid ground, I began to crack. I was struggling; I needed time to mourn and sit with my pain. And I had to be honest with myself--I could not, at that time, give Samantha what she needed from me. Not time, not affection, not attention. Nothing. As much as it pained me to do, I did the only thing I felt would save us both and made the difficult decision to send her to live with her father for the remainder of the school year. I figured this time apart would be good and give us some breathing room to reflect on how we could be better for each other and to each other.

After Samantha moved out, there was no way I could live alone in the emptiness of the place I had, until just recently, shared with her and my mother. Within weeks, I found a small two-bedroom home for rent and moved out of the place I had once called my home but could now no longer tolerate or even look at. I was ready for a fresh start, a do-over, an opportunity to shake off the pain in which I had been trapped.

Living on my own was a bit strange, and while I never fully got used to it, it was everything I needed at that time, not only for my emotional healing but for my mental healing too. I was ready to begin this new chapter in my life and was hopeful that things would soon turn around. Beyond anything, I was quite proud of myself for getting out of my comfort zone and being open to doing something I'd never done before, like adulting all by myself. I felt like such a big girl! The place was perfect for me--and for Samantha when she came home on the weekends. It looked like a cabin snuggled up against the hillside surrounded by trees. Inside, there were beautiful cherry hardwood floors and windows wrapped around the entire living room, overlooking the city below. I will admit that I didn't fully appreciate all the greenery around me because it attracted wildlife, but as long as they kept their distance, I could learn to coexist with them. All I cared about was the fact that my place felt like a sanctuary in the middle of a city, and I had the best of both worlds.

Once I finished unpacking and got all settled in, my twin and I spent a weekend decorating the second bedroom for Samantha so that she would have a special place that felt safe and happy to come home to. Not having her with me on a full-time basis was difficult, but we were slowly beginning to recover, and she was doing really well at her new school, which comforted me. She also admitted to me that she actually liked staying with her father because he gave her a freedom she had not always had when she lived with me since I was an overprotective and sometimes overbearing mother. I obviously never intended for that to be the case, but as a young mother carrying around the heaviness of my traumas, I projected a lot of my fears onto her, and I was slowly starting to recognize that.

One of the few good things that came from losing my mother was that it gave me an opportunity to step back and reflect on my own parenting. I could see that I had been doing to Samantha everything that had been done to me growing up. For instance, I wasn't giving her the space to be young and free or to live and learn from her own mistakes. I didn't trust that I was doing enough to protect her and with that, I didn't trust that she was capable of making healthy choices. In my attempts to protect her from the world, all I really accomplished was making her world small, and she didn't deserve that. I also realized that I let her down when I didn't listen to her all those times she attempted to express her own pain and sorrow. Instead, I dismissed her because I expected her to be tough and resilient just as I had been forced to be at her age. I was modeling my upbringing, which had in many ways damaged me, and now I could not allow myself to do that to Samantha, too. I became determined to change the narrative by learning to trust her.

Looking at the ugly parts of ourselves is never an easy thing to do, especially when our children reflect our fears back to us. But if I was going to heal myself and Samantha, I had to be willing to go deep within myself and face my shadow. I had my work cut out for me, but I was okay with that. For the time being, I was content with simply learning to survive without my mother and learning to become a different kind of mother myself. With each new sunrise, I welcomed the opportunity to heal my heart just a little bit more.

"That really became the moment
I set her soul free, and in doing so,
I also freed myself."

27

Over time, life began to take on a new form of normalcy and as I was coming back to life, I was learning to channel my pain in a healthy manner. I was no longer consumed by my grief and anger. Whenever I'd see an elderly person now, I felt nothing but love and compassion for them. I recognized that to get to live to be of a certain age is a gift, but with that gift can sometimes come a lot of pain and suffering. *How can I look into the face of an elderly person and not see that with each wrinkle is a story? How can I be angry at anyone who's endured and overcome, possibly, the unthinkable? I certainly cannot.*

Reflecting on my mother's life and death allowed me to see that she manifested her departure. I don't mean to suggest that she wanted to die, because I don't believe that, but I do know she didn't see herself living into her elder years. In fact, I cannot recall a single time when my mother so much as mentioned growing old. Perhaps it was because she had lost both her parents and her husband before the age of thirty-five, and she either didn't want to or didn't know how to live that long without them. Either way, my mother always rejected anything that reminded her she was aging or made her feel old in any way, like being called a grandma. She was so opposed to any grandparent reference made toward her that she insisted on being called *mama*. I can see how, as a woman who had worked as hard as she had, she would not want to lose her independence, much less her youthful looks, which kept her feeling young at heart.

That got me thinking. If we have the power to manifest relationships, health, wealth, and everything else with our thoughts, why can't we also manifest our departure? Much like an artist who retires while they are still at the top of their game, I believe my mother left while she could still be fully present and able. As a spiritual being, this didn't sound the least bit crazy to me, and it was in coming to this conclusion that I began to feel relieved that she had not left us before she was prepared to do so. Perhaps that is why she never cried throughout the six months she had been ill. If she was at peace with it, there was no reason for me to not be at peace with it, too. I suppose I will never know for certain whether she was ready to go, but the thought that my mother could have actually chosen to depart on her terms was like stepping into a bath of tranquility. Suddenly I knew with all my heart that if I continued to suffer, my mother's soul wouldn't be fully resting in peace, and I couldn't live with that. That really became the moment I set her soul free, and in doing so, I also freed myself.

I knew I would forever miss my mother, and the anniversaries of her passing would never get easier, but I decided I'd rather spend the rest of my life celebrating hers instead of mourning it. What sense does it make to have lived some of my most beautiful moments with her and not remember them with joy in my heart? Now when I think about her, I cannot help but smile because I know she's with me; I see her everywhere. She's the sweet hummingbirds who visit me while I sit quietly in my backyard and the butterflies that have started coming around ever since I started writing this book. She's also the white feathers that magically appear in my house from out of nowhere, which I know because a psychic medium told me that is how she lets us know she is near. There is something profoundly beautiful and healing about choosing to remember my mother with joy in my heart rather than with sorrow. I am comforted in knowing that when the time comes, and I am ready to go, I will once again see her beautiful face.

I would not have been able to come to this conclusion had I not been willing to sit with my pain; it helped not only to heal my heart but to begin finding bliss in the simplicities of life that we can sometimes take for granted. My newfound joy came by way of going for long walks around the city or going to my favorite coffee shop and having my favorite drink, a Mexican Mayan Mocha, made with Mexican hot chocolate. The coffee shop, which is still there today, is located on the corner of the busy intersection. I would sit there for hours; if it was a chilly evening, I'd sit inside and read a book or have a nice conversation with a complete stranger. But, if the weather was pleasant, I'd sit outside for a good people-watching experience and savor every moment as I narrated the story of each passerby in my head. On my walks back home, I'd stop in at my local church whenever it was empty. I spent time meditating in the quietness of the beautiful space that had been Samantha's school for eight years and my mother's favorite church; it had become my sanctuary. There, sitting in my solitude, I not only felt close to my God but also close to my mother and Samantha, which always nourished my soul.

During this time I, the girl who once failed Physical Education, even took up running for the first time in my life and actually grew to love it. Going for daily runs at the Rosebowl in the neighboring city of Pasadena really helped me get back into a healthy weight and mindset. There was something about jogging outdoors surrounded by nature that felt incredibly freeing and therapeutic. I guess it's a lot like being forced to read in grade school and hating it, then growing up and realizing how much you actually love to read.

On Samantha's sixteenth birthday, we decided to spend the day out for a shopping and dining experience. It had been a lovely day, and as it was coming to an end and we headed back to our car, we crossed paths with a young girl walking her very cute dog. We stopped to admire the dog and asked the young owner if it was okay for us to pet her, and she said it was. Little did I know that the young dog owner was reeling us in to ask if we wanted to see the puppy she was selling. *Yeah, no, I just want to pet your dog, not buy one.* I thanked her and let her know we were on our way out and not interested in getting a pet. As though she had not heard me, she extended her arm toward us and in the palm of her hand was a tiny, furry puppy sleeping soundly. *Oh my gosh! Look at that sweet little thing. No, wait! Get ahold of yourself, Karen. Take a step back and walk away. Do it now.* This girl was a pro, and if I didn't know any better, I would think she and this puppy had been rehearsing what happened next. She set the puppy down, and as though the puppy had been trained to do so, she immediately walked over to me and cuddled up next to my foot. This was one of those slow motion moments when you want to run for the hills screaming, *Nooooooo!* But I couldn't look away, much less walk away. I wanted to. Believe me, I did. But I couldn't. I was the sucker who had just gotten tricked into buying a puppy I had no intention of ever buying.

I was so blindsided that before I knew it, I was at the bank teller pulling out cash, paying this random girl, and driving away with a puppy in my arms. *What have I done? I've never owned a pet before. My place isn't even puppy proof. Does this mean I have to pick up poop now? I kill plants, what if I kill this poor unsuspecting dog?* A few hours and a couple hundred dollars later, I was finally headed home from the pet store. She was so sweet, this puppy, and even though I had not fully processed what I'd gotten myself into, I instantly knew my mother had sent her to heal Samantha and me, and to bring us closer together. And in many ways, she did just that. We named our sweet girl Darla, after the female character in the classic show, *The Little Rascals.* As sweet as she was, I soon discovered having a pet was a lot more work than I anticipated, but Darla was ours now and I couldn't get enough of her.

This little girl who couldn't speak or tell us she loved us filled our home with laughter and was the breath of fresh air Samantha and I had been in such desperate need of. It was as though our puppy was filling the void in our hearts and we felt complete again. On the weekends when Samantha was home from her dad's, we spent every waking moment playing or cuddling with Darla, and would have lazy days of doing nothing but catching up or watching movies. And, just as my mother and I had once co-parented Samantha, she and I were now co-parenting our fur baby. It felt so good to have this bonding experience with Samantha and something to smile about again.

I don't know whether it was the puppy or the immense sense of peace that had recently come over me, but I started to feel a real shift in the energy surrounding me. Everything that had appeared hazy and grey suddenly appeared bright and colorful, and I could feel everything with such intensity and vibrancy. The sky appeared bluer than ever, the trees seemed taller and greener, and the air smelled fresher and more crisp; I could see the beauty in everything and everyone, and I felt alive, so very alive! As my heart healed, I began to make room for all the goodness life had to offer, and I was ready to receive every bit of it with open arms. I even started to give some thought to letting love in again. I didn't know how or when it would happen, but simply being open to the possibility felt really good to my soul. For the first time in a long time, I was overflowing with hope, and I was ready for every possibility that awaited me.

28

One evening, after another exhausting day at the office, I got home and felt the need to stay in rather than go for a run. It was a warm day in late spring and I thought it would be nice to step outside and sit on my porch, something I'd hardly had a chance to do in the year I had been living at my place. I changed into something cool and comfortable, poured myself a glass of wine, and took Darla outside to play. Sitting there in my deliberate stillness, I took in the scenery around me and allowed the outdoor air to fill my lungs. It was all so beautiful and peaceful, yet it somehow provoked a surprising and sudden flood of emotions. *This is unexpected. Where is this coming from?* In my attempt to connect with my emotions and understand where my tears were coming from, I closed my eyes and allowed myself to sit still. As I searched my heart, I realized that although I was not unhappy, my soul was nudging me that there was something more I needed to be doing with my life to feel truly fulfilled and in my purpose. *What is my purpose?* I wondered. It certainly wasn't working in my cut-throat corporate job, that's for sure. It had become an increasingly toxic work environment and I was spending so much time there that I could feel it sucking the life out of me.

With my eyes still gently shut, I lifted my face up toward the sky and felt a light summer breeze dance around me, brushing my hair away from my face as if to say, *Open your eyes, my beloved, and see the vastness of life all around you, waiting to be lived with everything you've got. Take my hand and dance with me. Give yourself permission to be free and do everything your mother didn't get to do in her lifetime. What are you waiting for? Your time to live is now.*

I opened my tear-filled eyes. That was a great question indeed--what was I waiting for? I had been so busy hiding behind the monotony of work and school and the walls of my home, that I had not at all focused on making future plans for myself. Yes, it was important to live in the present moment, but living as though I had no future was not in any way honoring my mother's life and the countless sacrifices she had made for me. Perhaps it wasn't my soul nudging me at all but rather my mother's spirit lifting me up from out of the small, protective box I had put myself into. Then, I thought about Samantha and felt grateful that at least her immediate future had been planned for. Together with her father, we decided that because she was thriving at her new school and making close friendships she did not want to part with, it would be best that she continue living with her father for the duration of her high school career and return home upon graduating. Although for now we decided to leave her college options open, she seemed to be leaning toward starting at a local community college and working her way up. I wasn't entirely happy with this plan, but whether I agreed with it or not, I decided to support whatever decision felt right to her. For now, I needed to get comfortable with the fact that for the next couple years I would remain the part-time parent, which was not at all what I had envisioned for us. Nevertheless, I figured that if I was going to make lemonade with the lemons life had thrown my way, I had to at the very least focus on the one thing I had been neglecting: my own future!

The time had come for me to get serious about laying out a plan and setting some goals. I had never really done that before, but as someone who made lists for everything, I figured I'd start there. I stood up, took the last few sips of my wine, and wiped the tears and snot off my face like any big girl would. After taking a few deep breaths, I gathered my thoughts, marched into my place, pulled a notebook and pen out of my desk drawer, and spent a few minutes intently writing down my top five goals. The list looked something like this:

GOALS!

Finish school - three semesters left. Yippee! Samantha and I will graduate the same year... class of 2010. So cool! Graduation trip? Maybe.

Buy a home. At least two bedrooms, two baths. Check savings account balance. Need to possibly downsize to save for down payment, moving expenses, appliances, new furniture. (Don't want to move again but will if I have to.) Credit score good to go. Hire realtor. Want to stay in Eagle Rock but it's too expensive. Research safest cities in surrounding areas.

Marriage? Yes! Need to get serious and be intentional. Stop dating younger men (not for you), or guys you meet at clubs or bars (not likely to want marriage), or hot guys with no substance (not everything pretty on the outside is pretty on the inside), and stop hanging out with exes (cannot meet your future husband with your exes still hanging around).

Children. Definitely. Two more, preferably boy and girl. Would love twins!!

Career. Unhappy and unfulfilled, but provides financial stability (10 years - time flies). Can't make a move until after home purchase. New career path? Open to it.

Let's do this!

That was my list in a nutshell. It was short, sweet and to the point, yet it was also quite revealing. While my goals were straightforward, it seemed I had some cleaning up to do when it came to my lovelife. Aside from my ex-husband, I had the terrible habit of remaining friends with my exes long after our break-ups.

I figured there was no harm in it if I wasn't dating anyone and I thought it was a perfectly healthy thing to do. But my notes were right. If I was determined to meet my future husband, I couldn't very well continue hanging out with my exes. If I did, then people would assume we were still together, and what if they knew of a good candidate to introduce me to? Besides, if I was really serious about moving my life forward, I couldn't keep holding on to my past. It was time to eliminate any detractors or distractions. *Wow, I feel so good! I should spend more time writing down my goals!*

As I looked over my list, the one topic I felt most excited about was buying a home. This was one of my mother's greatest dreams which she never got to accomplish, but there was no reason I couldn't. My home would be hers in spirit. I began to daydream about what my place would look like, how I would furnish it, and how good it would feel to have something Samantha and I could call our own. The thought filled my heart with so much joy that I decided right then and there that this would be my top priority and everything else on my list would have to take a backseat.

My mother had now been gone for a year and yet she continued to inspire me in the most amazing ways. All along, she thought she was raising me to grow up, get married, and have children, but unlike my older sisters, that was not the order in which my path was meant to unfold. What my mother hadn't realized is that while she had always encouraged her daughters to find a good man to marry, she had been demonstrating the power of independence. She had been a single parent and an independent woman, my entire life, getting stuff done like a boss. My journey was meant to look more like that. Yes, I wanted marriage and more children, but first, I had some pretty big dreams I wanted to accomplish on my own, because the one thing I had learned from my shero is that I didn't need a man to make it happen.

In the days that followed, I went all in. I immediately hired a realtor who had been highly recommended but who, unfortunately, turned out to be a great disappointment. Besides being flaky, he seemed to ignore my communication with him and only showed me properties that were the opposite of everything I had asked for. It felt as though from the moment we met, he had decided to put me in a box and would only show me homes that he thought were suitable for me yet were nowhere close to what I had described. From the neighborhoods he took me to, to the condition of the homes themselves, they were all wrong.

He insisted on showing me rejected homes nobody wanted to buy. A couple of the homes were in such poor condition that it would have cost just as much to fix them up as it would to buy them. I was not an investor looking to flip a house; I was a single woman looking to buy a home, one which offered safety, tranquility, and joy, and none of what I was seeing made me feel any of those things. After months of failed attempts to redeem himself, I had no choice but to fire him.

I couldn't believe that after all those months, I was back at square one. I had no realtor, no prospects, nothing. Actually, there was one good thing that came from working with him. In one of our conversations where he'd taken a look at my finances to ensure that everything was in order, he advised that although I did have a solid financial history and enough savings, he was concerned the banks would not feel I had enough to cover the down payment in addition to any unexpected or emergency expenses that could arise. He had asked whether I would be open to downsizing to a more affordable apartment, which would allow me to put more money away while we searched for my home. He was right. If I was going to do this on my own, I needed to consider moving out of my very cute but very costly rental, and save as much money as I could.

As I thought about where I might find a cheaper rental, I recalled a recent conversation I'd had with my eldest sister about what she would do with her spare bedroom now that my nephew had gotten his own place. *That would be perfect.* I decided to reach out and ask my sister whether she would be open to having me temporarily move into their spare bedroom in order to save up for a house. I didn't know what to expect, but much to my surprise, she and my brother-in-law got back to me quickly and agreed to let me and Darla move in rent-free. It honestly felt as though I'd won the lottery because their generosity meant I would soon have my very own home! That was a pretty big deal for a girl like me. With Darla in tow, and a select few pieces of furniture and clothing to get by for the next year, I moved back into my sister and brother-in-law's home for the third and final time.

As I packed my belongings and prepared to have them taken to storage, I was humbled by the fact that in my determination to make my dream a reality, there wasn't a sacrifice I wasn't willing to make. It felt strange for me to be going back to the house I'd previously moved into twice before because I had been homeless with nowhere to go. But then I realized how symbolic it also was. This time around, I was moving back into my sister's place to begin a new cycle--a cycle which would be the beginning of my legacy of generational wealth, which would secure Samantha's future and ensure that neither she nor her children would ever be without a place to call home.

Sadly, not everyone was as happy for me as I'd hoped. One day while I was at work, a colleague with whom I had become close personal friends asked about the status of my house hunting. I shared with her what had transpired with my now former realtor and that I was in the process of looking for somebody new. My colleague was a few years younger than me, had grown up in an affluent neighborhood, and was a graduate of an ivy league school, so I knew it would be difficult for her to relate to my struggle, but at the very least, I thought she would for sure offer some empathetic support. Instead, all she said with a chilling indifference was that not everyone was meant to be a homeowner. *Wait, did I hear her correctly? Did she think homeownership was not in the realm of possibility for a brown, single mother such as myself? I didn't realize she thought so little of me.*

After shaking off the initial shock, I realized that just as my *so-called-friend* had, by her own admission, thought I was not worthy of homeownership, my former realtor was also under the impression that I was somehow not capable of living outside "the hood," which is why he had been unwilling to show me anything outside of that. All my life, I have dealt with envious people--*the haters*--who don't want to see anyone but themselves succeed. But this went deeper than that; this was bigotry, the white superiority complex rearing its ugly head in an attempt to make me feel small, and worse, to convince me that I was meant to stay small.

In my younger years, I would have let others' limiting beliefs of me limit me, but I couldn't let that happen now. This dream I was carrying in my heart was too big and too important for me to allow any naysayers to take it from me. Instead, I took their negative energy and used it to fuel my dream. I decided that I would never again hire another non-Latino to do the work a Latino could do just as well. In fact, I wanted to take it a step further. I decided I would hire a Latina realtor who could understand my needs, from one woman of color to another. That was the first time I truly understood the importance of being intentional about who I give my business to, and it became a decision I still proudly practice to this day.

29

Ask and you shall receive--isn't that what we're encouraged to do? It is certainly what seems to have happened to me; some might call it a coincidence, I call it serendipity. After taking some time to decompress and clear the negative energy of the realtor I'd just fired, I asked the universe to send me a new realtor, someone I could fully trust and who would have my best interest at heart. Then one day, I went to lunch with a colleague whom I had spent some time training when she started a few weeks prior. She was a kind soul with an outgoing personality and we clicked almost instantly. Our conversation over lunch was flowing so naturally that I felt comfortable enough to share with her my recent experience in searching for a home and how dreadful the thought of having to look for a new realtor was for me. Like any good listener, she let me go on and on, venting about my frustrations and when I was done sharing, she looked at me with a smile on her face and said I needed to look no further because she was a realtor on the side.

Hearing this was music to my ears. My face lit up and my eyes opened so wide that I must have looked like a kid in a candy store because she burst out in laughter. I had asked the universe to send me a Latina realtor, and there she was having lunch with me. If this was not a serendipitous moment, I don't know what is! I was so excited that without even asking her for references, I expressed interest in working with her. Within days of our initial conversation, she began sending me listings to consider. I knew I was in good hands when she took me to see properties that were much nicer and in better condition than anything I had been shown prior. While

I liked almost everything we saw, I wanted to take my time until I knew for certain I had found *the one*. She was incredibly patient and understanding, and she offered one important piece of advice: I should take my time with this process and go with my gut instinct because I would know when *the one* came along. She could not have been more right.

One Friday evening just as I'd arrived home from work, I got a call from my colleague/realtor indicating that she had just gotten a lead about a condo that was about to go on the market the following week. If I was up to make the drive and drop by that evening, the sellers were willing to let me take a look at the place. Of course I was open to seeing it because if I liked it, it meant that I'd get to make an offer before it went on the market and there would be no other buyers to compete with. I was, however, somewhat disillusioned by the fact that the place was outside my desirable geographical area, in the San Fernando Valley, where I knew nobody. But, I had agreed to keep an open mind and went anyway. Because my twin had always been good about giving me an objective opinion, I invited her to come along.

As we pulled up to the condo, which faced a tree-lined street surrounded by single family homes, I noticed it had a white picket fence. *Oh my gosh, I've always wanted a white picket fence like the ones I read about in my childhood books.* Trying my best not to get too excited, I gained my composure and followed my realtor into the home. Upon entering, all I could think about was that my realtor was right. From the moment I walked through the front door, I felt a sense of lightness and peace come over me, and it was almost as though I could feel my mother's spirit surrounding me. I had not felt this feeling in any other place we had looked at, and I knew right then and there that this would become my home.

The sellers were a nice couple who'd just retired and were moving closer to their children and grandchildren. After a brief conversation with them, they invited us to take a look around. The place reminded me of homes I'd seen in San Francisco because it was three stories high and had many steps to get to each level. I figured this would be a good daily workout for me. On the first level was the living room, which had a fireplace in the corner and a sliding door that led to a cute little patio. *I can plant some pretty flowers and put a bench with lots of pillows out there to sit on and read.* To the right were stairs that led down to the garage, but we would look at that last. The second level had the dining area and kitchen, and the third was where the bedrooms were. I loved that the second and third levels also had balconies where we could sit outside and enjoy the cool breeze on a warm summer's night, or where I could sit quietly to meditate. The more I looked around, the more I became certain this place was the perfect fit for my little family. I looked over at my twin and I saw approval in her eyes and a smile on her face, which only confirmed what I already knew: this was in fact *the one*. I didn't want to waste any time and gave my realtor the green light to make an offer. Within days, I received word that my offer was accepted and we officially opened escrow a week later.

The Spring of 2010 brought me one of the most life-changing and pivotal chapters of my life. In addition to my first home, it brought me much to celebrate, like Samantha's high school graduation and her eighteenth birthday; that is the age I was when she was born. It was hard to believe that she had moved in with her father as a fifteen-year-old teenager and was now returning home as a young woman, old enough to date, drive, vote, and even enroll herself in college. It was strange coming to terms with the fact that she no longer needed me to parent her the way a young child does, but eventually I did. The most important lesson I have learned about parenting is that the relationship between a mother and daughter can be full of complexities and still be profoundly beautiful in its own way. Seeing Samantha grow up to become her own person has been one of the most rewarding experiences of my life, and as difficult as some of our chapters were, I wouldn't trade any of it for the world.

It was in this springtime that I also got to celebrate my own college graduation. It had taken me a long time, and I had faced many obstacles along the way, but I had finally arrived. I wished with all my heart my mother could have been there to witness this accomplishment, but having Samantha and siblings there was also immensely special. As I put on my cap and gown and the rope that signified I was graduating with honors, I closed my eyes to keep the tears welling up in my eyes from streaming down my made-up face. I thought about the little girl inside me, the one who'd never been told she could be anything she wanted and who'd once questioned her existence. *We did it, little one! Together, you and me. Never again will you doubt yourself or your purpose.* On that day, I was flying so high there was quite literally nothing that could bring me down.

I spent the days that followed celebrating this momentous occasion with my family and friends. It was really the first time I'd heard many of my family members express their pride in me. At one point, one of my nephews even shared that I had inspired him to continue his college education and that he'd written an essay about me. It meant so much to me that I could inspire anyone at all--most of all my own family. Being in survival mode makes it easy to forget that you always have an audience even when you think nobody is watching. Realizing this not only made me want to always do my best but, most importantly, to be my best--for myself and everyone around me.

Then, just when I thought the celebration was over, we closed escrow on my new place and I was handed the keys. I cried tears of joy and I wanted to hold on to this amazing feeling for as long as possible. I was so happy that I called my family and asked them to take a drive out with me so they could all see the place. It was late evening and despite there being no power, I opened all the windows and doors and gave them the grand tour. We sat on the floor with nothing but the moonlight and street lights shining in and laughed about who would have to help me move yet again. They were as tired of helping me move as I was tired of moving (I didn't blame them), and they made me promise I would stay put for many many years to come. With confidence, I promised, and I was sure to make good on my word.

Samantha and I spent the next several months settling in and making our place feel like home. I was fortunate enough to have an awesome support system to help me with things like arranging and rearranging furniture, hanging up wall decor and window treatments, and even with a few DIY makeover projects. Setting up my very own house was intense and sometimes overwhelming, but it was also tremendously rewarding and meaningful. Seeing our place come together the way it did was everything to me. I went for vibrant colors that made our place feel full of life while also cozy and inviting. The walls were painted yellow and I incorporated lots of reds, dark greens, and other earth tones to compliment one another. I made an altar by the fireplace with pictures of loved ones and my all-time favorite artist, Frida Kahlo, along with Day of the Dead figurines, known as *calacas* and *calaveras*. Samantha's bedroom was adorned with a beautiful chandelier and leopard print bedding because she went through a phase of being obsessed with all things leopard print. I even let my twin convince me to have a red accent wall painted in my bedroom because she'd heard it attracts love. *Hey, if painting a red wall in my bedroom will invite love into my life, I'm willing to give it a shot.*

All in all, our home became my sanctuary, where I felt happiest, safest, and most at peace. There were countless mornings I'd get up, make a cup of coffee, and sit in my living room in total silence to look around in awe and gratitude. If you ask the people who know me, they will tell you my first home was a condo. If you ask me, the woman who'd been homeless on more than one occasion, my home was my castle--with a princess, a mascot, and a queen who ruled it. The only thing missing was my king, my Prince Charming, my knight in shining armor.

"You'd be surprised at what some people will conceal just to get a first date …"

30

As I have come to learn, timing really is everything. With Samantha enrolled in college and working part-time, me, finally done with school, and our place all together, I had a lot more time on my hands than I was used to. Until then, I had felt a lot like a hamster, running in circles all day every day, jumping from one task to the next with little to no time for rest and relaxation. Now, I had so much time that I'd started to wonder whether I'd get bored. But, the blessings continued to pour onto my family, and my twin got engaged to marry her longtime love and partner. Having what seemed like all the time in the world made it easy for me to jump at the chance of lending my twin whatever support she needed in the wedding planning.

Unlike me, my twin is a total DIY (do it yourself) enthusiast who loves making things with her hands and enjoys the process of seeing her ideas come to life; her wedding was the perfect opportunity for her to do this. With her vision for a romantic, vintage feel, we did everything from purchasing vases at local thrift shops to spray paint and make into centerpieces, to visiting the garment district in downtown Los Angeles and purchasing burlap to cut and use as table runners. At one point, we even set up shop in my garage and created a mockup to take photos of the set-up, which would ensure that everything would look precisely as my twin had envisioned. It was a lot of work, but it was also quite a fun learning experience for me.

Beyond her wedding day, the most special moment we shared was the day we shopped for her wedding gown. My twin had purchased many bridal magazines to get ideas, but I guess she failed to read up on the fact that bridal shops require that you make an appointment to try on gowns. What did we know? Our sisters had gotten married in the 1980s, when we were kids and brides still went to local bridal stores to have their gowns custom-made. As we stood there with our tails between our legs feeling clueless, the nice saleslady took pity on us and said we could at least take a look around the shop after we made an appointment for a future date. We happily accepted.

When I tell you there was some kind of divine intervention working its magic that day, I am not exaggerating one bit. After a few minutes of browsing, the saleslady approached us and said the wedding party they had been expecting was a no-show and asked whether we'd be interested in taking their place. Without any hesitation, we accepted. My twin instantly became nervously excited as we began picking out sample dresses from the various racks for her to try on. I couldn't believe how heavy some of the gowns were, but I could see now why brides always glow on their wedding day. It's all so magical.

After trying on a handful of dresses, my twin's excitement slowly became disillusionment; nothing she had tried on thus far was to her liking. Determined to help keep the momentum going, I asked whether she was open to having me pull a few options. Much to my surprise, she quickly said yes, and I knew that was my one chance to show her something she would love. There was a rack we had not yet looked through because those gowns were over her budget, but I didn't see the harm in taking a look and trying on something a little more high-end. Besides, unbeknownst to my twin, I'd already decided that should we find a dress which exceeded her budget, I'd pay the difference as part of her wedding gift. I pulled out a beautiful satin gown and handed it to her. Although she seemed skeptical, she went ahead and put it on, walked out to stand in front of the mirror, and as soon as she saw herself, she began to cry. *Wait, what's happening? Is she crying because she loves it or because she absolutely hates it?*

Although I had been married before, I had not been a traditional bride and was out of my element; I didn't know whether to console my twin or celebrate with her. Then, as if the music had been cued, one of our mother's all-time favorite songs, Andrea Bocelli's rendition of "Amapola" began to play over the speakers. My twin, still in the dress, turned to me with disbelief on her face and we both began to cry. Upon seeing herself in the mirror, she was pretty certain this was the dress she wanted, but hearing our mother's song begin to play at precisely that moment was the confirmation she needed that it was absolutely *the one*. In spirit, we knew our mother was there giving my twin her blessing and approval and rejoicing in this beautiful moment. To top off this already beautiful experience, the saleslady informed us that the gown had been marked down, which meant it was within a budget my sister could work with. It was truly one of the most magical days I'd ever experienced.

My twin had set her wedding date for a few days after our birthday, and with all the commotion, we decided it was best to forego any birthday celebrations and focus solely on the wedding. A few of my colleagues had a different idea; they wanted to celebrate my birthday over margaritas. Frankly, I was happy to oblige because with all the wedding planning, I had earned myself a drink or two. We agreed to go out for happy hour on Thursday, October 13th, three days before my birthday. I remember it clearly because thirteen happens to be my lucky number, and as luck would have it, this would be one of my luckiest days yet.

Down the street from my home was a family restaurant with a bar that had a reputation for good margaritas and freshly made flour tortillas. I was happy to suggest that place because it was a family environment where we could avoid having any drunk guys trying to talk to us and disrupting our girl time. We arranged to leave work a little early that day in order to beat traffic and make the most of our happy hour time. We didn't get a chance to change out of our work clothes and we were probably a little overdressed for a family restaurant, but we didn't care. Upon arriving, we took the table farthest from the bar and immediately ordered a round of drinks and a basket of warm flour tortillas with butter. This was already turning out to be the most perfect low-key birthday celebration--from the food to the drinks and conversation, everything was flowing quite nicely and I could not have been more grateful to my friends for encouraging me to step out and enjoy some much needed girl time.

A couple hours into the evening, our server, Bonnie, approached the table with a margarita in her hand and said a gentleman at the bar had sent me a drink. *Aw man, this is everything I was trying to avoid. I don't want to get stuck having to talk with some guy just because he bought me a drink. Especially not on my girl's night out!* Not wanting to sound rude or ungrateful, I expressed my appreciation to Bonnie and asked whether she would politely tell the nice gentleman I could not accept the drink. My friends disagreed and said I should take the free cocktail and just enjoy it. Bonnie agreed, said not to worry because there were no expectations, and set the drink down in front of me. The bar was directly behind me and I couldn't see the nice man who'd sent the drink, but my friends all assured me he wasn't staring or anything, which made me feel better because I didn't want him to perceive my acceptance of the drink as an invitation to come over and talk to me.

A short while later, my friends noticed the gentleman getting up from his seat and said it appeared as though he was closing out his tab and getting ready to leave. I let out a sigh of relief because that meant the coast was clear and I could now enjoy my margarita with no obligation. As it turned out, they'd spoken too soon because he wasn't leaving at all but rather making his way toward our table. *What? No! I don't want to have to talk with a stranger. Is he cute? Oh, who cares! Shoot, I hope I don't have any food between my teeth!* Having nowhere to run or hide, I sat up and the next thing I knew, he was standing next to me.

Looking up at him, I was pleasantly surprised to find a tall, dark, and handsome Black man, even if he was dressed a little more casually than I prefer--in a ball cap, jeans, and a t-shirt. Next, I noticed the tattooed biceps bulging out of his t-shirt, which gave a whole new meaning to the term eye candy. *Okay, Mr. Biceps, I guess if you're going to interrupt my girl time, the least you can do is let me admire your nice physique.* As I discreetly glanced over at him, he introduced himself as Mike and went around the table to ask each one of my friends their names. I was impressed by his politeness, and my friends, well let's just say they were like tipsy schoolgirls, giggling and smiling so hard all their teeth were on full display. *Women are such suckers for a nice looking man with a good smile and some manners. But I don't blame them, he is definitely nice to look at.* After exchanging some pleasantries with them, he paused, made eye contact with me, and said that while it was very nice meeting everyone, he'd come by to specifically talk with me. *Oh, that's a very direct thing to say, but also kinda sexy. Who is this smooth operator? Ugh, probably just a player looking for his next playmate. Can we just get this over with so I can get back to my friends, please?*

As I turned to face Mike, who was now almost kneeling next to me so as to not hover over me, I put on my best fake smile and hoped he didn't notice my blushing cheeks, because being put on the spot definitely brought out the rare shy side of me. Our eyes met and as I got my first good glimpse of his face, I could immediately feel he had a gentle and calming energy about him. He didn't look like a player at all but rather like a man going after what he wanted. How could I hold that against him? We should all be so bold. He shook my hand and said I was beautiful and that he liked my outfit. It was a warm day and I was wearing a beige lace top with pretty short sleeves; a white, knee-length poofy skirt; and beige open-toe heels. After introducing myself and thanking him for the compliments, I also thanked him for the drink and told him I appreciated the nice gesture. Awkwardly, and with a shy smirk on his face, he confessed he'd actually not sent the drink. *I'm confused. If you didn't send the drink, who did?*

Noticing the confusion on my face, he quickly explained that he was friends with the restaurant owner and was a regular there, which meant he was friends with all the staff. Upon noticing me, he casually mentioned to Bonnie that he found me attractive, and unbeknownst to him, she took it upon herself to play matchmaker by sending the drink on his behalf, then later told him what she'd done. While he admitted to being somewhat embarrassed by the whole thing, he also admitted to not wanting to waste the opportunity to say hello and tell me how beautiful he thought I was. Still trying to digest the whole thing, I looked over at my friends, who were all eavesdropping, only to find them all smiling big and nodding their heads with excitement and approval. The entire encounter felt as though everyone was in on some hidden camera matchmaking show and I was the only one not in the loop.

As cute and funny as it all was, I really just wanted to get back to enjoying myself and closing out the night with my friends. They, on the other hand, wanted in on the matchmaking efforts. When Mike asked whether I was single or in a relationship, they all jumped in and said I was very much single. *Wow, okay! Thanks for* that… *friends!* After he was done expressing his disbelief that I was single, he admitted it was music to his ears and said it must be his lucky day. *Is it though? I mean, you technically didn't even send the drink, let's be honest. And I'm still not one hundred percent sure you're not a player. Oh, Karen, be nice. He seems perfectly harmless and actually quite sweet. Just talk to him. Your friends don't seem to care anyway.*

When it was my turn to ask him some questions, I started by asking his full name and he said it was Michael Scott but that most people just called him Mike. I liked Michael way better than Mike and asked whether it would be okay for me to call him by his given name. He said he would like that because it's what his family calls him. *This guy says all the right things, doesn't he? I'm still not ruling him out as a player.* As we got to talking about ourselves, Michael didn't waste any time with small talk and dove right in; he said he was a man of faith and was very involved in his church and was a police officer who was divorced with three kids--two sons and a daughter, to be exact. *Hmm, a divorced police officer with three kids. Sounds complicated. Not sure I'm interested in going down that road.*

I realize it may sound strange for a divorced single parent to not want to date another divorced single parent, but I had been there and done that, and from personal experience, it was almost always complicated for one reason or another. For example, I once had a boyfriend whose ex was so not over their break up that to get back at him for moving on, she would send their daughter home for the weekend wearing a Disney costume without any additional clothes to change into. I'd have to either lend her Samantha's clothes, which were two sizes too big for her, or we'd have to go out and buy her clothes because her mother would never return Samantha's clothes back to me.

Needless to say, that experience left a bitter taste in my mouth and I swore I'd never do that again. However, as my conversation with Michael continued, I kept trying to find reasons to dislike him, but I simply couldn't find any. Not only was he funny and kind and had mustered the courage to approach a table full of women just to talk to me, he'd also been the most honest man I'd met in a very long time, which I found immensely refreshing. You'd be surprised at what some people will conceal just to get a first date, like denying their own children--but that's a whole other story in and of itself.

I don't know whether it was his sincerity or his confidence, but I found this man very attractive and I was thoroughly enjoying everything about our conversation. Nevertheless, it was getting late and I really needed to get back to my friends. He was very understanding and agreed I should get back to them, but not before asking for my number. *He is very sweet, but I really don't know if I should. I mean, what if he's got baby-mama-drama in his life. I don't want to deal with that.* Noticing my hesitation, one of my friends nudged me and said I should go for it. *She's right. Okay, let's do this.* After Michael was done storing my number in his cell phone, he looked up at me and said that he'd be calling me soon because he'd like to take me out. I smiled and said I looked forward to it. When I got home a short while later, I noticed he'd sent a message saying that it had been a pleasure talking with me, that I was a beautiful lady, and he wished me sweet dreams. His message brought a smile to my face and I wished him a good night.

In that moment, I don't think either one of us could have predicted that my birthday happy hour would mark the beginning of the most beautiful love story I have ever known, my own.

"… our partners are mirrors who reflect back to us what we cannot always see in ourselves…"

31

Still feeling tired the next morning, I was grateful it was Friday which meant it was a casual day and also usually pretty light at the office. I was looking forward to getting home that evening and vegging on the couch with Darla when I remembered that I'd made plans with an ex-boyfriend who'd recently resurfaced and had asked to see me that evening. *Ugh, why do I keep getting myself in these situations? They're called exes for a reason, Karen. Move on!* I decided I'd tell him I couldn't make it after all whenever he reached out.

As the day went on, I had not yet received a call or message from my ex, but I did receive a message from my new friend, Michael. He wanted to know whether I was available to meet for a drink later that evening. I wasn't sure whether to make plans with Michael when I had not even officially canceled my plans with my ex, but I figured, *What the heck, why not?* If I was serious about continuing to build the future I envisioned, I had to stop looking backwards and start looking at what was ahead of me. To be on the safe side, though, I told him I had plans that evening and could only meet for a short while, which he was okay with because he had to work the next morning anyway. *Perfect, I'll run home, freshen up and go see whether he's still the nice guy I met last night.*

On my way home from work later that day, I received a call from my ex, and while I felt somewhat guilty for being flaky (because I very much dislike flaky people), I told him we should not see each other again because I knew he wanted to reconcile and there was no chance of us getting back together. He was disappointed to hear this, but we both knew it was for the best and that was the last time we ever spoke.

My impromptu first date with Michael took place at the bar of a chain restaurant, which I was totally fine with because I wanted to avoid all the first date formalities. I had worn jeans to work that day, but since I had time to stop by my place, I took the opportunity to shower and change into a cuter pair of jeans, which showed off my curves a little better, an off-the-shoulder top to show a tiny bit of skin, and some casual high-heeled sandals to complete the look.

Michael arrived at the restaurant before I did because he wanted to grab some seats before the bar got too crowded. I hoped to remember what he looked like and easily spot him in a crowded bar, but there was no mistaking him. He was still the tall, dark, and handsome man I'd met the evening before, except tonight he looked even better, with a long sleeve collared shirt and a paperboy hat, and he smelled amazing. When he saw me, he stood up and gave me a warm, welcoming hug, and as soon as we sat down, we picked up right where we'd left off the evening prior. There was not a single awkward moment and our conversation flowed naturally and effortlessly. Like most first dates, we asked a lot of the initial getting to know each other questions and found that we had several things in common. We were both the youngest in our families, we'd both lost our mothers to cancer, we'd both married young, and our kids were all close in age. The men I'd dated over the last several years had all been younger than myself, and it was a nice change of pace to talk with somebody I had more in common with. More importantly, I really liked how attentive Michael was the entire night and how he made me feel like we were the only two people in that entire restaurant; it was definitely a connection far deeper than just physical attraction.

I was having such a great time that I'd completely forgotten I had told him I needed to leave early to meet with friends. When I was finally ready to go home, he walked me to my car and asked whether he could see me again. Of course, I said yes and told him I'd really like that. As I grabbed my keys out of my purse and thanked him for a lovely evening, he asked whether he could give me a goodnight kiss and without hesitation, I once again said yes. Like the true gentleman he had been all night, he reached over, gently grabbed my face and leaned in for one sweet peck, then another and another. His lips were soft and so electrifying they shot butterflies into the pit of my stomach. *My God, this man is sexy*. It was the perfect ending to a perfect evening and when I arrived home, I realized I was still wearing the same giddy smile I'd had on my face when I left the restaurant.

Over the course of the next several months we became inseparable and our romance flourished into something quite beautiful. First, he met Samantha, who approved of him almost immediately, followed by my family, who adored him and appreciated how happy he made me, which of course made me even happier. Although it took a little longer for me to grow close to his children, particularly his daughter who was a daddy's girl and understandably kept me at an arm's distance, I knew it was only a matter of time before they'd warm up to me. I wanted them to know that as an extension of their father, I cared deeply about their feelings and I made sure to give them all the space and time they needed to come around. This is why in the initial months of having our kids come together, we planned family outings in neutral spaces where they could be themselves and get used to one another without feeling any pressure. For me, this was incredibly important because I had witnessed Samantha's feelings get ignored and hurt by the women her father dated, and I wanted to ensure I didn't make the same mistakes. As I knew would happen, his kids eventually let their guard down and we became good friends; I couldn't have asked for more.

Seeing my life fall into place so beautifully felt like a dream, especially when I realized that I'd actually manifested this beautiful man. You see, until that point, I had completely forgotten that when I was a child, I had an imaginary friend. He was a boy who lived in the living room wall of the apartment we once lived in, not literally, but in my imagination. I remember how much my siblings would taunt me and say I was crazy because they couldn't see how real my friend was to me. Whenever I close my eyes, I still see him standing there, a skinny Black kid with an afro, wearing plaid pants and a short-sleeved shirt. Then I remembered that like my new love's name, the boy's name was also Michael. *Oh my gosh, is that why subconsciously my mind immediately wanted to call him Michael instead of Mike, like everyone else did?* The memory of that boy and making the connection with the man I was now in love with felt so surreal. To make matters more interesting, it turns out that Michael's parents had gotten married in 1952, on October 13th, the same day we met. There were too many coincidences for us to have met by chance, and I felt more certain than ever that fate had brought us together.

From the moment we started dating, what I liked most about Michael was that he was always up for a fun adventure. We went camping with my family, took road trips to Las Vegas or Arizona for Dodgers Spring Training, and we loved Halloween time because we enjoyed dressing up in a couple's costumes. No matter where we went or who we were with, we thoroughly enjoyed each other's company. For close to a year, life went on feeling like a dream, until it didn't.

When the love dust began to settle, and as we grew closer and more in love, I began to feel painfully vulnerable and my unhealed traumas began to resurface. As I struggled to keep my demons at bay, I began reverting to old ways, mainly self-sabotaging. I'd heard that our partners are mirrors who reflect back to us what we cannot always see in ourselves, and that's exactly what was happening with us. Before I knew it, I was confronted by all my unhealed trauma: my abandonment issues, the sexual abuse, and my former husband's infidelity. In an attempt to protect myself, I did the only thing I knew how to do well: I pushed Michael away with everything I had. I became distrustful, controlling, jealous, and very angry. Everything he did and didn't do bothered me and I made sure he knew it.

Our once dreamy relationship soon turned into something I hardly recognized, a battlefield which no longer felt sacred or safe. *Karen, you love this man. Why are you so hell-bent on pushing him away? Why do you do this every time you start to feel your happiest? All men are not the same--don't be afraid. Who am I kidding? All men may not be the same, but all the men who were supposed to love me have either abandoned me, cheated on me, or have hurt me in some awful way, and I can't and won't let this man hurt me the same way. I can't stick around knowing how this story will end, with my heart broken and my self-esteem shattered. Push, Karen, just keep pushing until he breaks. That way, you can justify why you ended things when you did.*

The more I reflected my pain onto Michael, the more he pulled back and reflected his own unhealed wounds back to me, because he too was carrying baggage from his own childhood traumas and his previous relationship, which he had not entirely sorted out. It was obvious that we were both in a great deal of emotional pain, because neither one of us wanted to admit that our love for each other could no longer sustain the relationship itself. Despite our troubles, we stuck it out for as long as we could, until we came undone. Just days before our one-year anniversary, we broke up and went our separate ways.

I was not at all prepared for what would happen next. My past unexpectedly caught up to me and I was forced to confront my biggest demon of all: the sexual abuse I'd endured at the hands of my eldest brother.

As I shared earlier in my story, I had made a promise to myself that I would never reveal the sexual abuse to my family because I wanted to protect my mother from learning the awful truth. With my mother now gone, and some family drama relating to my eldest brother surfacing, I was left with no choice but to finally speak my truth about what he'd done.

I remember the day as though it were yesterday. It was a cold January afternoon when I received a call at work from one of my sisters who wanted to inform me of some devastating news. I braced myself because although it was not unlike her to call me at work, I could tell by the tone in her voice that it was something serious. She said that one of our nieces who had been in town over the holidays was alleging that one of our nephews had touched her inappropriately. I sat there stunned and in disbelief. I couldn't believe that one of our nephews could be capable of such a thing since all our children had grown up together and were extremely close. She then revealed that it was my eldest brother's son who'd committed the offense. As I listened to her cry about how devastated our eldest brother would be to learn that his son was a predator, I became angry that anyone could think our brother was somehow an innocent victim in this story. *Speak up, Karen. I know it will hurt you and potentially even destroy the only family you've ever known and loved, but you have to speak up. Breaking the silence is the only way to break the cycle. You cannot let this sickness continue to plague your family. You cannot live with the guilt of not speaking up when you had the chance.*

With my knees shaking and my voice cracking, I began to speak my truth right there over the phone in the middle of my workday. I was in a daze, a dream-like state and it all felt so surreal, but I couldn't stop now.

I didn't go into detail, but I wanted my sister to know that the brother she was attempting to defend was a predator himself and had victimized me, along with several others in our family. Although it wasn't my place to tell her who those other family members were, I wanted her to know that if he was capable of victimizing us, I believed he was capable of victimizing his own children. My sister, who thought she'd called me with devastating news, had just received the most shocking news of all, and for the first time ever, she was left utterly speechless. I felt guilty about breaking the news to her in such a manner, but as I've come to realize, there is never a good time or place to share such ugly things with those you love, especially not when they happen to love the person who committed the horrific acts against you.

After we hung up, I was so shaken up I had to leave work and I cried like a baby the entire way home. I was ashamed of my silence and not being able to prevent the cycle from continuing, and I was also ashamed that my dirty little secret was now out in the open for everyone to hear about--because at the time, I still blamed myself as though I had somehow provoked it. I immediately fell into a deep state of depression, not only because I was hurting for my niece and my family but because I was also hurting for my inner child who now had to revisit that painful past she couldn't seem to get away from. All I could think about was how much I wished Michael was around and how much his love and support would have meant to me during these difficult times.

Sadly, as I suspected would happen, my family learned of my truth and immediately became divided. There were those who believed me, those who wondered why say anything at all after all these years, and those who not only turned a blind eye but also their backs on me and chose to say nothing at all. I'm not angry with anyone for how they chose to handle the situation, because I recognize that I'd had years to process it all, while they were only just learning the awful truth; perhaps, just like me, they would also need years to process it all. That is, in my opinion, the worst thing about feeling ashamed is that there is no one way to overcome it except to face it, and sometimes people just can't face what is in front of them because in doing so, they must acknowledge that much of what they've believed their entire lives was a lie. In their own way, they loved me, but they loved their brother more, and that is something I'd always known. That was why, even as a child, I was intuitive enough to know that silence was the only way to keep my family close.

As a divorcée, I knew firsthand how painful separation of families could be, but somehow this separation felt a thousand times worse. In an instant, I lost the only family I'd ever known and loved, including two Godchildren, nieces, nephews, and brothers-in-law, all who'd meant the world to me. My holidays, which had always been filled with fun family gatherings, were now quiet parties of a few. Samantha, who'd always had many cousins to play and talk with, had now only the memory of them to hold on to. I mourned the loss of my family for a very long time, but as painful as walking away from them was, I was really proud of finally having the courage to stand up and fight for me in a way nobody had ever done. Since then, I have been freer and more myself than I'd ever been my entire life, and for that, I could not be more grateful.

Of my eight siblings, I remain in contact with only two, my twin and the middle of the three boys. A couple of my sisters have made attempts to reach out, but as long as they want to go on pretending that the painful truth does not exist, I cannot be a part of their illusion, and I choose me over them. My eldest brother did, at one point, reach out to me and his other victims in a group text message to say he was sorry. I would think that if you have the gull to victimize a young child and rob them of their innocence, you would at the very least pick up the phone to apologize, but of course he was too cowardly to do such a thing. Undeserving of a response, I simply deleted the message just as I've chosen to delete him from my life.

The most wonderful thing to come from all the pain is that I can now say to my inner child what I'd wished my family could have said to me, *I'm so proud of you, Karen. As ugly and painful as the truth is, by speaking up, you have broken a generational curse that can no longer continue because you finally found your voice and used it for the greater good. You sacrificed your family for the sake of your future generations and for that, you will be greatly rewarded in ways you cannot even begin to imagine. Go on and continue healing yourself, then help others do the same. You are so brave, my little girl, and I am so proud of you.*

32

As time went on and I had started to think I would never see Michael again, he began reaching out again. I didn't want to get ahead of myself and assume this meant we would reconcile, but it did make me hopeful. It started with the occasional hello, then more frequent messages about how much he missed me, then full-on conversations about how we could work on our differences because the six months we'd spent apart had been utter torture and we were ready to make peace and find a way back to each other. Within a few short months of reconciling, we were ready to take our relationship to the next level and decided to move in together. Logistically, it made the most sense for him to move in with me, and with Samantha's blessing, we soon began preparing to make it happen.

As I rearranged furniture and cleared out some things to make room for Michael, I couldn't help but feel excited about how bright our future looked, especially because he had always been a great source of inspiration for me. Seeing him do what he loved and was passionate about lit a fire in me I didn't even know existed. I, too, had philanthropic goals I wanted to accomplish, but until I'd met Michael, they'd simply been dormant dreams I had never considered making a reality. Now, having a life partner whose moral support I could count on, I knew I could do it all, and that excited me to no end.

The first few months of living together were bittersweet, because while I was happy to finally have Michael settled into our place, acclimating to the changes was a little more challenging than I anticipated. Until then, I had been both the woman and man of the house, and learning to relinquish the masculine energy I'd been exerting as an independent woman was not easy for me. You have no idea how many times Michael had to remind me that he was now the man of the house, and he was right; however, rewiring my brain to think in such a way after growing up watching my mother do it all, and having to become independent at a young age myself, was no easy task. But, I was committed and willing to do whatever unlearning I had to do in order for him to feel like my equal partner in life.

As life began to take on a new normal, we settled in nicely and got into a routine that worked for us. Because we were all adults with busy schedules, we divided the household chores and learned to work as a team to help things run as smoothly as possible. Days turned into months, and as the seasons changed, I became more certain than ever that Michael was not only the man I wanted to spend the rest of my life with but also the man I wanted to bear children with. Despite our kids being grown, I still found myself longing for babies, which is something I'd never kept secret from Michael. In fact, in the initial stages of my relationship with him, I was very honest about what I wanted if things got serious between us, which were marriage and babies--two babies to be exact. Without hesitation, he said he was all in, and even though he'd had a surgical procedure to no longer produce children, he was more than willing to have it reversed if it was something we both really wanted. Knowing that he loved me enough to do that for us meant the world to me and I held on to that hope with all my heart.

A couple summers after we'd moved in together, Michael had a baseball tournament on the east coast that we were very excited for because I'd never been to D.C, Maryland, or Virginia, also known as the DMV, and he wanted to take me around the different towns to see all the historical sites. One of Michael's sisters had recently retired in Maryland with her husband, and she offered us a place to stay while we were there, which we graciously accepted. We decided to arrive a couple days before the tournament started in order to get settled in and get a chance to explore the different towns. Little did I know this trip would change my life.

On our second day there, we woke up early because we were scheduled to visit the Lincoln Memorial in Washington, D.C., which I was very excited about. My excitement, however, soon turned into concern when I noticed that Michael had woken up not looking at all like his usual happy self and seemed on edge. He is usually the calmest and most laid back person in the room, but on that day, he seemed nervous and tense, and when I asked him whether he was okay, he simply answered, "Yes." I could feel in my gut that he wasn't being honest, but our day was just getting started and I didn't want to ruin it by pushing the issue.

Aside from being visibly tense, Michael also seemed overly concerned with what I would be wearing that day, which was also very much unlike him. In our relationship, I was the fashionable one always helping him put his outfits together, so I questioned why he cared. All he said was that he just didn't know what to wear because I'm not typically a casual person and he knew it would be very hot out. He was right, it would be hot, but I hadn't packed anything other than summer dresses, so I decided to go with a strappy, long, salmon colored cotton dress with pretty blue flowers embroidered on the front of the bodice, and flip flops. My hair was only shoulder length at the time, but as humid as it was, I knew it would frizz, so I made sure to pack something to put it up with, just in case. He decided to go in jeans, a long sleeve baby blue shirt, and a fedora. *Maybe you're just grumpy because you know it's going to be hot out and I know how much you hate being hot. Don't worry, my love, we'll find a way to keep cool.*

When we got downstairs and walked into the kitchen, I noticed Michael's sister and brother-in-law had already left for the day, so we grabbed a quick, light breakfast and headed out. The minute we walked outside, we knew it really was going to be a very hot day, but we couldn't pass up the opportunity to see the sites and were just going to have to manage.

The drive into D.C. was a little hectic because we'd hit some morning traffic, but I was glad that at least Michael seemed a little more at ease. That was, until he parked the car and suddenly seemed tense again. *What's wrong with him? I should ask but I don't want to upset him. Did I do or say something wrong and he's just not telling me? Why won't he talk to me? I can tell his mind is a million miles away and I'm so confused right now. We had been looking forward to this day and now he feels like a stranger to me.* I noticed his cell phone had been ringing off the hook since we'd arrived, but he wouldn't answer it and I couldn't understand why. All he kept saying was that whoever it was could leave a message and he would call them. For now, we had to hurry because it was a far walk to the site and we were late. *Late? For what? I thought we were here to walk around and see the sights?* Then, as we got out of the car, he said he needed to get something from the trunk but asked me not to follow him. *Huh? What the heck is going on with you? Why are you being so weird? If I did something to upset you, I wish you'd just tell me so we can hash it out.* But he said nothing.

After he was done doing whatever he needed to do in the trunk, he walked up to me and grabbed my hand, which is when I noticed that he was perspiring like I'd never seen him perspire before. I mean, it was warm, but he was drenched and his cheeks were bright red. I became immediately concerned that perhaps he might not be feeling well or was having an episode because he suffered from vertigo. Maybe he was so determined to make this day fun and special that he was trying to put on a brave face for me despite not feeling well. I was staring at him so intently that I didn't realize we were actually running and he was pulling me alongside him. As I tried to keep up with him, I asked him to tell me once and for all what was going on, and all he said was that we were supposed to meet with some of his teammates who were also there for a tour, and we were running late. *Oh, is that it? Well, why didn't you just tell me that to begin with? So we're a little late--your friends will understand. You put way too much pressure on yourself. It's okay, my love.*

As we approached the steps of the Lincoln Memorial, I became less concerned with how Michael was acting and simply enjoyed the amazing view. I wanted to stop and take a moment to acknowledge what this place meant to me. Growing up I'd read about these very steps in my history books and heard all about Martin Luther King, Jr.'s "I Have a Dream" speech, and I couldn't believe I was standing there in the very same place. This was, to me, a dream in and of itself. But Michael was so anxious to find his teammates that I didn't get a chance to really let it all sink in.

We made our way up to the top of the steps, and Michael was anxiously looking around. *Can he let this moment be about us instead of his friends? I mean, he never said this was going to be a group thing and now I feel like this was never about us, but only about his friends. This sightseeing trip is not at all turning out to be what I'd envisioned. Oh well, I'll try to make the best of it and capture some good photos to show Samatha when we get back home.* I grabbed my camera and pointed the lens toward the long water fountain in front of the steps, where thousands of people had gathered on August 28, 1963, to listen to that historical speech I'd read so much about. I then heard Michael's voice in my ear, asking me to turn around and look over at the statue of Abraham Lincoln, which left me speechless because it was enormous. I asked him if we could walk over and take a closer look, but he said we should stay put a little longer because his friends were on their way to meet us. *Ugh, fine, whatever. I'll just keep taking pictures of this amazing view.*

Because it was summertime, there was a sea of people everywhere I looked, which made it challenging to get a clear shot of anything, but I was determined to enjoy myself despite whatever was going on with Michael. As I continued snapping pictures, I heard Michael's voice in my ear again. He asked me to look down below toward the bottom of the staircase and read to him what the signs said. *What? Where? What signs? I don't see them. Oh, there they are. Who are those kids and what are they doing? Wait, what does that say?* A large group of kids formed a line across the steps and each one of them was holding up an oversized cardboard sign with a red letter on it. People kept walking in front of them and stopping, which made it difficult for me to read, until I finally got a clear view and read the words out loud, "Will… you… marry… me?" *Oh my gosh, the cards read "Will you marry me!" Someone is getting proposed to! This is so exciting!! Where's the couple? I want to make sure I get pictures of them and we can exchange numbers so they can have pictures of their special moment. That's what somebody did for my best friend when she got engaged in Central Park! This is so beautiful!!* When I turned around to tell Michael, he was on one knee with his arm extended, and in his hand was a small red box. *Wait, what's happening? Is that sign down there for me? How? When did he do all this? Is this really happening? Oh my gosh, everyone is staring. Wait, what's happening?*

Between every thought crossing my mind and all the chatter around me, I faintly heard Michael's quivering voice say, "I love you, Karen. Will you marry me?" His hands were shaking and he had tears welling up in his eyes. *Oh my gosh, this IS really happening.* At that moment, I didn't care that there were cameras and hundreds of people all around us, and I began to cry the ugliest and most shameless cry ever! So much that I couldn't speak and had to simply nod my head, *Yes, yes, yes!* He put the beautiful, sparkly ring on my finger and I hugged him harder than I'd ever hugged anyone before. All I could hear was Michael yelling, "She said yes!!!" Everyone began clapping and cheering and cameras were flashing all around us. *I can't believe this is happening. This explains why you've been acting so crazy today, my love! How did you do this? You know, I don't even care. This is so magical. How I wish my family was here.*

As it turned out, Samantha and my twin had attempted to fly out to be there for this momentous occasion, but they couldn't find flights that would accommodate a quick turnaround at an affordable enough price. But, Michael did make sure to ask Samantha for her blessing, which she gave wholeheartedly. She was the first person I called and we cried together on the phone. Then I called my twin and cried some more. Finally, I looked up at the partially cloudy sky and smiled because I knew my mother was rejoicing wherever she was. *Mamita linda, how I wish you were here to witness this moment, but I feel you in my heart and know you're here with me.*

As I wiped the tears and I looked around, I started seeing many familiar faces. Michael's sister had actually been the one who'd come up with this grand idea and had, along with her church friends, solicited help from a group of visiting choir kids to pull it all off. Her husband was there as well, along with several of Michael's teammates and their spouses and kids, all who'd taken pictures and video to capture it all. For a moment, I felt like Cinderella because I had kids running up to me wanting to hug me and congratulate me and tell me how beautiful I was. I'd never been made to feel this special in my entire existence, and that moment, seeing the man I love ask me to spend the rest of my life with him, was by far one of the most magical and memorable moments of my life.

33

Without skipping a beat, Michael and I spent the next six months planning our wedding day. From finding the perfect Spanish style venue, to finding my beautiful wedding dress, a strapless vintage white lace gown paired with a mantilla cathedral length wedding veil, everything was coming together almost effortlessly. It was a time of such joy and much excitement in our household that we hadn't taken notice of the giant dark cloud that seemed to be looming over us, threatening to rain down on our happiness and wash it all away.

As our wedding date neared, Michael and I began looking ahead into what our future as a married couple looked like and we started making big picture plans, like buying a bigger home and making some investments. Although we seemed to be on the same page about most things, I was slowly beginning to learn that we weren't on the same page on a few things that were of great importance to me.

The first thing was that he'd had a change of heart about wanting to have more children. I was confused to learn this because leading up to our engagement, that was something I had been looking forward to and was one of the reasons I wanted us to get married. To learn of his change of heart was crushing to my soul. How was I supposed to reconcile that the man I wanted to spend my life with was now unwilling to take part in making one of my dreams a reality. Obviously, I didn't want to force him to do something he didn't want to do, so I said little about it, but deep down inside, I was confused and hurt, and also quite angry with him for not having said anything to me before proposing. He'd cornered me and I didn't know what to do.

As I slowly came to terms and accepted this new reality, I figured that not all was lost. If I wasn't going to be able to create life with my soon-to-be-husband, I would at least have his support in my future endeavors. He was, after all, a source of great inspiration for me, as someone who loved his job and loved doing things for the communities he served. I wanted that so badly and until I'd met Michael, I didn't think it was possible for me to do everything I wanted. I started with mapping out some of my personal goals, which I shared with him for feedback. First, I would use my reserves to pay off my remaining school debt, which would allow me the freedom to search for a job that felt more rewarding to me, even if it meant taking a salary cut. Once I secured a new job, I'd start doing some volunteer work because it's something I'd wanted to do since graduating college. I also really wanted to go to cosmetology school and get licensed to work as a freelance makeup artist, which is something I'd always loved doing. My plan was attainable and realistic and would be a great way for me to do something more personally rewarding to me. I was done wasting my talents in my corporate job that didn't always see or value my potential.

Excited about the future, I felt confident Michael would be happy and excited for me as well, and offer his full support. But sadly, and to my great surprise and disappointment, he was unwilling to support my endeavors. In fact, he thought so little of my plans that any time I wanted to discuss them, he seemed disinterested and questioned how I could be so foolish to consider leaving my stable and good paying job after all the years I'd spent establishing myself there.

With Michael's blatant lack of support, I became more conflicted and confused about our future than ever. How was I supposed to feel excited about marrying a man who not only unexpectedly changed his mind about having children with me but was also unwilling to support me in my personal and professional endeavors. He wasn't the only one one with goals and ambitions. He wasn't the only one who deserved to live for his purpose. In the years we'd been together, Michael had reaped the benefits of my unconditional support but was now unwilling to reciprocate it. He failed to see that each time he crushed one of my dreams, I felt less valued by him.

I don't think Michael was intentionally trying to keep me in a box, but the more I gave into his wants and did not advocate for my own, the more it felt like I was living in his shadow rather than in my light. As someone who'd never felt safe or supported in my relationships with men, I needed Michael to show me that he was different, but he wasn't doing that; and the more insecure I felt, the more I pushed him away.

Is this cold feet? Am I just looking for reasons or excuses to push him away? I finally got what I wanted--the man, the ring, the wedding, so why am I not happier? Please Karen, don't self-sabotage again. But is it self-sabotaging when I don't get to have my happy ending? Yes, a life partner will contribute to my happiness, but happiness is about so much more than that. You held off on marriage this long, you declined other marriage proposals for a reason--don't you dare sell yourself short now. Stop dimming your light for the sake of others and speak up. If not now, when?

As the wedding plans progressed, I couldn't shake the feeling that our marriage was doomed before we even got to walk down the aisle. I began having nightmares and my anxiety was so far off the charts that I was constantly on edge and every little thing would make me fly off the handle.

Then, I realized that in the time Michael and I had been apart, I had only just begun to scratch the surface of my healing and I needed more time. Also, I was beginning to see that Michael was completely oblivious to the fact that he had a lot of healing and growing of his own to do. By his own admission, and based on things I'd heard from others, I knew his selfishness had been an issue in his previous marriage and I could not take another step forward knowing he would be repeating some of his old patterns, especially as it related to his loyalty and fidelity. Around this time, I discovered that Michael had not been entirely forthcoming about some of his friendships with women from his past or with women who were interested in more than just friendship. He knew what I'd been through in my previous marriage and also knew I had no tolerance for dishonesty.

Leaving me with no other choice, I did the only thing I could think to do: I handed Michael my engagement ring and called off our wedding.

"I also forgave myself for all the self-loathing I'd done, for not always being gentle with my mind and body, and for not always knowing how to advocate for myself."

34

When I was younger, I often wondered why some people come into our lives for a lifetime while others come and leave soon after. But over the years, I learned that in one way or another every person in our lives is a teacher. And while some are meant to stay permanently, others come for a specific reason or season to either deliver a message or help us get through a difficult situation, or to simply restore our faith in God and ourselves. My life has always been sprinkled with messengers from God whom I believe are guardian angels, and this chapter of my life was no different.

In the weeks and months after calling off my wedding, I was in such a state of sadness I could hardly function. I spent weeks putting on a brave face at work, pretending the wedding was still on, then running home and crying myself to sleep after numbing myself with a pint of ice cream or a bottle of wine. Things only got harder in the days after I picked up my wedding gown. It was a Saturday and Samantha had left for work, so I decided to get dressed and go alone. I cried the entire way there and I knew the young girl who handed me the box preserving my gown and the bag carrying my veil could feel my pain; it was palpable. I was grateful when she didn't ask any questions and just let me go on about my day. On my drive home, which seemed eternal, I cried so hard I could have really used some windshield wipers on my eyeballs, but instead, I let the tears flow. When I arrived home, I took the box and bag upstairs to my bedroom. I could no longer contain my pain and I fell to the ground and sobbed like a child who'd lost her favorite doll. It was a pain so deep even my soul was aching.

At that point, I decided it was best to take a few days off work and begin to rip the bandaid off by notifying family and friends that the wedding was off. It was a difficult thing to do, but something interesting happened along the way. With each message I sent and every call I made, I felt my faith growing stronger than ever. I knew I'd overcome far worse and that just as God had not abandoned me before, he wouldn't abandon me now. *Okay, Lord, you take the wheel and drive. Whatever lesson I'm supposed to learn from this, my heart and eyes are wide open, and I leave myself at your mercy.* I decided that instead of giving energy to my problems and blaming myself for the failure of my relationship, I wanted to gain a better understanding of how I came to be in this place and how I could find a different way to protect myself without feeling the need to push away the people I love most.

I started by going to bookstores and getting my hands on whatever I felt could help me grow spiritually and emotionally, from self-help and relationship books, to coloring books (because my inner child loves to color and we were in serious need of some joy). After that, I began to get back in touch with my support system, my twin and friends, who'd been reaching out wanting to lend their love and support, which I now felt ready to receive. Until then, I'd been leaning solely on Samantha, my biggest angel of all, who was doing the best she could to help cheer me up. But it was time to let her get back to being her young and carefree self, and time for me to find my way out of the darkness I'd buried myself under.

I'd also always heard that hair carries energy, and with me being ready to call in some fresh new energy into my life, I cut my waist-long locks into a bob. Then, I realized it wasn't short enough and cut it even more, just in case there was any old energy holding on for dear life. It's amazing how liberating cutting off your hair can be when your soul is so desperately in need of healing. With that out of the way, I was ready to step out into the world a lighter me.

One day, a colleague and friend, the one who'd convinced me to give Michael my number at the bar a few years prior, invited me to join her at a women's empowerment event happening over the weekend. I didn't know whether I was entirely ready for something like that, but I figured it couldn't hurt to be surrounded by positivity and I decided to join her. At that event, I met a wonderful woman, a healer, who would help change my life.

The woman's name was Angelica, and she and I instantly connected from the moment our paths crossed in the hallway where we checked in for the event. The connection was so strong, it was as though our souls had been friends from lifetimes before. She was there with her best friend, who raved about how much Angelica had been helping her heal from her past traumas. Feeling intrigued to learn more about this woman's healing abilities, I asked what she did for a living. Just as we were beginning the conversation, an announcement was made that the event was about to start and we were asked to enter the ballroom to take our seats. In a matter of seconds, I lost sight of her. *Oh well. If it's meant for me to cross paths with her again, we will find each other.* Lo and behold, as was destined to happen and much to my great surprise, we were seated at the same table.

After initial introductions around the table, Angelica shared her story. She was a divorced mother of two who'd left her abusive husband and had, in the process of it all, found Reiki energy healing. Until that moment, I'd never heard of Reiki, but I knew I wanted to know more about it if it meant I could reach the same level of inner peace she was displaying. It was magnetic. I also came to learn the name Angelica means angelic messenger of God. This only confirmed what I already knew: meeting her had been no coincidence at all but a divine intervention ordained by God himself.

She explained that Reiki was an ancient Japanese healing practice which, in simplest form, is life force energy. More than a holistic healing approach, Reiki is a deeply spiritual healing practice when used in combination with healing crystals, essential oils, sound healing, and calling in spirit guides and archangels. Listening to her speak so passionately about this practice brought me to tears, perhaps because I knew in my heart that she could help me find the healing I was so desperately seeking. *I wonder if she can feel my pain? Is she the lifeline I have been searching for?*

After the event was over, I walked over to her and we began to talk. I don't know what compelled me to do this, but in those few minutes of talking, I poured my heart out to her. I admitted that my life seemed to be falling apart, and I was dragging Samantha down with me. She was witnessing all my pain and I believed that was contributing to her personal struggles. Angelica reminded me that as the matriarch, I was the foundation of my home and that if I could not find inner balance and harmony, everything within and around me would continue to crumble. Until that moment, I had not connected the dots and realized that just as my mother had been the foundation of our family, I was now the foundation of mine. It was up to me to regain strength in order to get our lives back on track. Samantha needed me, but I needed me too. I don't think Angelica knew this at the time, but with her words alone, she had already begun to heal me. A few days later, I went in for my first Reiki session with her, and from the moment I put myself in her healing hands, I knew my world would be forever changed.

As I prepared to see what Reiki could do for me, I decided to do away with any expectations and simply allowed myself to be open to Angelica's guidance. When I arrived at her home, where she had her Reiki practice set up, she greeted me with a gentle smile and a loving hug, then welcomed me into her space and asked me to make myself at home. She was a petite woman about my age, dressed casually in denim jeans and a t-shirt, and she wore her long black hair in a ponytail. Her place was warm and inviting, with colorful images on the walls, of God, angels, and her favorite artist, Frida Kahlo. I could smell sage and essential oils in the air and could hear meditative music playing softly in the background. In the middle of the room was a massage table with a pillow and warm blanket draped over it.

After I sat on the massage table, we began to talk about how I'd been feeling and what I'd been feeling, and then she went into how the session would go. She first asked whether I was comfortable with touch since Reiki energy can be transmitted with or without the practitioner touching the client. I opted for touch in case that would optimize the experience. She then explained that she would be working with the seven main chakras, also known as energy portals or openings throughout our bodies, and would be placing crystals and essential oils on and around me. Finally, she asked me to set an intention, and without really knowing what to expect, I kept it simple and to the point: *I want peace of mind, body, and spirit, and I want to feel whole again.* She then asked that I lie back, close my eyes, and take a few deep breaths to relax and be one with my body. She also asked that I allow myself to acknowledge and connect with whatever emotions came up for me during the session and explained that it wasn't unusual for clients to feel the presence of spirits and ancestors, but I should not be afraid as she had already called in divine protection. I was not afraid. On the contrary, I could not have been more ready. I closed my eyes and began to pray, *Thank you, God, for Angelica and for this sacred space she has so lovingly created to bring healing to myself and others. May she, her loved ones, and her beautiful home be forever blessed with abundance and prosperity. I receive your healing energy with all of me.*

The session went on for about forty-five minutes and while I didn't quite know what she had done, by the time it was over, I felt my spirit overflowing with an immense sense of peace, love, and gratitude. She explained that unlike traditional Western medicine, Eastern medicine was not about prescribing a pill that could magically take my pain away, but a practice that would take time because the goal was to get to the source of the pain and begin to heal it from within. I was to wait a few weeks before I could see her again, and those weeks could not have passed fast enough.

Over the course of the next several months, Angelica took me under her wings and not only became my healer but also a teacher. She taught me about archangels, spirit guides, healing crystals, cord cutting, the power of manifestation, and so much more I'd never known about. I wondered how I'd survived this long without any knowledge that these practices even existed--no wonder I'd felt so lost for so long. With her love, guidance, and help, I began shedding layers of my painful past and rebirthing a new me.

As for my shame, anger, and resentment, it slowly began melting away, and I gave myself permission to make peace with and forgive all those who'd ever hurt me, intentionally or not. I also forgave myself for all the self-loathing I'd done, for not always being gentle with my mind and body, and for not always knowing how to advocate for myself. This incredibly freeing feeling inside me was so beautiful that I wanted everyone to get to experience it firsthand. I started by encouraging Samantha to go to Angelica. When she did, I soon began to see her beautiful transformation unfold. I also encouraged friends and colleagues and anyone who trusted me enough to listen to give it a try. Angelica could have continued to reap the benefits of my referrals but instead, she encouraged me to become a healer myself. She strongly felt that I, too, had the gift of healing.

All my life, I had been told I was wise beyond my years, but I had never considered myself a healer. Yet here was this woman healer telling me I had the gift, and this was a message I could not and did not want to ignore. The seed was planted and it was up to me to water it, nurture it, and watch it bloom. It was then that the biggest and most life-changing shift began to take hold in my heart. I was ready to make radical changes, and now I knew exactly which direction to go.

35

There is an American actress named Emma Stone who said that she couldn't think of a better representation of beauty than someone who is unafraid to be herself. That is exactly what I became, unafraid, and unapologetic for being myself. All the things I'd felt I needed permission to do, I finally began to pursue without needing anyone's validation.

The first thing I did was take my reserves to pay off my school debt once and for all. My gosh, that felt so good! When I finished college, I had promised myself that I would have every last dime I owed to the government paid off within ten years, and now I had paid it off in only six. I was so proud of myself! Once that was done, I was open to looking for a new position, possibly at a non-profit, where even if I took a salary cut, I could be happier and more fulfilled. The thought of leaving the workplace where I'd spent close to twenty years of my professional life was frightening but also exhilarating. I knew I had many talents that were going unnoticed and unappreciated, and it was time for me to find a place where I could shine.

While I waited for the stars to align and the universe to bring me just the right place, I became a volunteer ESL (English as a Second Language) teacher at a non-profit in the San Fernando Valley, where working adults attend courses to help them advance in the workplace, or where they simply go to learn new skills. It was incredibly rewarding to do something selfless for my Latino community and I know my mother would have been so proud.

The final thing I did was give my home a much needed makeover to clear out any remaining bad juju left from all the hurting and crying I'd done in that space. I needed my home to feel like my sanctuary again, and in order for me to do that, I had to clear out and remove all painful memories, from family photos to some of Michael's belongings, which he'd left behind. I was in no way trying to erase anything or anyone from my past, but I was a woman unlearning that I needed others to feel whole or happy, and I was finally learning that all I ever needed to be either of those things was myself. I was taking my power back and never again would I hand it off to someone else.

It had been nine months since I'd called off my wedding, and while in that short period of time so much pain and suffering had transpired, I'd also experienced tremendous healing and transformation, so much that I could hardly recognize myself anymore--in the most amazing way. I loved who I was becoming, but more than that, I loved that I was finally creating a life for myself I knew was on my terms and no one else's.

After a few weeks of searching and interviewing at different organizations, I was beginning to think that perhaps I'd gotten ahead of myself because nothing seemed to be panning out for me. Feeling disheartened by the reality that I may have to stay in a toxic work environment longer, I decided to start taking daily walks to a local church up the street from my office. One day, I walked in there feeling a sense of desperation and I cried out to God to help me once again because I knew I was ready to take a leap of faith, but I also knew my fate was in his hands.

As it is written, "Ask and you shall receive." Again, this is exactly what happened to me. When I arrived home that evening, I went online once again to search for a job, but this time I felt more determined than ever. As I scrolled through all the job listings I'd already looked at, one I hadn't seen yet caught my eye. I read over the job description, and even though I was not entirely certain I was qualified for the position, I went ahead and submitted my application anyway. By the next morning, I received a call to schedule a phone interview and I knew this would be my chance to hit the ball out of the park. The interview, which was only scheduled with the hiring director for thirty minutes, went on for over two hours. She was one of those guardian angels God had sent my way and we hit it off instantaneously. She not only found my credentials impressive but wasn't at all concerned that I didn't know everything there was to know about the position because she could tell I was a go-getter and was confident I would pick things up quickly. We scheduled an appointment for me to meet the team I would be working with and just as I hoped would happen, we were a perfect match.

Within a couple weeks, I left the company I'd grown up in and ventured off to greener pastures. Working with a team who actually appreciated me, celebrated me, and welcomed me with open arms meant everything to me. That alone made me want to give the organization and the team everything I had. As I blossomed and received promotions, I regained confidence in myself and my ability to do anything I set my mind to--something I'd always known about myself but had forgotten over the years.

As my healing took hold and my life began to take on new meaning, I was more certain than ever that I was ready to love and be loved in a healthier, happier, and more compassionate way. It was still not entirely easy for me to accept that I had pushed away the only person I could envision that life with, but something in my heart urged me to remain hopeful. In each other, Michael and I had found a once-in-a-lifetime kind of love, and I didn't want to believe that either one of us was willing to let that go to waste. For now, all

I could do was give time a chance to mend the broken road and hope that somehow, someway, it would lead Michael back to me.

"… I had never established boundaries in any of my relationships, with anyone in my entire life, and that needed to change immediately."

36

This may sound a bit cliché, but you know that old saying about setting the person you love free and if they come back to you it was meant to be? Well, that is quite literally what I did; I set both Michael and myself free. I freed him from the burden of feeling as though it was his job to complete or fix me, and I gave him all the space he needed to decide for himself whether or not he wanted to give our love another try. One of the things I learned--albeit the hard way--is that love doesn't need to be put into a pressure cooker, it isn't something you chase, and it is definitely not something you should ever beg for. Real love happens on its own terms in the most organic way. I freed myself because I recognized that whether or not Michael and I got back together, I would be just fine. Feeling this much in control of my emotions was not only a first for me but was a truly empowering feeling that I never wanted to lose.

Over the nine months Michael and I had been apart, we had never entirely cut off communication, but our messages and conversations were usually brief and never addressed our issues or the hurt we both felt. We were not friends but also not enemies, and being in limbo after close to a year was not my idea of moving forward. The more I pulled away, the more I felt him making an effort to connect. While I was open to hearing what he had to say, I'd grown tired of the small talk and I wanted him to know that I'd forgiven him and hoped he had forgiven me too. We had both caused each other a great deal of pain over the years, and it was time that we either put the past behind us and start over, or cut off all communication and go our separate ways.

Once again, I surrendered to God and asked him to do as he sought fit. The minute I did that, Michael returned of his own volition. It started with late-night song dedications which quickly evolved to "I miss you" and "I still love you" messages. Sometimes I would respond and others I would simply sit with the song lyrics and allow the words to wash over me. I still loved this man, deeply and completely, but he needed to show me that he was ready to confront our problems so that we could find a resolution.

One early November day, Michael unexpectedly reached out and asked whether I would be open to meeting him. I responded, *Yes*. Of course I wanted to meet; I had been waiting for this moment for what seemed like forever. We decided that because it was going to be a warm sunny day, it would be nice to head out toward the coast. Over the course of our relationship, Michael and I had always enjoyed going to Third Street Promenade in Santa Monica, grabbing a nice lunch, and sitting out on the benches and people watching while enjoying a warm cup of coffee or a sweet treat. I figured this would be a nice way to spend the afternoon reminiscing and talking. He picked me up at my place early in the afternoon and even though it was a fairly relaxing drive, there was some awkward silence. I stared out the window most of the time wondering what he would say or who would start the conversation because we had a lot to sort out and much of it was heavy. Sitting there next to him after all that time was bittersweet and I hoped our meeting would mark the beginning of something better for us.

When I saw Michael, I realized I had let go of a lot of the hurt and resentment I thought I was still holding on to. I was not excusing any of his hurtful and selfish behavior, but throughout my healing journey, as I gave myself the opportunity to sit with my pain and examine myself deeply, I had come to realize some very important things. With Michael, I was on a completely different playing field than I'd ever been on with anyone else. With him I wanted to roll up my sleeves and be in the trenches, fighting for our love instead of just calling it quits or walking away for good. I was well aware that if we did work things out, we had a long road ahead because we had to rebuild trust from the ground up, and that would be no easy task considering everything we had been through. But, despite everything, I was fully prepared to do my part, which is something I would not have not been willing to do with anyone else ever before.

Also, I could see now that subconsciously, I had been punishing Michael for all the pain the men in my life had in one way or another inflicted on me. I was literally holding him responsible and expecting him to right everyone's wrongs, as though it were his responsibility to clean up a mess he had not even created. Not only was that unfair to him but, whether it was my father's abandonment, the abuse I'd endured at the hands of my brother and ex-husband, or other heartbreaks I'd experienced throughout my life, the only person responsible for healing those wounds was me. I could no longer pawn off my pain onto Michael expecting him to fix me, because I didn't need to be fixed; I simply needed to heal, forgive, and let go.

The most important and eye-opening realization I came to was that I had never established boundaries in any of my relationships, ever, with anyone in my entire life, and that needed to change immediately. Growing up with that feeling of desperation to please everyone in order to feel loved and never being taught about the importance of boundaries, I had always gone all in and given so much more of myself than I ever received in return. Whether it was my love, friendship, support, money--you name it--I was giving it away like hotcakes and taking whatever scraps were thrown my way. Then I wondered why I always felt so depleted and unfulfilled. Now, I'd come to understand that by not setting boundaries with others, I was not only selling myself short but I had no right to be upset with anyone for crossing boundaries I had never bothered to establish any in the first place. *Hello?!?!*

As I poured my heart out to Michael about all the hard lessons I'd learned during our time apart, I could see he was remorseful for the role he'd played in adding to my pain and distrust of men. But I also saw a sense of pride in his eyes. He was witnessing a far more evolved woman than he'd known so far. More than anything, I could see that my words had lifted a big weight off his shoulders because he knew I wasn't holding him solely responsible for the undoing of our relationship. I recognized we had both played an equal role in that.

Michael expressed his sincerest apologies and his deep regret for his mistakes and for not having been the man I deserved. He promised that if I would have him back, he would spend the rest of his days making it up to me. Hearing Michael take responsibility for his actions and feeling the sincerity in his voice made me feel really proud of him--and also of me. Nine months prior, neither one of us could have done that. Now, we were the kind of people who could look in the mirror without shame and look into each other's eyes without guilt but rather love and compassion. I was ready for a fresh start and excited to begin a new kind of love story.

"… while the road got bumpy along the way, we recognize that overcoming the hard stuff early on helped us build a strong foundation."

37

Three months after Michael and I reconciled, he proposed. Believe it or not, it was almost as much of a surprise the second time around as it was the first--not because I didn't think he would propose, but because he proposed on the one day he'd always sworn he wouldn't: Valentine's Day.

This particular year, Valentine's Day landed on a Tuesday, which meant we both worked and needed to schedule plans accordingly. As we had done many years prior, we decided we would go to one of our favorite spots in Pasadena where we could always get an early reservation and be done before the late-night dinner crowd came in. At the time, we worked in completely different parts of town; he was in the San Fernando Valley and I was in downtown Los Angeles, so we arranged to leave work a little early and decided it would be easiest to meet at the restaurant. Because I typically attended meetings, I always made sure to look sharp, but on this particular day, I wore a dress that was both professional and that I knew Michael would like seeing on me. It was a form-fitting light grey pinstriped dress with a ruffled bottom, matched with maroon shoes for a splash of vibrant color.

When I arrived at the restaurant, he was standing by the entryway, holding a card and a dozen red roses in his hands. I never expected or pressured Michael to buy me roses on Valentine's Day because I knew it was something he'd been pressured to do in the past. This was why, for the first several years of our relationship, he preferred to send chocolate-covered strawberries, which I enjoyed but were bad for my waistline. I think not feeling pressured by me actually made him want to buy me roses, which made them that much more special. I also couldn't help but notice how good he looked standing there like a gentleman in love. He was a lot more dressed up than I'd expected him to be, with grey slacks, a button down shirt, and dress shoes; I couldn't take my eyes off him and the icing on the cake was that he smelled as good as he looked.

I didn't know whether it was the way he looked or the fact that it was our first Valentine's Day since we'd gotten back together, but this felt a lot like a first date and I was quite nervous. I managed to keep my cool, though.

After getting seated and comfortable, I excused myself and made my way to the ladies room. When I returned, there were two champagne glasses sitting on the table. *He ordered champagne? This is a first. Does he even like it?* I sat down, smiled at him, and asked what the champagne was about. He said he was really happy and wanted to celebrate that we were there once again, together, and he looked forward to countless more dates in the years ahead. *He's not a man of many words, but he always gets it just right.* We picked up our glasses and toasted to his heartfelt words.

As I started to take a sip of my champagne, I noticed something shining at the bottom of the flute and I pulled it away to get a better look. My engagement ring was inside the glass. *Oh, hi there, beautiful. I haven't seen you in a while… Hold on a minute, did Michael clean the ring or wash his hands before placing it in my drink? I don't even want to know. Let's just get the ring out of there and onto my finger, because this time, I'm keeping it on for good.* Michael took the champagne glass and pulled the ring out with a utensil, dried it with his napkin, and was about to get down onto his knee when I stopped him. *I know what you're thinking and no, don't worry, I am not going to run away or say no.*

If you've ever gone out to dinner on Valentine's day, you probably know how overcrowded and busy restaurants can get, and this day was no exception. Unlike the first proposal, with all the hoopla and people around us, I wanted this to be just for us and nobody else. When I told him how I felt, he agreed and sat back on his chair. Then, still holding the ring in the tips of his fingers, with the sweetest and most loving look in his eyes, he expressed his love for me and asked me to marry him. We giggled quietly and I said, "Yes, a thousand times yes!" Then we kissed and hugged as discreetly as we could without making a scene, and I could not have felt happier. It was a proposal in total contrast from the first one, but it was so much more meaningful because this time around, I had not a single fear or doubt and was ready to commit to this man once and for all, until death do us part.

Unwilling to put off our wedding any longer, we were married eight months later, on Friday, October 13th, the same date his parents had been married sixty-five years prior. We exchanged vows before our children, our extended families, and some of our closest friends and colleagues. On that day, Michael did something else he swore he would never do: he got emotional when he saw me in my wedding gown for the first time as I walked down the aisle to our favorite song, "Another You," by Brian McKnight. Until that moment, I had been holding it together quite nicely despite the fact that just before my brother walked me down the aisle, he too had cried. But seeing my future husband standing before me with tears of joy in his eyes, I could no longer contain my own emotions.

In few but deeply meaningful words, our vows told our story of trials and tribulations and of immense love and heartfelt promises. I don't think there was a dry eye in that garden. I meant every word I said: Michael has been and will forever be, one of the greatest loves and teachers of my life.

Once we got through the emotional stuff, we joined the party and celebrated our milestone--Michael and I were officially husband and wife! I think a lot of people there didn't know whether we'd ever actually get to this point, but there we were, happier and more in love than ever before. I danced until my shoes came off, we smiled so hard our faces hurt, and we enjoyed every single moment of the entire evening. My most favorite part of the reception (besides being with our family and friends and dancing the night away) was hearing Samantha, who'd been my maid-of-honor, give the most heartfelt and deeply emotional speech. She talked about how much she'd dreamt of this day and how happy she was that I'd found love with a good man. She also welcomed her new siblings into her life. Believe it or not, we were so moved by her words that we completely forgot to make a speech of our own. But we were absolutely okay with letting her have that moment because it meant everything to Michael and me that, despite having witnessed so much of the pain, she was still rooting for us and giving us her blessing.

Before leaving for our honeymoon, Michael and I made one important stop. We paid my mother a visit at the cemetery and delivered all the flowers from the wedding venue, including my bouquet, to her. I wanted to decorate her space with the beautiful flowers the same way she had decorated my life with love. Plus, the deer and other wild animals who lived in the cemetery would appreciate the nice treat.

Since the day we got married, Michael and I have continued to grow in love in ways I didn't even know were possible. We are complete opposites--him being the soft spoken bear that he is and me being the feisty firecracker that I am--yet somehow we are the perfect match, accepting each other's imperfections as much as our virtues, and believing in each other's dreams as much as our own.

Occasionally, we'll reminisce about the first years of our relationship, and while the road got pretty bumpy along the way, we recognize that overcoming the hard stuff early on helped us build a strong foundation. I always thought relationships had to be this big explosive thing like fireworks, but what I have discovered throughout my marriage is that there is so much beauty in the subtleties. Like having your person there next to you as you close your eyes at the end of a long day, and as you open them upon beginning a new one.

I'm not saying that life is a fairy tale, because if you've been reading my story you know it's anything but that; however, I do believe happy endings can exist.

And while my story is far from over, with countless chapters still left to write, there was one missing puzzle piece I needed to find for me to feel complete: my father, Leon Katz.

38

You know those long questionnaires your doctor's office hands you when you check in for an appointment and you're asked to fill in information about your family's health history? I'd love to take a poll to see how many people who know both their parents actually appreciate having the ability to accurately complete those forms. As the child of a single parent who knew close to nothing about her father, this is something I have given great thought to my entire life.

Several years before my mother became ill, I had experienced some minor health setbacks of my own, and I can't tell you how absolutely frustrating it was when my doctors asked about family history and I could only provide fragmented answers. Immensely frustrated, I confessed to my mother that I had been giving some thought to looking for my father. I felt it would be highly beneficial for me to get his family history in case there was anything I needed to alert my doctors about. I was surprised when she didn't hesitate at all to give me her blessing and actually wished me luck in finding him--I was grateful for it. I reached out to a couple attorney friends who suggested I speak with a private investigator.

Unfortunately, I learned that without a social security number or last known address, which my mother could not provide after all those years, searching for a man with a very common Jewish name like Leon Katz was nearly impossible. Or, as the investigator put it, "It would be a lot like searching for a needle in a haystack." This was the mid-nineties, a time when genetic testing was really only used by hospitals and private labs for medical research and paternity testing but was not available to the public at large. Feeling defeated, and with little else left for me to do, I threw in the towel and decided to just accept that I would probably never get the answers I was seeking.

As new technology emerged and the mapping of the human genome occurred in 2003, genetic testing skyrocketed and became available to the public worldwide. This meant I could finally go in search of some long awaited answers, which both excited and scared me. In doing my research, I found countless stories of people finding family members they never knew existed. While some stories ended happily, other stories tore families apart.

Reflecting on this fact, I decided to do whatever I could to avoid destroying anyone's life. I have always wanted my existence to serve a happy purpose and be a blessing for others, not a living nightmare; also, I was not trying to force my way into anyone's life. So, I set the intention to go on this journey for the sole purpose of my own self-discovery and nothing more. If during my genealogy journey, fate brought my father and I together, I was open to it, but I wasn't going to make that my focus. *Who or what I will discover on this journey I am about to embark on remains to be seen, but no matter what happens, remember that you are your why.*

As I searched online for a reputable and established DNA service, I came across Ancestry. They offered testing to help me create my genealogy story, which was exactly what I was looking for. They would also match me with relatives who'd been tested through Ancestry and were a match, but that was the least of my concerns. I had also learned that over time, DNA results can change because as more people get tested, experts are better able to determine the specific regions people migrated from. This was all so fascinating to me, and the more I researched, the more intrigued and eager I became to move forward with getting tested.

Michael and I had only been married a couple months when Christmas arrived that year, and I thought it would be really cool if we got tested together. Although Michael had been raised by both his parents, there was a lot of curiosity about why he and his six siblings, who all share a mother and father, hardly resembled one another. With little to no information provided by his parents before their passing, I figured he would enjoy coming along with me for his own adventure of self-discovery.

I was happy when the kits arrived just in time for Christmas. I wrapped Michael's kit and stuffed it in his stocking and hid mine in my desk until he could open his and we could submit our tests together. I was so anxious and eager to get my test in, but if I was going to go on this journey with Michael, we might as well do it at the same time. When Christmas finally arrived, I was unwilling to wait a minute longer than necessary and we initiated the process on that very day. It was a lot simpler than I imagined it would be. When I opened the package, I found a small box with a booklet providing full instructions, a saliva collection tube, and a prepaid return mailer. First, I went onto the Ancestry website and activated our accounts so that once the DNA results were available, we would receive electronic notifications. We then took out our kits, spit into the tubes and gave them a little shake as instructed, and placed them inside the return envelopes, which I mailed the very next morning. That was the easy part. The hardest part was having to wait six to eight long weeks to get my results; the anticipation was torture.

Exactly one month after I mailed in my DNA, I received an email notification that read: *Your AncestryDNA results are in!* I couldn't believe the moment of truth had finally arrived--far sooner than I expected, actually. My heart began to flutter. *Okay, Karen, this is the moment you've been waiting for your entire life. Take a deep breath and open the message.*

Reading through the results, I couldn't help but smile nervously. They confirmed a few details I'd already known, but much to my surprise, they also provided some new information I never suspected to find. As it turns out, I'm made up of some of the most beautiful cultures that have ever existed. I will break down the information in the order it was provided, and while I don't exactly know how the percentages are estimated, I will share that with you as well.

First off, the results confirmed that I am 26 percent Indigenous, specifically from the Yucatán Peninsula, a region made up of different Mayan tribes. Although I wasn't surprised to find that I am of Mayan descent, I was surprised to find that it was mostly from the Yucatán Peninsula rather than Guatemala. But, as I have come to learn, there was once a time when borders did not exist and people could travel freely throughout various regions. While this result was surprising, it helped me understand some recent nudges I'd been receiving.

Shortly before getting my DNA tested, I had been feeling urgently called to visit the city of Mérida, which made no sense to me because I've never been there, nor do I know anyone who lives there. Mérida is the capital of the Mexican state of Yucatán and has a rich Mayan heritage. When I started researching this particular city, I immediately fell in love with everything I'd read about it. I even mentioned to Michael we should consider retiring there, and to my surprise, he said he was open to it. These results answered the very question I'd been asking about why I had been feeling the need to visit that specific place--my ancestors were calling me home.

Next, my results confirmed that I am 16 percent European Jewish. Call it naivete, but until then, I had not realized that being

Jewish was considered an ethnicity; I had always thought of it solely as a religion. Specifically, my ancestors were from the Southwest regions, Lithuania and Latvia, areas that were targeted by the Nazis. Although millions of Jews were killed in the Holocaust, hundreds of thousands of others were able to escape to the United States and elsewhere, which is what must have happened with my father's family.

Of all the things I was discovering about myself while reading my results, the biggest and most unsuspected surprise was coming to find that I am also 14 percent African, specifically from the Cameroon, Congo & Western Bantu Peoples, located in the heart of Africa. As surprising as this information was to me, it felt so amazing to learn that I came from a culture that's been in existence for over three thousand years. While I am most comfortable identifying as a multiracial, which is all-encompassing of my diverse background, I feel proud and honored to know that I come from generations upon generations of African kings and queens.

As I looked back on my life, I thought perhaps it was no coincidence at all that I'd always been obsessed with certain aspects of the Mayan culture, like the vibrant colors and textures. Or that I'd always wanted a menorah in my home and was obsessed with learning about the holocaust. Or that my childhood imaginary friend was a Black boy and that my life partner is a Black man. Or even that the sister who took care of my twin and me in Guatemala would sing us a song called "Angelitos Negros (Black Angels)." The puzzle pieces of my life were finally coming together and I was both humbled and grateful to live in a time when gaining this information was possible.

The remainder of my results revealed smaller percentages from other Indigenous and European regions, so I will not list them all. But, as you can see, I am truly a mishmash of this, that, and the other, and I love everything about that. Sitting in my office, alone and filled with questions, excitement, and nerves, one feeling stood out above the rest: total and utter completeness. It was strange to feel so complete after living with a huge void in my heart, but there I was, holding the answers to every question I'd been asking for as long as I'd existed. I knew now exactly who I was and where I came from, which meant everything to me.

    I couldn't wait for Michael to get home so I could show him my results. But first, I needed to call my twin and tell her everything I'd just learned. *Will she be as happy as I am with the results? I can't wait to find out!*

"I was starting to think
the universe was playing
a trick on me."

39

When I decided to go on my journey of self-discovery, I didn't quite know what to expect or what I would find, but I never imagined it would help me reach a new level of peace deep within me. All my life, I had felt so much inner turmoil that my mental and physical being were in a constant state of fight or flight and I was like a volcano, waiting to erupt at any point in time. Learning who I am and who I am made of has been one of the most beautiful gifts I have ever received. It was as though God or the universe had taken my hand after a very long and exhausting journey on my own and assured me that everything from this point forward would be alright. It was now safe for me to let go of all the false narratives I'd been told about or had believed about myself, and I could now embrace everything I knew to be true. All I could hope was that my twin would find the same peace in her heart that I had found in mine.

For most of our lives, my twin and I were looked upon and treated as two halves of one person; we shared most of the same happy moments as well as the heartbreaking ones, and experiencing our father's absence was no different. Because our mother was the only one who knew who our father was, we were told many contradicting lies by our siblings, like that our father was a Hindu who wore a headscarf, or that he was Jewish and wore a yarmulke, or that he was bald and that's why my twin had been born bald. Being young and impressionable, whether or not something makes sense or is false, one tends to believe what they're constantly told or teased about enough that it shapes their opinion of themselves and is also deeply scarring. Now, with the answers about our ancestry,

I could share the knowledge with my twin in hopes that she would also embrace who she is and let go of everything she too had been told she was. At the time that I had purchased mine and Michael's DNA kits, I had also decided to give one to my twin, but for whatever reason, she had been putting off sending hers in and I wanted to be mindful of that in case she wasn't ready.

I gave her a call and when she picked up the phone, I cut right to the chase and eagerly shared that I'd received my DNA results but I would only share them with her if she was prepared to receive them, and then I paused and waited for her response. The phone went silent for a few seconds and then she asked whether I was open to sharing the results with her. *Yay! I was hoping you would say that! Of course, I will share them.* In anticipation, I had already taken a screenshot of the results and immediately sent them to her so that we could read through them together.

Her overall reaction was pretty much the same as mine, some things were confirmed for her and some had come as a surprise. But, mostly, she had questions about how we had come to be mixed with so many different ethnicities across the map. I, too, had many questions and told her I still needed to research the results further. It also seemed that talking about this subject piqued my twin's interest so much that she mailed in her DNA kit the very next day. As we waited for her results, I went searching for answers, and boy, was I in for a treat!

Beyond just DNA, Ancestry provides a wealth of information about the history of the regions and communities a person is connected to. As I dug deeper, I discovered that my father was not only Jewish but also African American and Creole, with family history in Louisiana dating as far back as the 1750s. As noted in my Ancestry profile: *...early Louisiana was home to a large African American and Creole population (people of color with mixed European, Native*

American, and African ancestry). I couldn't believe what I was reading because I had just purchased tickets to take Michael to the annual Mardi Gras in New Orleans, Louisiana, as a surprise birthday gift. *Had I also been called to visit Louisiana by my ancestors?* Once again my mind was blown by all the coincidences--or were they coincidences at all? I was starting to think the universe was playing a trick on me.

I was deep in my search when I came across the most precious piece of information I'd discovered yet. It was a copy of a Louisiana census from 1940 with my father's family all listed on it. My grandfather's name was Leon M. Katz and my grandmother's name was Albertine B. Katz, her maiden name was Diaz. According to this census form, my father had four older sisters and he was the first born son, also named Leon M. Katz; he was five years of age at the time of the census and his entire family's race was marked as *Negro*.

As I stared at this form, I was overcome with emotion for so many reasons. *That man*, as my mother had always called him, was now a real person with a family history of his own, and I had known nothing about it; I had grandparents and four aunties and probably lots of cousins. *Would they have accepted me more than my own family had?* I couldn't help but wonder. I spent a good part of that day crying, but they were mostly tears of joy rather than sadness. How could I not be grateful for the information that was helping me piece myself together more?

Based on the information in the census, my father would have been a year older than my mother and I wondered whether he was still alive or was also gone. *Did I have siblings? Did my twin and I cross his mind?* I realize that many would have looked at this and felt anger that our father had not only kept us from knowing him but also an entire group of people who were our family. However, as I sat there, examining all the emotions flooding me, I never felt anger.

I knew that I had every right to be angry, but I'd made such peace with all of it throughout my healing that there was no anger left in me to feel. The one thing I felt most at that moment was curiosity; the more information I got a hold of, the more questions I seemed to have. And, unbeknownst to me, another angel was about to enter my life with more answers than I could have ever asked for.

"… he co-created two magnificent lives with an amazing woman who was equipped to give us everything he couldn't."

40

Just two days after I received my DNA results, I also received a message in my Ancestry inbox from a woman named Brenda, whom I didn't know but had been matched with as a first cousin. I will be honest and say that because I wasn't familiar or fully comfortable with how Ancestry's messaging system worked, I was hesitant to want to connect with anyone. This was especially the case because I'd discovered my eldest brother had also been tested and we were matched as siblings. Fortunately, Ancestry also allows you to block people, which is what I did so that my brother would not be able to find me or my results. I wanted nothing to do with him, and while it may sound crazy, a part of me wished that somehow our DNA had not been a match at all. With him on the site, and in an attempt to shield my information from any other family members I'd cut ties with, I decided to remove my profile name and replaced it only with initials, which had changed since I'd gotten married.

Despite my hesitation to respond to this woman, Brenda, Michael encouraged me to. He thought perhaps she was the key to gaining more information about my father. The thought made me nervous, but Michael was right, and I decided to respond. The email conversation went like this:

January 27 - message from Brenda:

I just received this message a few days ago from Ancestry. I am curious as to where the connection is that leads us to being first cousins. I thought at first it was from my father's side but when I look at the DNA comparisons it looks like it might be from my mother's side of the family.

Don't know if you can see my tree or not and if any of the people on there match your relatives.

Brenda

January 27 - my response:

I am unable to see your family tree, as I only opted to do the genetic testing. My mother was Guatemalan and immigrated to the U.S. in the 70s. She met my father in the U.S., but I never met him. The only thing I know about him is his name and that he's Jewish.

Do you have family from Guatemala or who are Jewish?

January 28 - message from Brenda:

Hi,

Thanks for writing back to me. I do not have family from Guatemala. My Grandfather I believe had some Jewish background because his last name was Jewish, Katz!

As I sit here writing this to you I began to wonder if my mother's brother would have met your mother. Is your father's name Leon M. Katz?

Brenda

Blood rushed to my head and I thought, *Oh my gosh--this woman is my father's niece. I don't know how to feel about this! What do I do?* Shaking and sweating, I ran to Michael, who suggested I respond right away and confirm that it was my father's name. I was kind of freaking out, but once again, Michael was right. I had to remain open to this if I wanted to learn more.

January 28 - my response:

Brenda, thank you for your response as well. Yes, your uncle would be my father because that is his name. As you might imagine, I am completely blown away right now and don't know where to go from here. I have a twin and this will be as much a shock for her as it is me.

January 28 - message from Brenda:

I am in shock also. What is your name? Where are you now? Where were you born?! How old are you?

Do you know his middle name?

If this is correct you have a sister and two brothers. I have to talk to some other family members. Hopefully we can talk and get this all straight.

Brenda

Based on Brenda's last comments--*if this is correct* and *hopefully we can talk and get this all straight*--I guessed she was as skeptical as I was about the whole thing. *Could this really be? My father is her uncle and I have three more siblings?* My emotions were all over the place and I could hardly think straight or breathe. I was so glad Michael was there to lend me his support, although I'm not entirely sure which one of us was more freaked out.

January 28 - my response:

Is he still living? Leon Katz, that is? Are you close to his children? How old are they?

I don't know his middle name because my mother didn't share much about him. It appears he left her upon learning about the pregnancy. She did say he came looking for us when we were around 9, but she refused to let him see us. He was close friends with my uncle, I believe they were roommates, and that is how my mother and Leon met. My mother was temporarily staying with my uncle when she immigrated to the U.S. It sounds like for a period of time they all lived together somewhere in Los Angeles. I believe he worked in banking at the time. But again, the details were few because I think she carried a great deal of resentment about the whole thing.

Unless he spoke Spanish, there would have been a language barrier because at the time, my mother was still new to the country and would have understood and spoken very little to no English.

My name is Karen, I live in Southern California and I'm in my forties. I am hesitant to share specific details about myself online, but would be willing to speak with you. I just want to be sure that this does not harm anyone, because my sole reason for having my twin and I tested was simply to learn about our genetic makeup, not to search for someone who may or may not have wanted us to find him.

January 28 - message from Brenda:

Karen,

I have an appointment at 2:30. If you want to call me this evening I would love to talk to you. My cell number is 213-___ -____. I live in the Culver City/Fox Hills area about 3 miles from LAX. When we speak I can fill you in on everything or maybe we can meet. Look forward to hearing from you soon.

Brenda

I was stunned to discover that my cousin was local, or only an hour away from me. My mind was racing! *Is my father here, too? What if I've passed him up on the streets? This is crazy!* I have so many questions.

That evening, Brenda and I spoke for hours. It was only awkward for the first few minutes, but then the conversation flowed as though we had known each other forever. She is a very kind and personable woman, more than willing to share whatever she could offer. Naturally, she was also very curious about my mother and my twin and me, so we did a lot of asking and answering questions, so many questions.

She said that while our family carried a Jewish last name, they were not practicing Jews. In fact, they really only identify as African American. She also shared that unfortunately, my father was no longer living. He had died of a heart attack at a relatively young age. Although she was younger when he passed, she remembered that throughout her life, she had known him to be the fun, loving uncle who loved to dance and was the life of the party. I don't know why, but knowing that he loved to dance just as my twin and I have always loved to dance made me feel connected to him. He also seemed to be a ladies' man because he had apparently been married several times and had fathered three children with three of the different women. While Brenda had met all three of my siblings, who are all older than me and my twin, she was really only in contact with two, because the youngest of the three never really came around.

Based on our calculations, my father died when he was only forty-seven years old, the age I was when I started writing this book. I was only nine years old when he passed, which, ironically, is around the age my mother said we were when he'd come looking for us. I couldn't help but wonder if he had, in part, died from a broken heart or from having to carry the burden of knowing he had abandoned his twin babies and had waited too long to remedy the damage he'd done. Apparently, our grandmother, Albertine Katz, had also died young of a heart attack. While I was saddened to hear that both my father and grandmother's lives were cut short due to heart failure, I was so grateful that I now had a piece of information I could add to those long medical history forms at my doctor's office.

My favorite part of the conversation with Brenda that evening was when she sent me photographs of my father and his sisters. They were a beautiful family and my father had been a handsome man, with cinnamon colored skin, black hair, and deep brown eyes. I could clearly see my twin's resemblance to him. *No wonder my mother took a liking to him and, albeit briefly, they must have made a beautiful couple and had a lot of chemistry. Go mom! Did they make passionate love the night they created my twin and me? I sure hope so! Maybe that's why we turned out as cute as we did!*

A few weeks after exchanging calls and texts, Brenda and I set up a date to meet in person. We decided to meet halfway at The Cheesecake Factory in Sherman Oaks, just off the 405 freeway. Along with her, she brought our other first cousin, Andrea, with whom she is very close, and who is also quite a lovely woman. I brought along my twin, her baby, Samantha, and Michael. We spent a wonderful afternoon getting to know each other, exchanging more stories about our lives, and just as I'd suspected they would, they embraced us with open arms. I could not have asked for more. We made plans to see each other again in the near future, especially because they hoped to arrange for us to meet our siblings and only surviving uncle, my father's youngest brother. I didn't know what would come of it, but I figured I had already gone this far and it wouldn't hurt to welcome these very loving people into my life.

Words cannot begin to express how grateful I am for my ancestry story, and while I will never get to meet my father in person, the fact that I can now put a face to his name means the world to me. He is no longer a stranger or just *that man* but rather an imperfect human who made mistakes, one who, despite everything, I am grateful for because he did something extraordinary: he co-created two magnificent lives with an amazing woman who was equipped to give us everything he couldn't.

Today, I have a beautiful relationship with the spirit of my father, whom I have grown to love in my own way, and with whom I get to connect when I go deep into meditation and prayer. I feel his presence and those of my ancestors in my heart and all around me, protecting and guiding me, and also reminding me that the spirit goes on to live far beyond this human experience.

Now that I had healed and closed many of my wounds, my heart was bursting with endless joy and I felt more compelled than ever to live my purpose. The old me would have questioned what my purpose even was, but now, after all the healing and growing I had done and was continuing to do, it was time to answer my lifelong calling to be of service to others. I could not think of a more beautiful way to do that than to dedicate my life to helping others discover their inner light and grow to heal themselves.

41

I first learned about coaching when I came across a Netflix documentary called *I Am Not Your Guru*, a behind-the-scenes look into a seminar thousands of people attend every year, including high-profile celebrities. It is said to be immensely transformational. The man behind this seminar's success is an American author, coach, and speaker known as Tony Robbins. As I watched the documentary, I was impressed with Tony's ability to look into a person's eyes and speak directly to them in a way that was honest and heartfelt but also compassionate and inspiring. Once Tony struck a chord with somebody, you could immediately see that person's face change completely as they connected the dots and the lightbulb went on inside them. All I could think was, *That is exactly what I want to do. I am going to help women discover the light within them.*

That moment marked the beginning of my journey as a life coach. Immediately after watching that movie, I went online and searched for a life coaching school. I came across Life Purpose Institute, an accredited school for coaches in San Diego, California. After researching their coursework and speaking with their staff and founder, I was all in and went on a yearlong journey of immersing myself in studying, learning, and practicing life coaching.

I still remember the very first day I sat in class, not fully knowing what to expect. The founder, an elderly woman named Fern who had taught coaching for years, walked downstairs from her office to greet the new class and said we were about to embark on "God's work." The moment she spoke those words, I knew I was exactly where I was meant to be and any doubt I may have had immediately dissipated. I was fortunate enough to have some of the best teachers and mentors who are masters at their craft. I was also grateful for my classmates, a diverse group of women from across the nation, many whom I bonded with while we allowed ourselves to be vulnerable and practice coaching one another. Needless to say, coaching school was, among many other things, a deeply personal and emotional experience for me.

The most wonderful thing I realized throughout my coursework was that I had the innate ability to do everything required of a coach--I am an intuitive person, an exceptional listener, and a compassionate and empathetic communicator. I had finally reached a point in my life where I was absolutely in my element, because I was committed to showing each and every person I worked with that I was as committed to their personal growth and success as they were. My greatest reward would be getting to bear witness to my clients' evolutions. How amazing is that?

When my coursework was complete and I received all my credentials, I was ready to begin serving others. I decided my specialty would be working with women, specifically women of color, because I knew first-hand that we often lack mentorship and coaching, or are sometimes overlooked and not given the encouragement to use our voices and advocate for ourselves in our personal and professional spaces. I was a woman on a mission, to heal and transform the world, one woman at a time.

Initially, I transitioned to working part-time at my job while running my business on a part-time basis, but it did not take long for me to realize that being a beginner entrepreneur while also working a demanding job was nearly impossible to do if I wanted to have a personal life at all. I was coaching evenings and weekends, which did not feel like the ideal situation for me, and I knew eventually something would have to give. After one year of trying to balance it all and not feeling like I was giving anything one hundred percent, I decided it was time to take the leap and gave notice that I would be leaving the organization at the end of the year in order to launch my business full-time.

I was so excited about being able to give my business all my energy and did everything I could to set myself up for success. To help me keep overhead costs down, I asked my best friend, who had recently taken up photography as a hobby and was pretty amazing, to take my headshots. Then, I hired a website designer to work with on my logo and branding, which turned out perfectly. Finally, I ordered my first-ever coaching business cards and registered for every networking event I could find in order to put myself out there and meet new people. I was ready to take the world by storm! The universe, however, had different plans.

When January of 2020 arrived, reports about a deadly flu-like virus called Novel Coronavirus, or COVID-19 for short, were beginning to surface, but with the public being told everything was under control, life went on as usual. I was excited, meeting with potential clients and signing on new ones; I was on top of the world and the year ahead looked very promising. By March, however, the narrative shifted when the World Health Organization declared COVID-19 a pandemic, which meant the outbreak had reached a global scale. The world as we knew it came to a complete halt and shut down almost entirely.

This would not have entirely affected me if the very nature of my business was not to connect with people. But making personal connections was what my business needed in order to thrive. I had not yet established myself on social media, and I don't sell a product. I sell an intangible service that often requires some explanation about how my specific coaching can help transform a person's life. I'd always found it easier to connect with people in person, especially because social media can often feel very inauthentic. But, with the pandemic and every single event I had registered for now cancelled, I had to roll with the punches and reimagine my business as a virtual one while also finding creative ways to connect with the outside world from behind the walls of my home office.

As winter transitioned into spring, more people became ill and lives were being lost in record numbers, and with that, worldwide fear and uncertainty continued to grow. Some of my clients lost their jobs or were reevaluating their priorities and wanted to put their coaching on pause, which was understandable. As clients began to drop, I could feel myself becoming worried and anxious about the future of my business. I realized I needed to provide myself with even more tools to be resilient and confident that I was on the right path despite the chaos.

I remembered how much Reiki had helped me in my time of need and how spiritually disconnected I was feeling with everything happening around us, and I knew I was not alone because so many were reaching out in need of support. As a believer of Reiki's deeply healing abilities, I felt called to go in that direction, and I could not think of a better time to learn how to provide more spiritually guided support to myself and anyone searching for a sense of connectedness to a higher power.

Unfortunately, when I reached out to Angelica, she indicated that with everything that was happening, her priorities had shifted and she had decided to put her Reiki practice on hold, indefinitely. *Without Angelica's help, I will have to go in search of a teacher.* This was the moment I came to realize just how powerful a tool social media is and how having a curated virtual space is essential in connecting with people from around the world who offer various services you may not have otherwise been able to find.

It did not take long for a friend to give me the number of a woman she'd heard about who was a Reiki master and teacher. When I looked her up on social media, I discovered that she and another Reiki master were collaborating and preparing to teach an online course. *Talk about divine timing.* But I wondered, *How can Reiki be taught virtually when it is a healing modality that sometimes requires touch?* Curious, I called and spoke with the teacher, who explained that Reiki is life force energy that transcends space and time. It can be used to heal people virtually or in person, and it can even be sent into the future. *That makes so much sense--how did I not realize that?* Hearing this teacher speak about overcoming her own traumas with the help of Reiki and how important it was for her to teach about this healing modality from a place of integrity and in honor of its Japanese origins was all the confirmation I needed to hear, and I enrolled in the course.

Much like coaching, Reiki is about connecting deeply with the person on the receiving end. I learned that as a practitioner, I would not be the giver of energy but rather the portal through which energy is transferred, and I found that so profoundly beautiful. Until I became a coach, I had not realized just how deeply intuitive I am, and I finally came to accept that I had a gift for receiving messages from the universe in order to deliver them as guidance to others. Being attuned to facilitate the transmission of healing energy along with the healing words I can offer was an honor. It assured me that I was on the right spiritual path.

When I completed my Reiki coursework, summer was coming to an end and fall was upon us. The world felt scarier than ever and I was fighting the urge to give up because I knew I had to keep moving my dreams forward. Everyone kept saying these were *unprecedented times*, but isn't life itself unprecedented? We never know what each day will bring. So I decided, rather than living in fear, I would live boldly and keep reminding myself that I had the tools to be resilient. *Stand firm like a lighthouse in the middle of an ocean storm so that you may light the way for others. And since you're not one to stand around for long, why don't you keep finding ways to heal and finally write that book you've been talking about writing for... well, ever?*

"They reminded me that the painful parts were as important to talk about as the happy ones."

42

As the final quarter of a long and heavy year arrived, so did my birthday season, and I could not think of a better time to breathe life into new projects and continue healing. For the remainder of the year, I set out to do three things I had been longing for: focus on healing my womb, where I carried much of my traumas; take a trip and connect with mother earth and my family; and finally start writing my book--yes--this book.

At the women's empowerment event I had gone to where I met my Reiki healer, I had also briefly met another incredible woman named Davina. She was one of the panelists who shared her story about coming to the United States at the age of seventeen from Colombia. She founded and created a bilingual lifestyle magazine called Alegría. The moment I heard her speak, something told me I would be working with her in the future and that I should approach her. I didn't know where this hunch was coming from, but I decided I had nothing to lose and went to introduce myself to her during one of the breaks. After exchanging a few words and still feeling inspired by her story, I decided to start following her on social media.

Four years later one late summer morning, I was scrolling through social media and came across one of Davina's posts. She had a call to action for Latinx writers interested in joining her fall publishing course. As it turned out, Alegría had now grown to become an independent publishing agency and she was ready to help those looking to become independent authors. Now, I wasn't a writer by trade, but I was definitely a writer at heart, and feeling the deep desire to finally tell my story, I reached out to get more information. After having a few of my questions answered, I was convinced the course was exactly what I was looking for and I enrolled.

That September, nine months into the pandemic, I and a group of other insanely talented poets, storytellers, and creators instantly became a family, and I began my year-long journey of making my dream of writing this book a reality.

I had always had a passion for writing, which is where I always shone the brightest throughout my education. Writing my own story, however, was far more challenging than I ever expected it to be, and it did not take long for me to realize that I had a lot of amends I still needed to make--with myself and the people I would be writing about in my story. My book wasn't just a story of love and happiness. It was more like a personal journal I was about to share with the world, divulging some of the deepest, saddest, and unhappiest moments of my life. This required that I revisit childhood memories that, despite all the healing I'd been doing, were still painful to recall and even more difficult to write about. I also felt guilty and somewhat ashamed, because in writing my story I knew I would have to air family secrets that would be very painful for some to read, especially those who love me most. Being so immensely vulnerable not only made me afraid but also made me want to give up before I even started.

Determined to not give up on myself, I had to continuously dig deep and find strength and courage to keep writing. There were days when I would show up to class with really heavy material to share. Sometimes, I would shake uncontrollably or sob. But after Davina and my classmates cried, got angry, or laughed with me, I would feel so much better and less alone. They reminded me that the painful parts were as important to talk about as the happy ones.

Week after week, for one entire year, Davina and my classmates sat through the roller coaster of my life story and listened with patience and love. It was like a weekly therapy session, but way more fun. Without them, this book would have probably been left unwritten and unpublished. I will forever be grateful to them for holding space for me as I relived the memories of turning my pain into power and my ashes into magic fairy dust.

With all the resistance and inner conflict I'd been experiencing during this time, I decided to finally make an appointment with a ceremonial healer I'd found through a mutual connection. I spent some time researching her, and after seeing images of her travels to the jungles of Peru to train with shamans (spiritual healers who practice divination and healing through rituals), I knew she was the real deal. I reached out hoping that she was available around my birthday. The timing would be just right for me to heal and connect with my womb and rebirth my sense of self and belonging. I was grateful that divine timing once again provided an opportunity for me to work with yet another healer who would change my life.

It just so happened that the healer was in town for a couple weeks and opened her calendar for me to schedule a private healing session. Because it was my first time working with plant medicine, I was not yet ready to work with psychedelics, but I did decide to work with a snuff called rapé, pronounced hap-eh, which is made up of sacred tobacco from the Amazon along with medicinal herbs. What makes communing with rapé so powerful is that it allows you to get out of your head and connect with your heart space. That, along with a ceremonial massage of the womb, where we carry ancestral trauma, was everything I needed to move forward with a greater sense of inner peace and healing.

What I have found throughout my healing journey is that it can be a very isolating endeavor because not everyone will understand the path you're on. And when people don't understand something, they tend to fear it or look at you like you've lost your mind. This is why, in order to avoid having anyone impose their fears or doubts or judgments on me, I have kept much of what I've done to heal myself, to myself. The payoff has been that, along the way, I have met so many beautiful souls who feel like kindred spirits and let me know I'm not walking this path alone. The beautiful womb healer I went to was one of those souls who helped open a door I didn't even know existed.

My womb healing session had been scheduled for a Friday, which was not at all surprising considering that Friday is ruled by the planet Venus, the Goddess of Love and Transformation. While I felt a little nervous because I didn't know what to expect or what would come out of it, I was also excited because I was ready for a breakthrough to elevate me to new heights.

I woke up that morning and decided to fast because I had been warned that rapé tends to make people purge. I dressed comfortably in loose cotton pants and a top, put on some flip flops, pulled my hair up, and wore a bare face to avoid having runny makeup--I knew I'd be emotional the entire time. I headed out early because the healer lived deep in the hills of Topanga, between Malibu and Santa Monica, and I wanted to take my time and enjoy the drive. When I arrived, I was greeted by a beautiful and warm young woman who welcomed me into her home where she had already cleansed and set up the space for my session. As we sat down, she said we would begin with a *platica* (conversation) so she could get to know me better and we could set an intention for the session.

After talking for over an hour, we went into prayer and the healer began to administer the plant medicine; then she sang, chanted, and prayed over me. The only purging I did was to weep like a child, and as the tears rolled down my face and onto my chest, they became symbolic of healing water washing over me, cleansing my soul, and renewing my spirit; I was releasing my old self and embracing all that I was and was becoming. I began to envision myself holding my inner child in my arms and rocking her back and forth, feeling her pain and fear dissipating. As I came back to my body, the healer's angelic voice filled me up with immense peace, gratitude, and love--for her, for the universe, and for the sacred plants that brought me back to life and helped me restore my inner child's innocence; she was now safe and whole.

When I arrived home that afternoon, I felt hungry, not so much for food, but for life! *I have this amazing life that I get to decide how to live, and I am ready to live it purposefully and intentionally, honoring my creator and my ancestors whose shoulders I stand upon.* What a gift it was to feel so alive!

Experiencing such profound healing made me realize that the deeper I go, the deeper I feel called to continue going. I imagine this is a lot like diving into the darkest part of the ocean and discovering a magical world that exists. Now that you've seen it, all you want to do is to swim up to the surface to catch your breath just so you can swim down deeper and discover what other treasures there are.

It was then that I asked Michael how he would feel about ringing in the new year somewhere on the beach, where we could disconnect from the world and connect with mother earth. I'm blessed enough to have a husband that is all about going with the flow, and we decided to head to the warm beaches of Los Cabos, Mexico. While Michael lay by the pool reading and relaxing, which was rare for him, I took time to be one with myself and the ocean waters. I spent my days meditating, journaling, crying, and reflecting on the sandy beach next to the water. As I reflected on the year, and years past, all I could feel in my heart was immense gratitude, which was a confirmation of all the healing I'd done.

On the evening of New Year's Eve, Michael and I sat on the terrace of the hotel restaurant, which overlooked the ocean, and had a romantic dinner. The universe had decided to grace us with the most beautiful and fullest white moon that seemed close enough to touch. We were mesmerized by all her beauty, and that of her companion stars, who together reflected their bright lights onto the vast ocean; it was a sight for sore eyes that made it impossible to catch your breath.

Witnessing all that beauty, tears welled up in my eyes. *What a profoundly beautiful time it is to be alive. In this great big world that can be filled with so much suffering, there is also immense magic all around us if we are only willing to take notice of it. I refuse to take any part of my life for granted, for it is a gift to be treasured and I know this now more than ever.*

At midnight, as I ate my twelve grapes for prosperity and luck in the year ahead, I put it out into the universe that 2021 would be the year I would finish and publish my book, and when I would return to the only place I could go to heal my ancestral wounds: Guatemala.

"At that moment, I was feeling my most uncomfortable because I was about to have my biggest breakthrough yet."

43

I was seven years old when I left Guatemala, hoping I would soon forget all about that place and swearing never to return. I could have never predicted then that forty years later, there would be nothing I wanted more than to return and make peace with her. The place had not only birthed my mother and ancestors but it was where I could reclaim the pieces of myself I'd left behind so long ago.

Throughout my journey of launching my business and of diving deep into my healing and writing, Michael and Samantha had always been my greatest supporters. I was happy that they also supported my wanting to go to Guatemala. They were both as excited for me to be going back as I was to be doing so, and the best part was that the two of them, along with Samantha's boyfriend, would be joining me for what I hoped would be the trip of a lifetime.

As we began discussing the logistics of our trip, we determined that nine days would give us sufficient time to explore some of my mother's favorite places she often talked about throughout her life. It wasn't until much later that I realized the synchronicities. We would be there nine days, and nine was the number of children my mother had birthed. *I know that's no coincidence.* Since my family knew how much our trip meant to me, they gave me free will to plan out the details. I was delighted until I realized that I had made it a point to know as little about Guatemala as possible, which meant I had no idea where to even begin. If I was really going to make this trip successful and memorable, I needed help.

I started by reaching out to a couple of my writing classmates who were both Guatemalan and had visited in recent years. Unlike me, they had many beautiful memories of their time in Guatemala and were quite fond of it. I hoped that would be the case for me, too. I, too, wanted to talk about my mother's homeland with the same pride and joy they did, and with their guidance, I was one step closer to making that happen. Once I compiled their recommendations, I made a list of the top five places I wanted to visit and was ready to go in search of a travel agent to help make it all possible.

As luck would have it, the universe once again conspired in my favor and arranged another serendipitous encounter through social media.

For some time, I had been following a young Guatemalan artist whose art is all about healing the divine feminine. I loved her work so much that I commissioned an art piece from her for a women's retreat I was manifesting in the not-so-distant future. One day, she posted an image of a beautiful new piece she had just completed, which I fell in love with, and just as I went to comment on the post I noticed a response from someone with a Guatemalan flag next to their name. *A Guatemalan flag! Cool! Could this be a sign of some kind?*

I don't typically stalk people on social media, but seeing that Guatemalan flag intrigued me enough to click on the handle, and lo and behold, next to the profile name read the words *Travel Agent - DM to start planning your trip to Guatemala with me.* I was and wasn't in disbelief, because this was not the first time I'd had a hunch about something only to discover it was precisely what I needed at the time. All I could do was laugh out loud as I thought, *If this is not divine timing or a serendipitous encounter, I don't know what is!*

As I looked through the young woman's account, I could see she was an avid hiker and adventurer, and she seemed perfectly legitimate, so I reached out to her through a private message. I mentioned that I lived in the U.S., was planning a trip to Guatemala with my family in late spring, and needed help putting it all together. She responded that she would be thrilled to speak with me, and we scheduled a virtual call. Once she checked out, I hired her. We spent the next five months planning out every last detail of my family trip, from beginning to end. Looking to maximize our trip, while also leaving room for rest and a couple healing sessions for me, we decided it would be ideal for us to spend three days in each city-- Antigua, Lake Atitlán, Peten, and the city of Guatemala.

With all the excitement about the trip and finalizing all the details, along with me frantically trying to write as much as I could before leaving, I had not been able to check in with myself to see how I was feeling about everything. Sitting at the airport, waiting to board our flight, I finally had a moment to decompress. I couldn't think of anything other than how nervous I was and how much I hoped this trip would be everything I wanted it to be and more, not only for me but for my family.

We took an overnight flight, which was surprisingly just under five hours long, and arrived in the city of Guatemala very early the next morning. We were exhausted from lack of sleep but still had to make our way to Antigua, one of my mother's favorite cities known for its cobblestone roads and colonial architecture and churches. On our drive there, my family slept, but I chose to stay awake and stare out the window. There was so much that looked familiar, yet somehow also quite foreign. Motorcycles with entire families riding on them, without a helmet in sight, flew past us. It was early morning yet businesses and shops were opening up and preparing for the day ahead. That is one thing I have always remembered about living in Guatemala; there are some of the hardest working people there who are willing to do whatever is necessary to keep food on the table. I have always found that quite admirable.

As we continued on and I remained glued to the window, unable to get any shuteye. I thought of my mother with a smile. *I'm here, mamita linda--beautiful mommy--and I know you must be so happy right now. I can feel you so close, but I want to see you. Will you please make your presence known, so that I know you're with us? I'll be looking for hummingbirds wherever we go.*

The minute we arrived in Antigua, I was in love. Many of the homes had the most amazing double wooden doors carved with such detail that I wanted to run up and down the streets knocking on each one and asking to be let in for a *cafecito* (cup of coffee). The streets of Antigua reminded me a lot of New Orleans, which I guess made sense since the Spaniards colonized both regions and left their architectural marks in each one.

Thanks to the recommendation of one of my classmates, we stayed in a beautiful boutique hotel nestled between private residences and shops. We were within walking distance of the Santa Catalina Arch, a landmark built in the 17th century, which we would see in the following days. At that moment, however, all I wanted was a traditional Guatemalan breakfast made up of eggs, black beans, and fried plantains, and a nice warm shower.

In the days that followed, we enjoyed walking the cobblestone streets, touring the different parts of town and learning of its rich colonial and Mayan history, talking with locals, and eating all the traditional Guatemalan dishes my mother used to cook for us. I looked for my mother everywhere we went, and I found her in an art gallery shown to us by one of our tour guides. As I walked through the maze of rooms, captivated and mesmerized by the imagination of each artist, I came across a room filled with nothing but the most colorful and radiant hummingbirds I'd ever seen. It was so magical, and I knew that each hummingbird was a representation of not only my mother but of all my ancestors accompanying her and celebrating my long-awaited return. My heart was overflowing with joy. *Gracias, mamita linda--thank you, beautiful mommy.*

My favorite part about visiting Antigua was getting to spend my mother's 85th birthday honoring her memory by visiting a local nonprofit hospital that housed orphaned children with special needs and senior citizens who'd been abandoned by their loved ones due to lack of financial resources. We could not think of a better way to celebrate my mother's legacy than by making a family donation in her name and paying it forward in her homeland, something I knew would make her spirit sing and dance.

A few days later, we drove to Lake Atitlán, which is about three hours west of Antigua. There, on a lake front property, my family would get some time to recover from all the adventuring we'd done in Antigua. I would also get the opportunity to travel into the neighboring towns where I would meet with a *curandera*, a healer trained in Indigenous healing practices, as well as a Mayan Priestess, who would conduct a private traditional Mayan and Temazcal ceremony for me to heal my ancestral wounds and rebirth myself.

I can barely find the words to fully describe how immensely healing my time in Lake Atitlán was. It was such a gift to connect with mother earth on the beautiful, lush grounds by the lake and to form a bond with the beautiful people we met along the way.

A couple days after arriving at the lakehouse and getting some much-needed rest and relaxation, my family stayed behind while I got up early and took a boat ride to a nearby town called San Pedro La Laguna--St. Peter Lagoon--where I was seen by the *curandera* introduced to me by a local herbalist. Much like the womb healer I had seen back home, our session also started with a *platica*. I shared with her about my personal traumas and my hopes that she could help me heal the parts of myself that still needed tending to; I felt I still needed to cut some energetic cords. After we spoke, she went and gathered plants and herbs, which she brushed over my entire body as she prayed for my healing. Interestingly, she spent quite a bit of time focusing on my womb, praying and rubbing the plants and herbs over and around my lower abdomen.

When she was all done, she told me that while I would not feel anything physical in the days ahead, I would energetically and spiritually begin to release all the trauma my body had been holding on to and was now ready to cut ties with. She closed out the session by lighting a white candle and using its flame to burn tobacco which released smoke all around me to purify my body and spirit. *I was led here, to this place and at this time. And as I receive the healing energy cleansing and purifying my soul, I am renewed; I am grateful for Señora Maria Cristina, and to the ancestors who bestowed her with the wisdom to heal those of us in need.*

Feeling my spirit light and airy, I enjoyed the rest of my day with my family, who had taken a boat to meet me. *I am so grateful for my family's willingness to sacrifice our time together for my healing. Now, I give them all of me by being present in these moments I get to share with them.*

On our final morning in Lake Atitlán, I arranged for my family to have breakfast at the lake house while I got up extra early in the morning to head to another nearby town called San Juan La Laguna--St. John Lagoon--to the home of Nana Maria Feliciana, the Mayan Priestess who held my private Mayan and Temazcal ceremony. In the days leading up to my trip to Guatemala, I had been communicating with her, a requirement she had to ensure my intentions were pure in seeking to heal myself and my ancestral traumas.

It wasn't until I was on the boat heading to my ceremony that I got nervous. At first, I thought I was shivering because of the cool morning breeze and splashes of cold, choppy water hitting my face, but then it dawned on me that I was shivering because I was embarking on a very serious journey of not only healing myself but my entire lineage, from past, present, and future.

As I began reflecting on my emotions, I recalled what I often share with my clients: it is when we allow ourselves to become our most uncomfortable that we often have our greatest breakthroughs. I imagine that is why a child lets out a cry when they are first born, because they have just broken through the tunnel of life to come out on the other side. At that moment, I was feeling my most uncomfortable because I was about to have my biggest breakthrough yet. *Am I ready for this? All I can do is trust that I wouldn't be here unless I was. Mom, if you're listening, I hope you're with me and I hope I'm doing the right thing.*

When I arrived, I entered the most beautiful and peaceful garden full of yellow Brugmansia bushes, flowers that hang like pendants known as Angel's Trumpet. In the middle of this beautiful garden was a petite Indigenous woman dressed in traditional Mayan clothing with her long black hair braided and a long beaded black necklace around her neck. I called out her name in a soft voice, Nana Maria Feliciana came to greet me with a warm hug and welcomed me to her space. Somehow, her embrace immediately took my fears and nervousness away. She sat down on a chair and asked me to sit next to her on a tarp she had placed over the grass. She began praying and I started to cry almost immediately. A short while later, she got up and walked over to a round firepit set up in front of me where she lit a flame, placed different colored candles for my healing, and called out to my ancestors and the Mayan gods. The more she prayed, the more I wept; it was a weeping that came from so deep down inside my soul that it made my chest and stomach tremble.

I was there, in my mother's birthplace, answering the call and representing an entire lineage of people, alive and gone, whose spirits were ready to heal and begin again. As I cried, Nana Maria Feliciana's voice got louder and spoke words I could not entirely make out, but which I knew were speaking to the gods for the restoration of my family's healing. As if the fire was listening and my ancestors were being rebirthed, the flames began to crackle and pop, and the white smoke danced and swayed with white butterflies that came out of nowhere flying all around us. We were so astonished that we gasped. It was proof that something truly powerful was transpiring right before our eyes; this was a moment that required belief in order to see and understand what is happening.

As we continued on, I looked for my mother and cried in sorrow that I could not see her. *Where are you mom, I need to see you. Please, please show me you are here with me.* Suddenly, as if to point my eyes in the right direction, a white butterfly came close to my face. I stared at it in awe as she flew toward a back wall I had not noticed because I had been captivated by the flames, and then I saw it. Just there, beyond the fire, was a large mural of a royal blue hummingbird. I sobbed even harder than before, because my mother's favorite color was royal blue, and there she was, revealing herself to me in her most favorite color of all. It was as if she were telling me, *Aquí estoy hija mía! ¿Me puede ver pintada en azul para que sepa que soy yo? No llore, mi niña, que aquí estoy. I am here, daughter of mine. Can you see me painted in blue so that you know it is me? Don't cry, my child, I'm right here.*

I can go on and tell you about the rest of my trip, but what I experienced in that moment, in that garden, with that Mayan Priestess, was everything I had gone to Guatemala for. The rest is just icing on a beautiful delicious Guatemalan cake, if there is such a thing. Just as I hoped would be the case, I fell in such love with Guatemala and healed so much of myself there, that I vowed to return very soon in hopes of helping other women heal on that sacred land just as I had.

A few days later, my family trip came to an end. As I sat in my seat preparing to return home a different woman, I looked to my left where Michael sat, then to my right where Samantha sat across the aisle next to her boyfriend, and I thought, *How blessed am I?* I closed my eyes and began to pray, and as I went deep into thought, I could hear the plane's roaring engine preparing to ascend into the early morning's sky.

Much like that aircraft was preparing to do, I too had broken free and become unafraid of what the future would hold, for I have come to learn that what lies ahead is a manifestation of my thoughts and actions. I know now that love--the kind we carry in our souls through each lifetime we come to live, the one that comes from a source so high and wide it cannot be seen with the human eye but only felt deep inside--that kind of love will always prevail. As for my actions, well, they speak loud and clear, for they are radical acts of self-love and compassion for the world; I am everything and everything is me. I love and forgive me, therefore, I love and forgive all.

I spent a lifetime running away from my darkness, concealing parts of myself because I was ashamed. But now I choose to share those same parts of myself with you and the rest of the world, so that in my vulnerability you can see yourself, so that through my pain and suffering, I can help you heal your heart, if only just a tiny bit.

My existence, the one I once thought of as insignificant, is, I discovered, absolutely indispensable. What I bring to the world is my one-of-a-kind gifts of healing, wisdom, love, and grace. Without me, there would be a lot less sugar and spice in the world, and everyone needs a little of both.

I am ascending into the light because I am not afraid of descending into the deepest and darkest parts of myself. Like the yin and yang, I coexist and do the dance of life between those two worlds of lightness and darkness; I no longer mourn the innocence my inner child lost, I now empower her to hold space in the world and unapologetically take her power back. You see, I am my shadow's lifeline as much as she is mine.

ABOUT THE AUTHOR

Karen Moreno Scott is a proud multiracial bilingual Certified Life Coach and Reiki practitioner, a wellness educator and motivational speaker, wife, mother, and now author. She was born and raised in Los Angeles, California, by her immigrant Guatemalan mother, Elsie.

In 2010, after returning to finish what she had once started, Karen graduated *cum laude* from Mount St. Mary's University in Los Angeles, California, where she earned a Bachelor of Arts degree in Liberal Studies. She holds a Life Coaching certification from Life Purpose Institute in San Diego, California.

Karen has served as a volunteer for numerous nonprofit organizations such as Habitat for Humanity and Homes4Families, and as an ESL (English as a Second Language) teacher at MEND Poverty, a nonprofit organization in Pacoima, California. For five years, she has served as the only female member on the board of directors for the Los Angeles Police Baseball Foundation.

As a coach, healer, and multiracial woman, Karen prides herself in serving her Spanish speaking community and women of color throughout the nation. Her dream is to expand her practice globally and open low-cost bilingual women wellness centers where women can feel safe, supported and empowered to change the narrative of their stories and create a path for generational wellness.

Karen currently lives in Santa Clarita, California, with Michael, her loving and supportive husband, and Rocky Balboa, their French Bulldog. Karen and Michael share a blended family of four amazing adult children, Michael, Jr., Samantha, Adriana, and Aaron. She is a self-proclaimed movie and eighties music buff. Karen enjoys hosting dinner parties and family game nights, traveling, the outdoors, live music shows, and dancing the night away. Of all her accomplishments, Karen's greatest and most favorite is having a loving home where her family and close friends can gather, share good food, and make beautiful memories.

Karenmorenoscott.com
Facebook.com/LifeCoachKaren
Instagram @karenmorenoscott

www.ingramcontent.com/pod-product-compliance
Lightning Source LLC
Chambersburg PA
CBHW020900080526
44589CB00011B/375